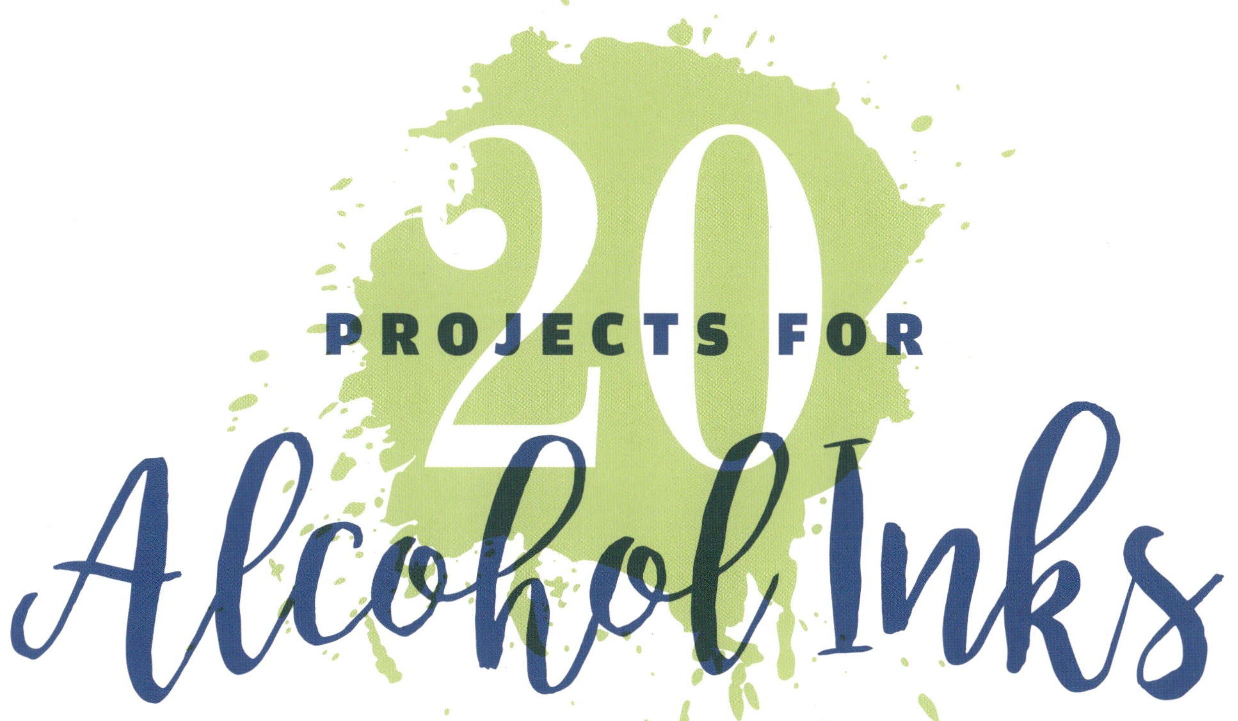

20 Projects for Alcohol Inks

A Workbook for Creating Your Best Art

KAREN WALKER

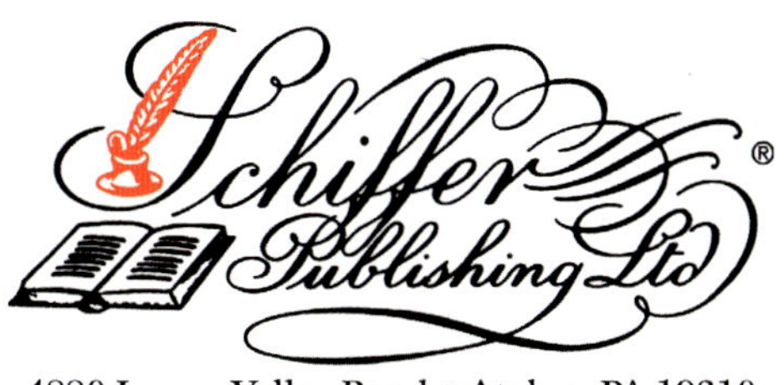

4880 Lower Valley Road • Atglen, PA 19310

Other Schiffer Books on Related Subjects:
Pigments of Your Imagination: Creating with Alcohol Inks, 2nd edition, revised and expanded,
Cathy Taylor , 978-0-7643-5133-4

How to Create Encaustic Art: A Guide to Painting with Wax,
Birgit Hüttemann-Holz, 978-0-7643-5416-8

Fire and Light: A Method of Painting for Artists Who Love Color,
Julie H. Hanson, 978-0-7643-5217-1

Library of Congress Control Number: 2018937206

Designed by Jack Chappell
Cover design by Brenda McCallum
Type set in Bromello/Amplitude/Avenir
ISBN: 978-0-7643-5646-9
Printed in China

Published by Schiffer Publishing, Ltd.
4880 Lower Valley Road
Atglen, PA 19310
Phone: (610) 593-1777; Fax: (610) 593-2002
E-mail: Info@schifferbooks.com
Web: www.schifferbooks.com

Dedication

With admiration and love to my husband, Patrick, and my daughters, Annie and Ginevra, whose support and encouragement throughout my artistic career I could not have done without. Also, a special thank you to all of my art friends and students who have brought such joy to the world of alcohol inks.

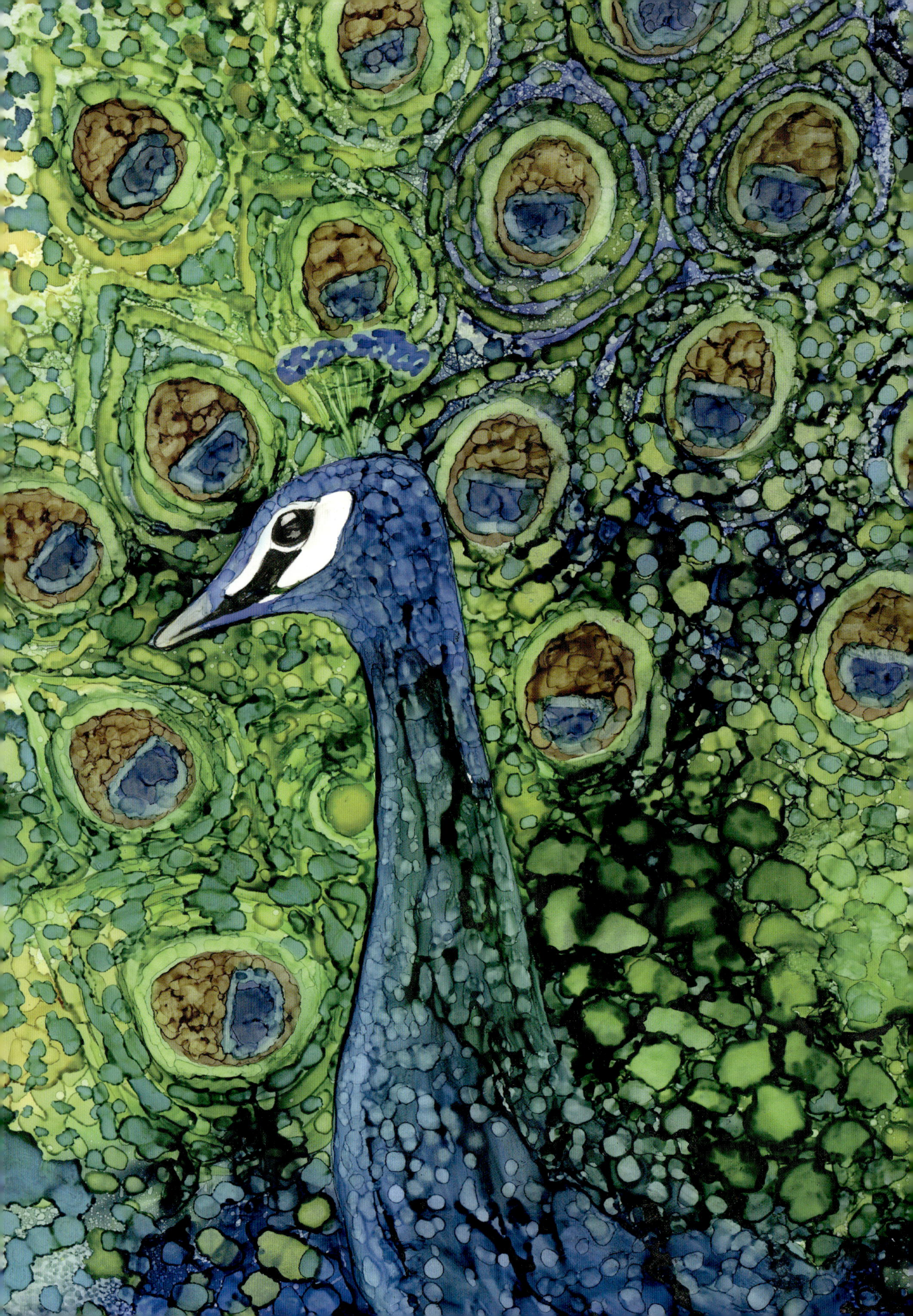

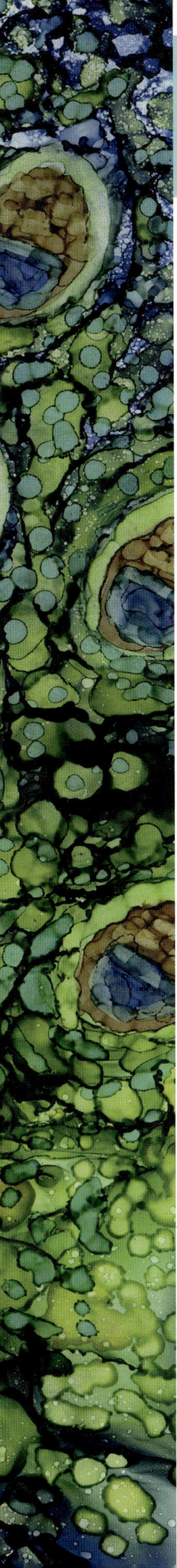

Contents

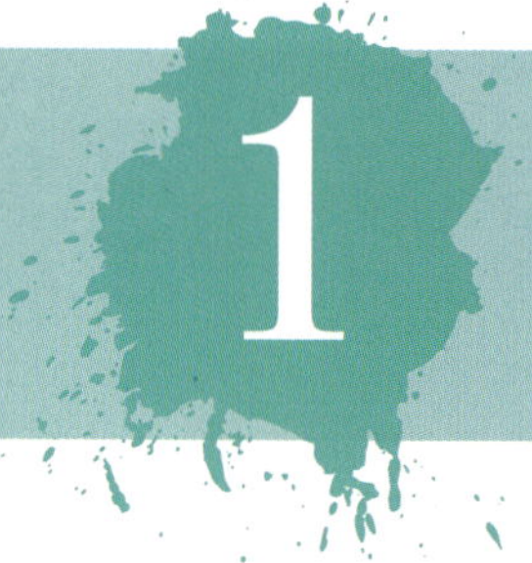

1 Introduction and Materials

Introduction

From the moment I first saw Sandy Scott's alcohol ink paintings at a local art show, I was hooked. I was captivated by the vibrant colors and the joyous, random fluidity. For me, the beauty of ink painting comes through allowing the color, flow, and spontaneity of the medium to become a central part of the art. Whether working abstractly or representationally, each painting is created not solely by artistic intention, but as a collaboration between the painter and the enchanting and unpredictable alcohol inks.

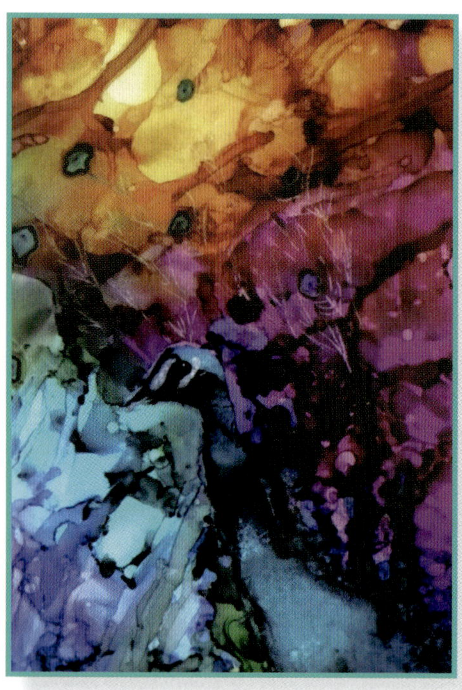

Karen Walker. *Peacock I.*
One of my first alcohol ink paintings, *Peacock I* became an inspiration for numerous peacock paintings, including its successor, *Peacock II.*

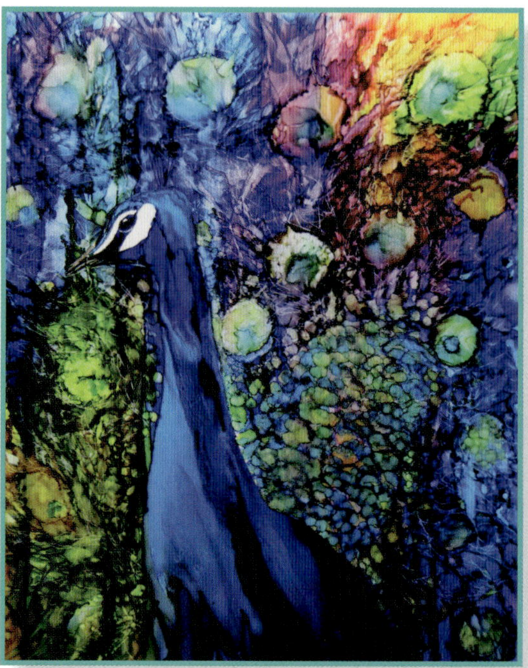

Karen Walker. *Peacock II.*
For me, *Peacock II* symbolizes the essence of my ink painting philosophy—a balance both between spontaneity and control, and abstraction and representation.

Materials

Alcohol Ink

Extremely fast drying and vibrant, alcohol inks are also dye based, acid free, and transparent. While there are a number of manufacturers, the projects in this book tend to use Tim Holtz® Alcohol Inks due to the consistency and flow of the ink. However, any alcohol ink would be fine—experiment to see which brands work for you!

Yupo® Paper

While alcohol inks flow on any nonporous surface, all the demonstration projects use white Yupo® synthetic watercolor paper, in weights ranging from 58 to 144 lb.

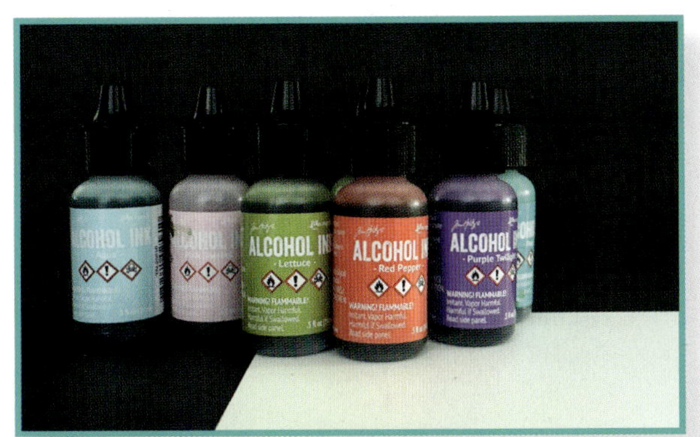

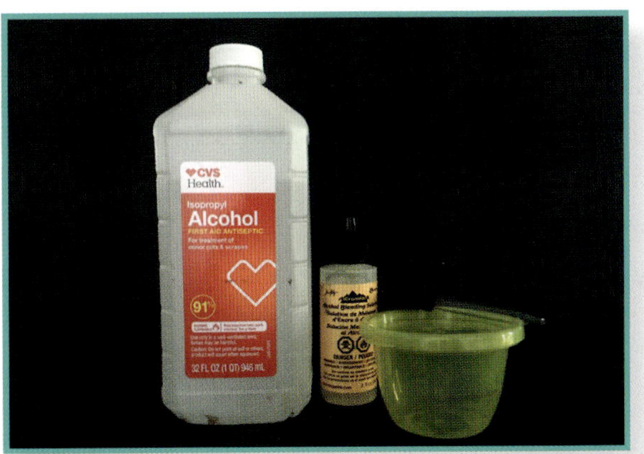

91% Alcohol or Blending Solution

Used primarily to lift ink, 91% alcohol is found in most drugstores. The major alcohol ink manufacturers also sell blending solutions or extenders that function similarly to the 91% alcohol.

Alcohol inks, 91% alcohol, and blending solutions all contain alcohol and should be used in a well-ventilated area with proper precautions.

For more information about safety when working with arts-and-craft materials, please take a look at the US Consumer Product Safety Commission's Art and Craft Safety Guide. Go to www.cpsc.gov and search for "art and craft safety guide."

Eyedropper and Lidded Container

Eyedroppers are a convenient way of dropping alcohol onto the paper. It is useful to keep a small amount of alcohol in a lidded container for this purpose.

Welled Palette

Both alcohol and ink may be dispensed into the welled palette for use with the small brush. For ease of cleanup, cover the palette with foil.

Masking Fluid

Masking fluid is used to preserve white areas of the paper. There are many brands available, including those with a fine-tipped applicator.

Small Brush

Many artists enjoy an angled or chiseled brush for lifting, but for most uses, any small, cheap brush is fine.

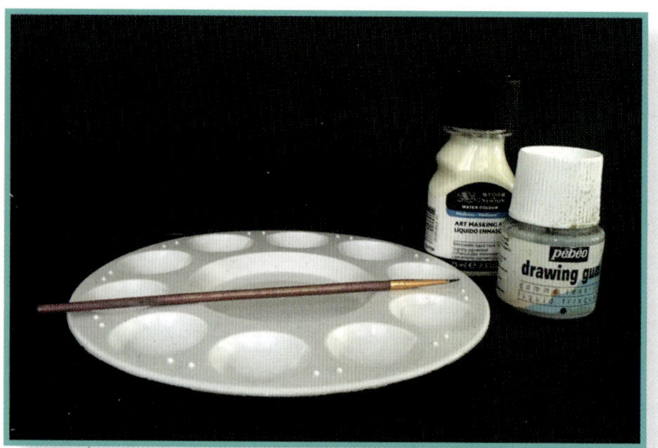

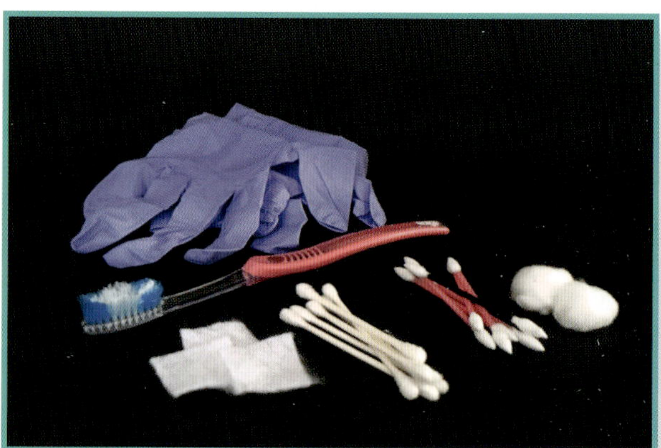

Cotton Balls, Cotton Swabs, and Felt Squares

Cotton balls, cotton swabs, and felt squares are used for texturing and lifting. There are an unlimited number of potential tools for texturing, including toothpicks, sponges, paper towels, and more. When using texturing tools such as the cotton swab, be sure to switch to a clean one as necessary.

Toothbrush and Tools for Air-Blown Effects

The toothbrush is used for splattering ink and alcohol. Many household items may be used for air-blown effects such as a straw, canned air, or an air compressor.

Gloves

Working with alcohol inks can be messy. Gloves are a great option to keep your hands clean. Additionally, several ink manufacturers offer specialized cleaning solutions.

Fine-Tipped Pens, Alcohol Ink Markers, and Pencils

For small details, opaque white pens and permanent fine-tipped pens in black or brown are extremely useful. Alcohol ink markers may be used in place of the small brush in many applications. The markers offer increased control and often come in a broader color range than the bottled ink. The pencil is used for creating the initial drawing.

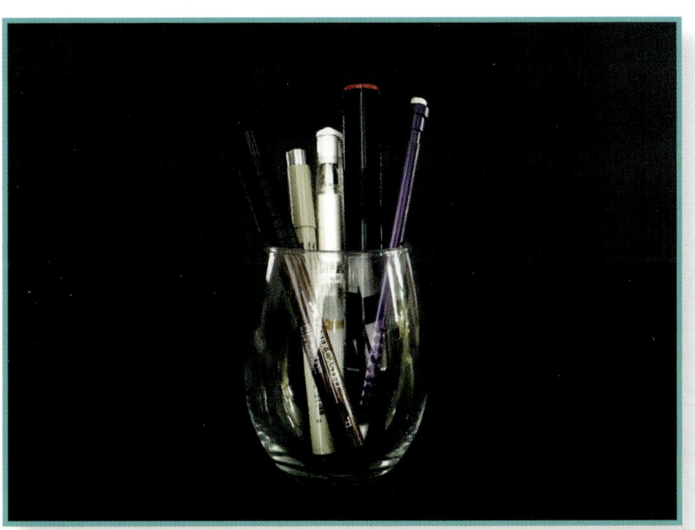

Mats, Backing, and Frames

I present my alcohol ink paintings matted, backed, and framed under glass. Many artists opt to seal their alcohol ink paintings. Refer to the ink manufacturer's websites for sealant recommendations.

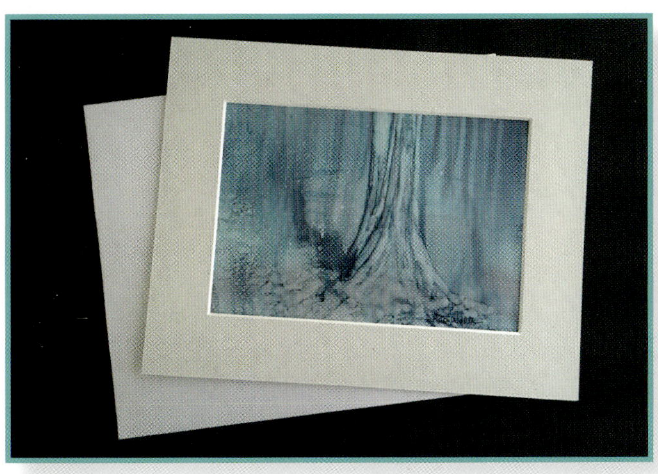

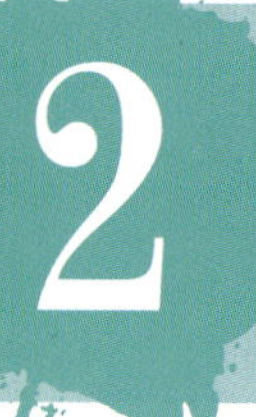

Spontaneity and Control

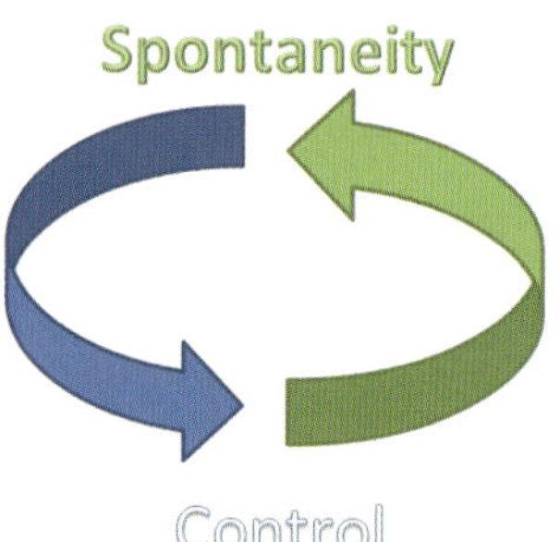

My general philosophy is to seek a balance between spontaneity and control. The magic of the paintings occurs with the fluidity and vibrancy of the inks. Creating recognizable subjects comes through control. As such, we'll use techniques for both. For me, the process is not linear, but cyclical, going back and forth between loose and tight control.

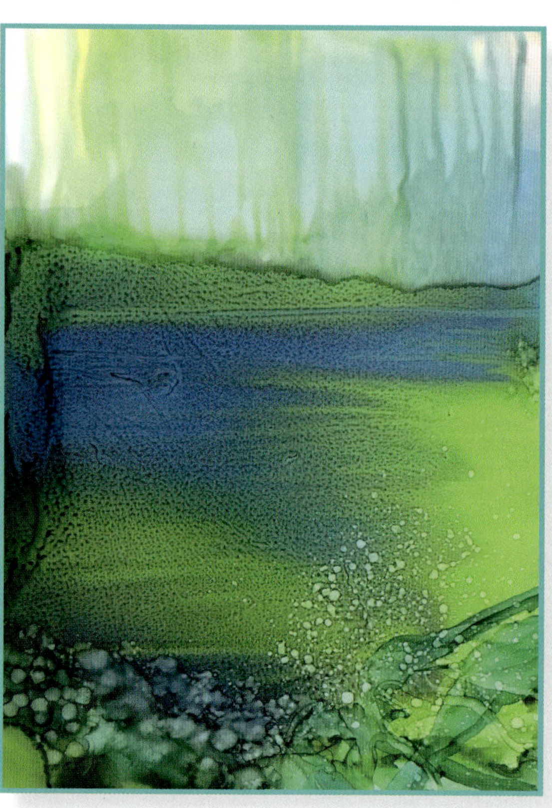

Karen Walker. *Secret Serenity.*

Karen Walker. *Lady Oriole.*

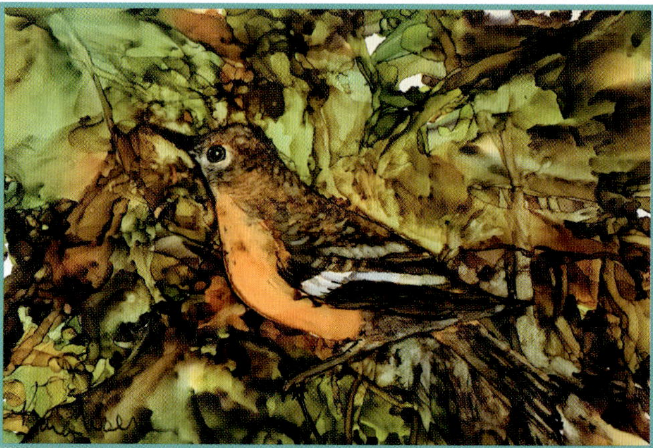

Project 1, *Secret Serenity*, presents the primary tools for spontaneity, including ink flow and textures, while Project 2, *Lady Oriole*, demonstrates the main tools for control: masking, lifting, and brushwork/pen work.

Project 1 - Secret Serenity

Secret Serenity demonstrates the techniques for spontaneity—primarily variations of ink flow and textures.

- Ink flow
- Alcohol flow
- Ink circles
- Textures
- Air-blown effects
- Splattered alcohol

Almost all of my ink paintings begin with an inky background created from these techniques.

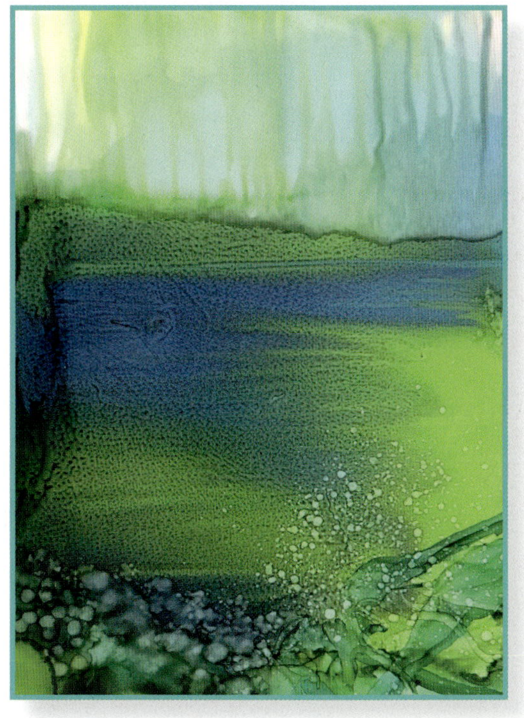

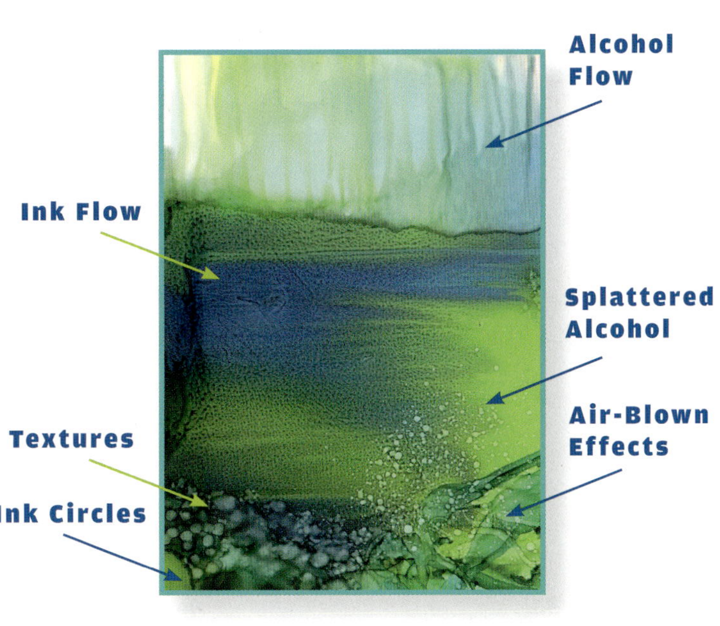

Technique: Ink Flow

1. Drop ink onto the paper to create the main landscape.

There are two approaches to creating ink flow: one can (a) hold the paper vertically and drop ink directly from the bottle or (b) leave the paper flat on the table when dropping the ink and then either pick it up to control the direction of the flow or let it dry flat. If the ink does not flow smoothly, wipe the paper with alcohol first.

Use the brush to direct the ink flow and tap out any white spots while the ink is still very wet.

For this example, hold the paper vertically and allow the ink to dry in this position.

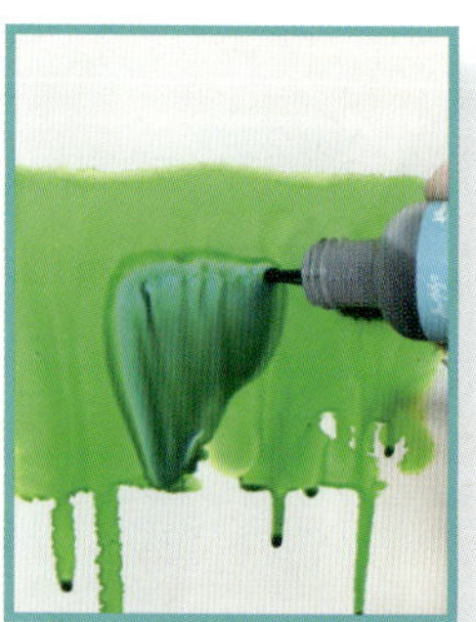

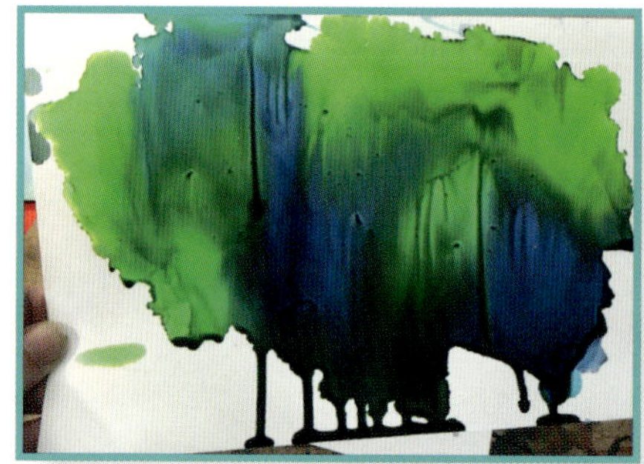

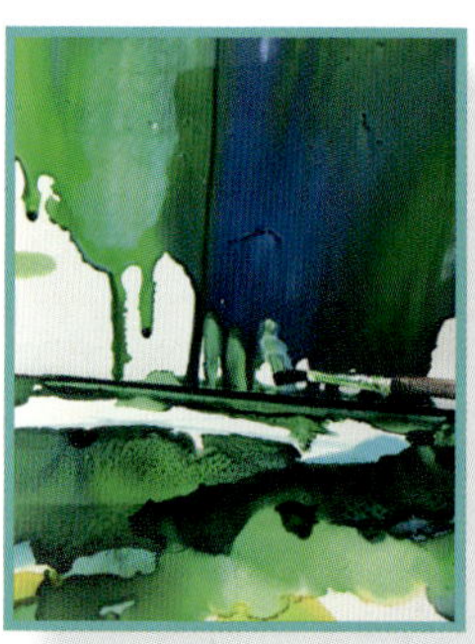

Technique: Alcohol Flow

2. To create the distant forest, turn the paper upside down and drop alcohol through the ink. Use the eyedropper and alcohol from the small container. Allow it to dry while it's still in the vertical orientation.

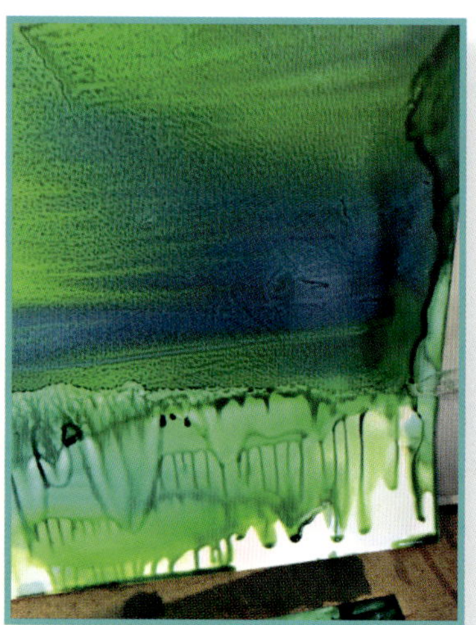

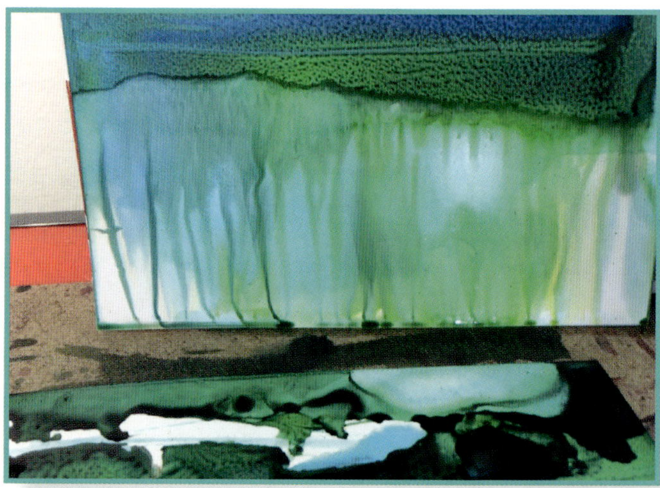

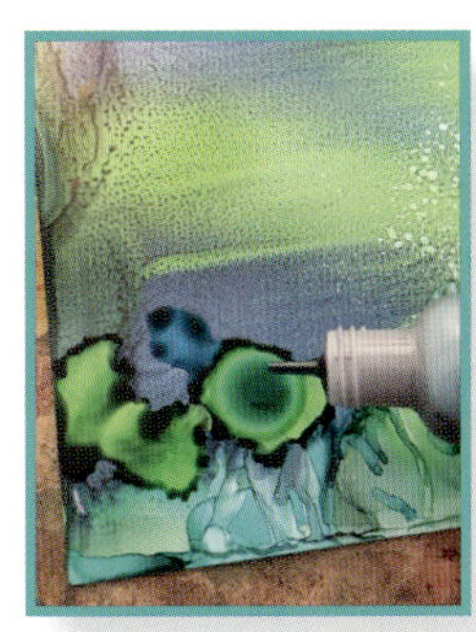

Technique: Ink Circles

3. To add ink to the foreground, lay the paper flat on the table and drop circles of ink. Depending on the dryness of each layer, the circles may nest or completely fill in.

Technique: Textures

4. To create a rocky textured foreground, use the cotton ball and cotton swab either with ink or alcohol, or both. Other texturing tools may include a sponge, felt, toothpick, and paper towel. The fineness of the texture is largely dependent on the amount of alcohol or ink used—textures are a wonderful opportunity for experimentation!

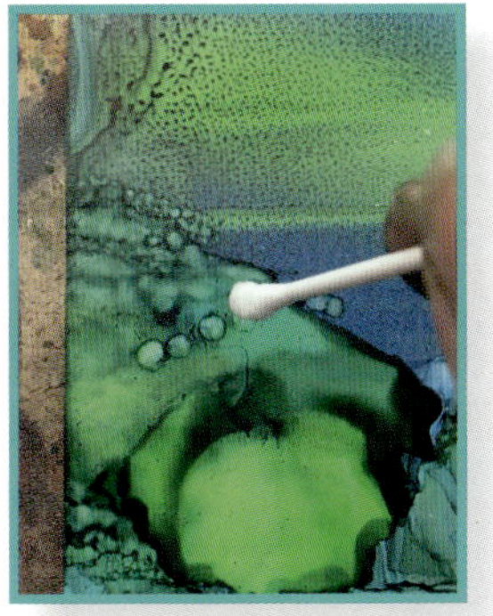

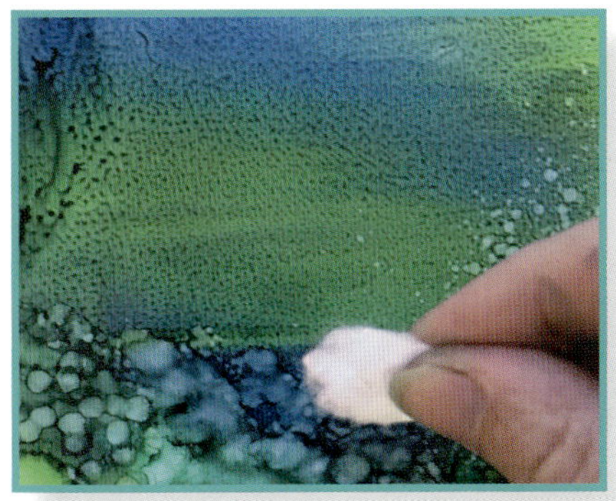

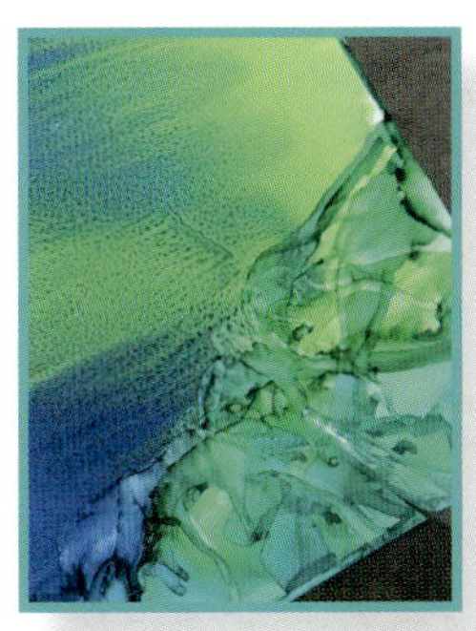

Technique: Air-Blown Effects

5. The grassy hillside is created by air-blown effects with both ink and alcohol. Use the eyedropper to control the flow of the alcohol. Experiment with straws, canned air, and more. This process can be a bit messy but fun.

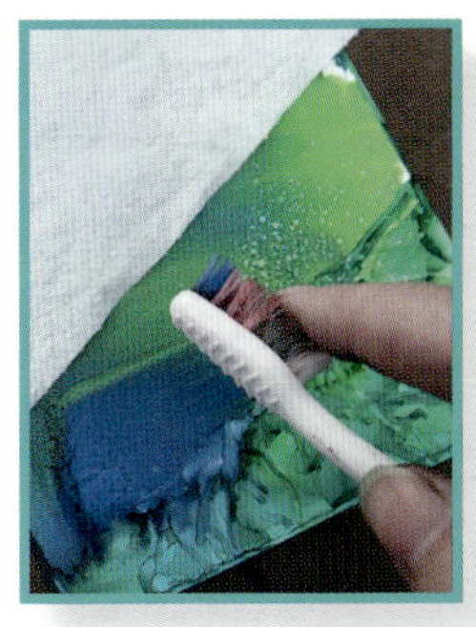

Technique: Splattered Alcohol

6. Create tiny dots by splattering alcohol or ink with a toothbrush. Protect parts of the painting by covering with paper or paper towel. Allow a few seconds in between splatters to see how the alcohol expands, since it is easy to oversplatter.

Project 2 - Lady Oriole

To create representational alcohol ink paintings such as *Lady Oriole*, it is necessary to direct and control the ink. The major techniques I use are:

- Masking
- Lifting
- Brushwork and Pens/Markers

These skills are used in conjunction with the techniques for spontaneity to create vibrant, inky pieces with specific identifiable subjects.

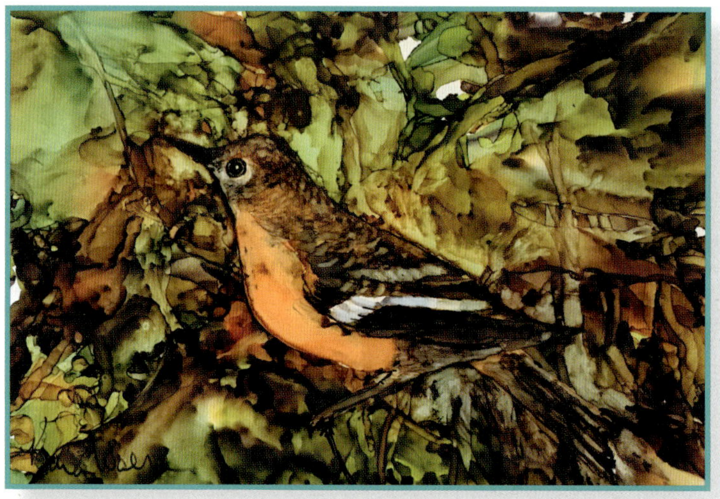

Karen Walker. *Lady Oriole*.

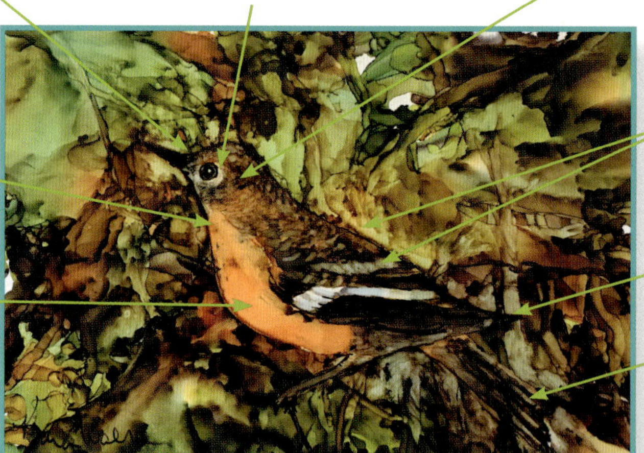

Technique: Masking

Masking is a technique that is used to protect the paper from ink. A fluid is brushed onto desired areas and then is allowed to dry to create a barrier. Masking will preserve not only the white of the paper but the lines of the drawing.

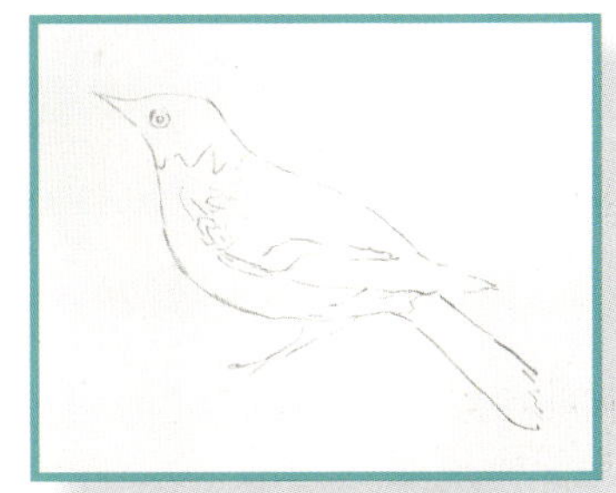

When masking, be sure to clean the brush immediately after, since it is difficult to remove dried masking fluid from a brush.

1. Use a pencil to lightly sketch key features of the oriole.

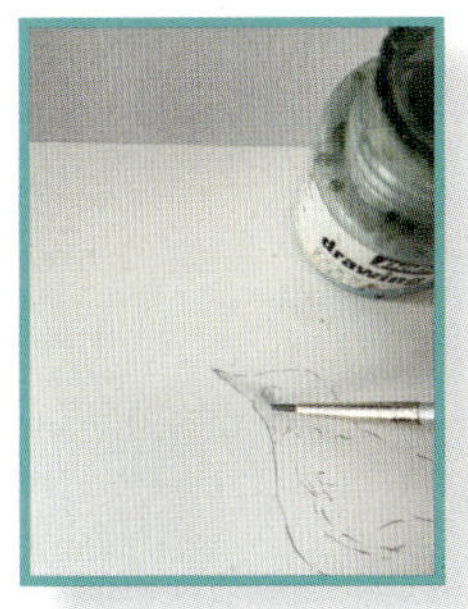

2. Dip a small brush into the masking fluid and apply over the areas to be masked. While one can mask an entire subject, there are advantages to masking only key elements such as the outline, white areas of the wing, details such as the eye, and areas requiring clear color. This strategy offers a more unified result, since the background ink will become part of the subject.

3. Let dry completely. Depending on the thickness of the masking, this may take between 10 minutes and several hours.

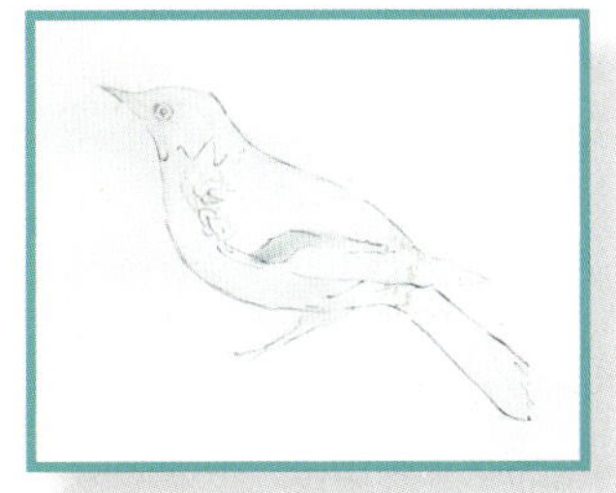

4. Create the background. Drop a variety of forest-colored inks on the paper and use the techniques for spontaneity (ink flow, textures, and air-blown effects) to yield an inky background.

5. Once the ink layer is completely dry, remove the masking fluid by running a finger across the masked areas to pull off the dried masking fluid.

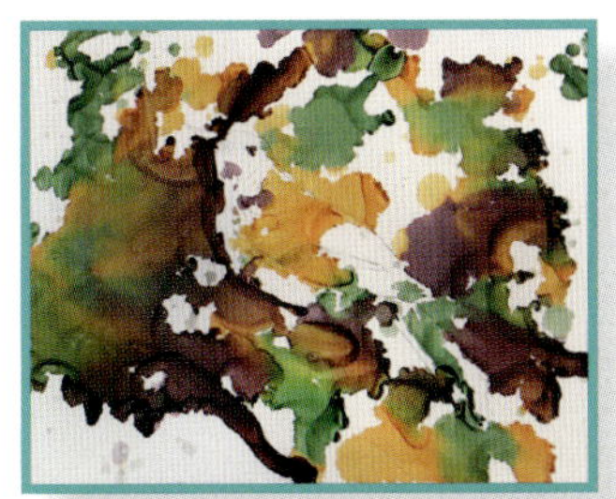

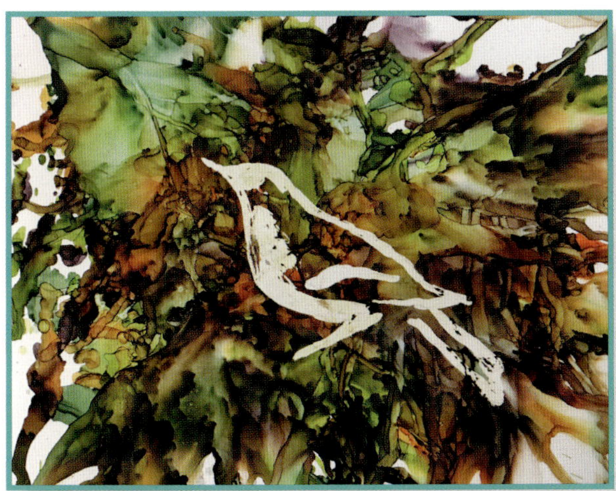

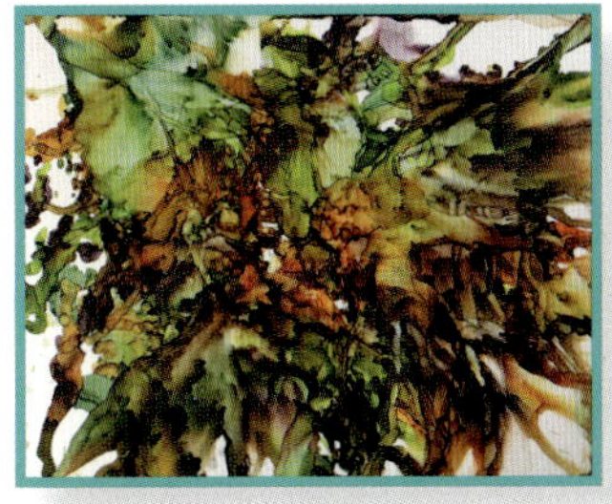

Technique: Lifting - Part 1

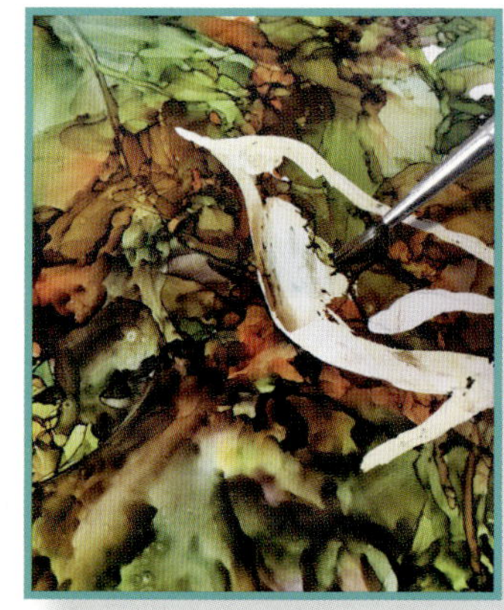

6. After masking, it is often desirable to use the brush and alcohol to blend in the masked areas. Be sure to leave those areas intended to be white untouched. To lift ink with the brush, pour a small amount of alcohol from the bottle into a separate container to avoid tinting the entire bottle. Use the brush and alcohol to remove ink. Periodically, wipe the ink off the brush onto a paper towel or other paper, and be sure not to use too much alcohol. The cotton swab is another useful tool to remove large passages of ink, particularly in areas where new ink will be painted in.

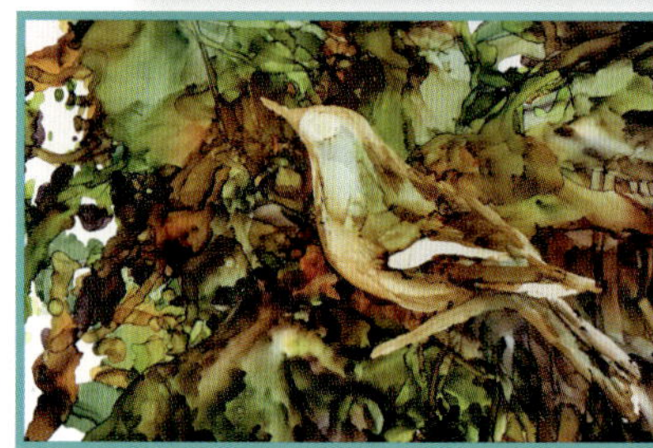

7. Lifting often leaves a stain on the paper. If an area needs to be pure white, it is best to use the masking technique.

Technique: Brushwork - Drop & Guide

8. To create an area of intense, brushstroke-free ink, use the drop and guide method, below.

Drop & Guide Method

In this example of painting an apple with the drop-and-guide method, ink is dropped directly from the bottle and allowed to expand. Instead of brushing through the ink, use the brush only to guide the edges until the shape is filled. For smaller areas, one may wish to drop the ink from a heavily loaded brush instead of the bottle. In addition to creating smooth ink passages in a subject, this technique is also useful for replacing or repairing inky areas in a background.

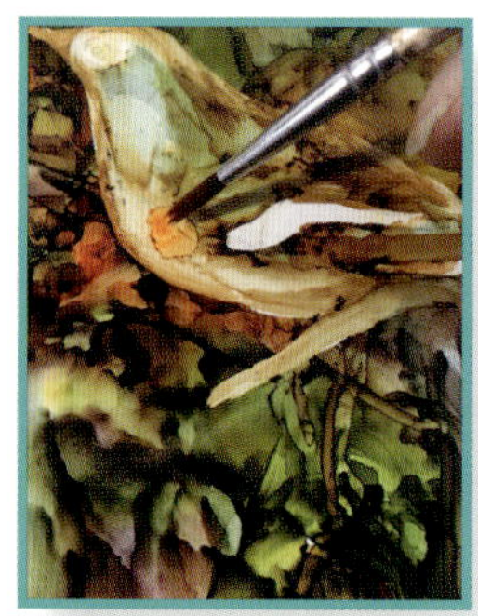

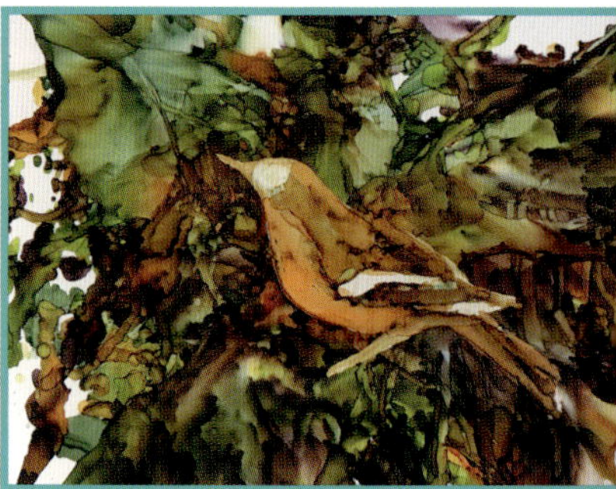

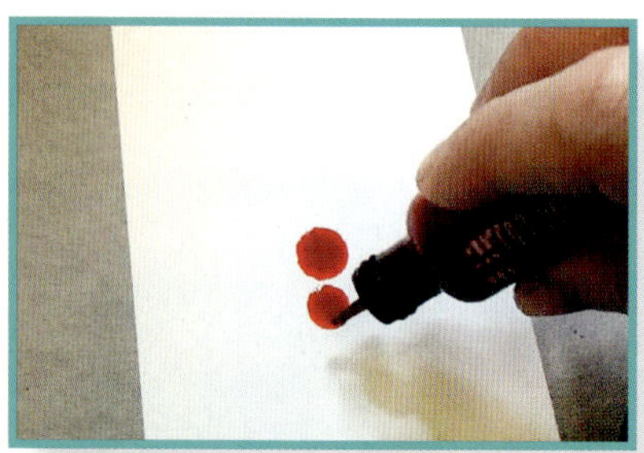

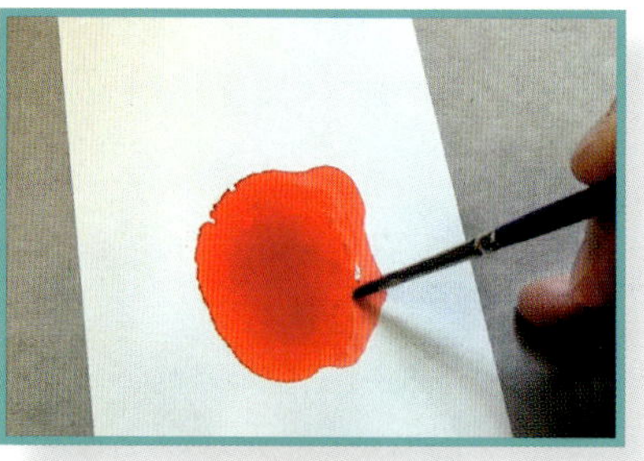

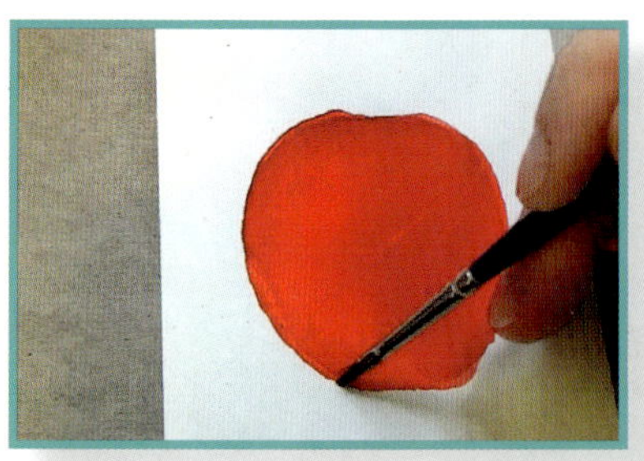

Technique: Brushwork - Direct Painting with Brush and Ink

9. Using a small brush, paint in the major features of the bird. To paint with the brush, dispense ink into the welled palette. Colors may be mixed in the palette or diluted with alcohol for lighter shades.

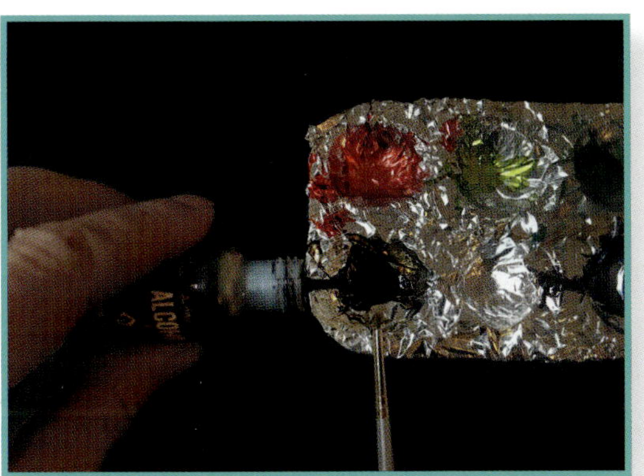

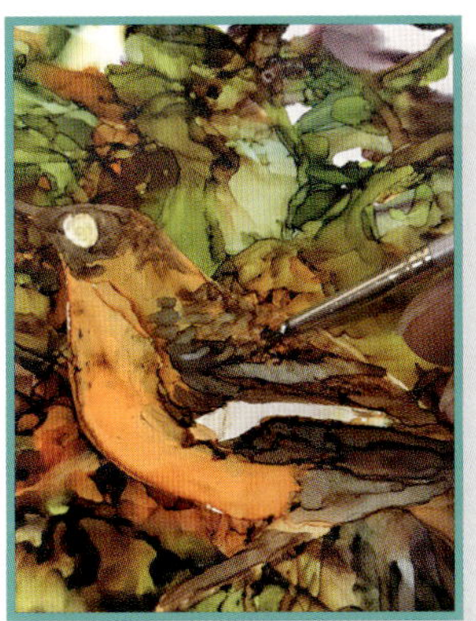

Technique: Fine-Tipped Pens and Alcohol Ink Markers

10. Fine-tipped pens allow for more precision than the brush will allow. They are often used for details such as eyes, shading (when softened with alcohol), and linear elements such as grasses. Projects in this book use black, white, and sepia pens. In most cases, the white pen is reserved for the final detail work.

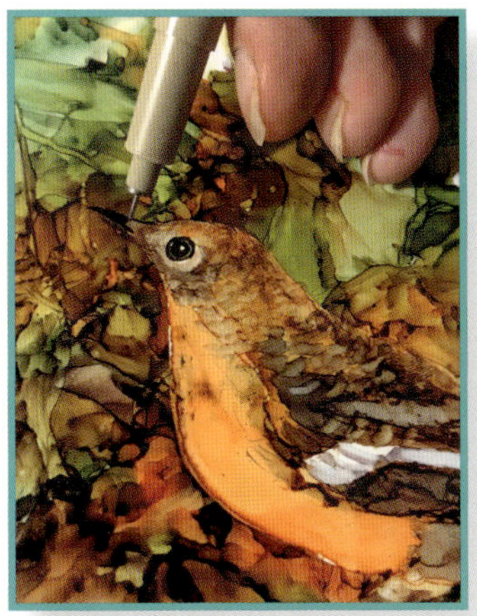

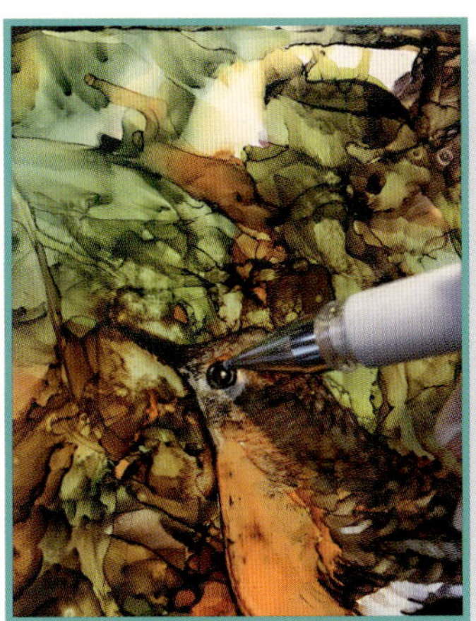

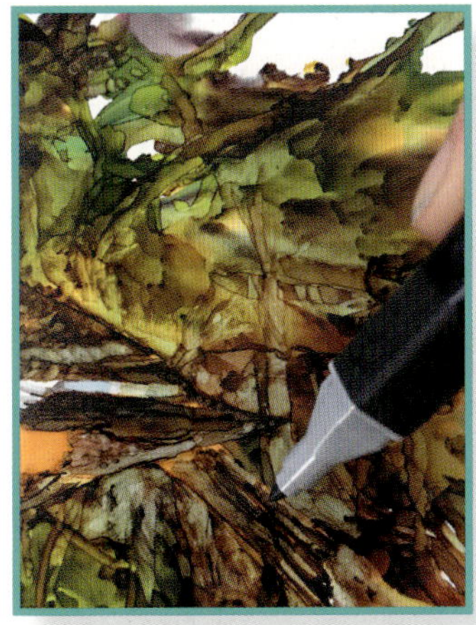

11. Use alcohol ink markers to add ink to small areas, such as the tail feathers. Alcohol ink markers may be used in place of the brush to add color in a precise and controlled manner. Pale markers may also be used to lift ink.

Technique: Brushwork - Dry Brush

12. Over time, the ink in the welled palette will thicken and dry. This thickened ink may be used with a dry brush to add tiny lines for detail in the feathers.

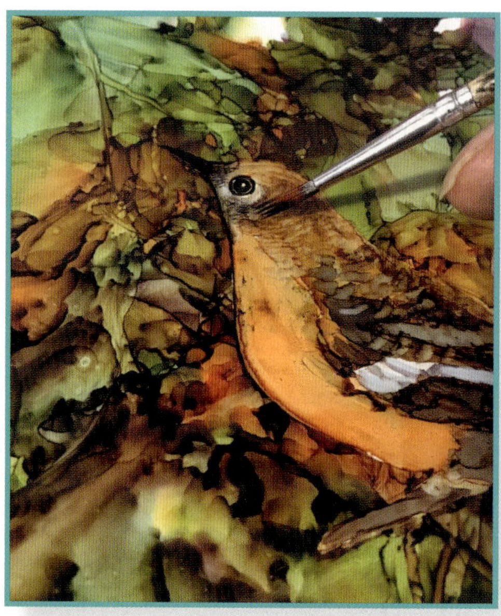

Technique: Lifting - Part 2

13. To make the subject more visible in this complex background, carefully lift ink around the subject, following the natural ink patterns of the piece. Details may also be "painted in" by lifting out ink with the brush, as in the feathers shown.

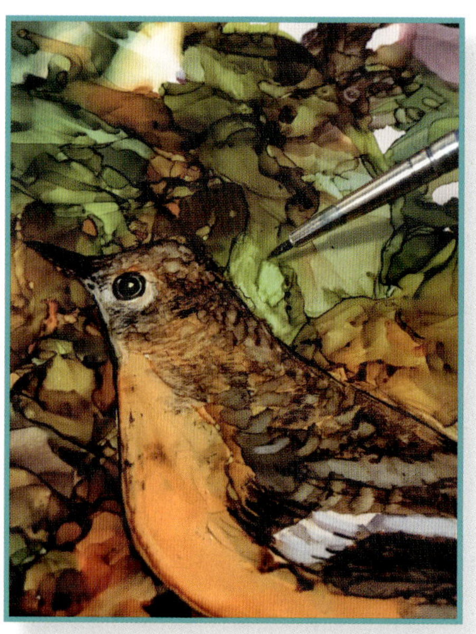

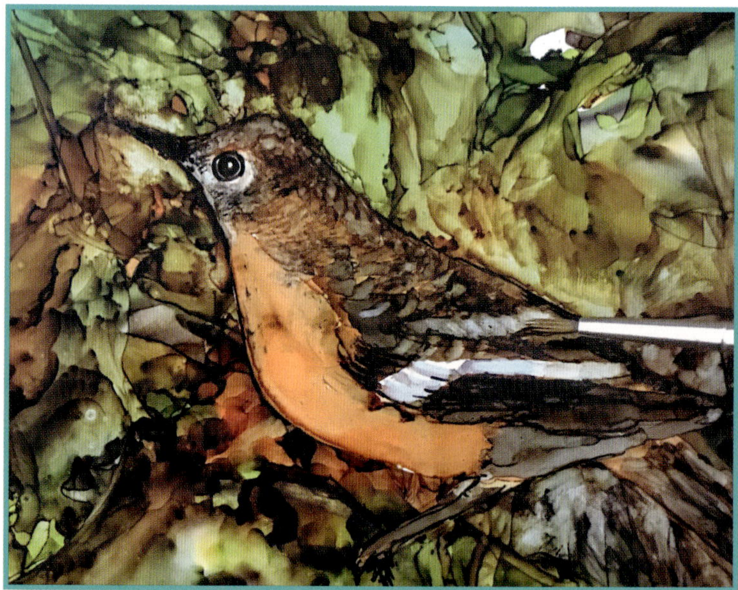

Techniques Gallery

Ink & Alcohol Flow

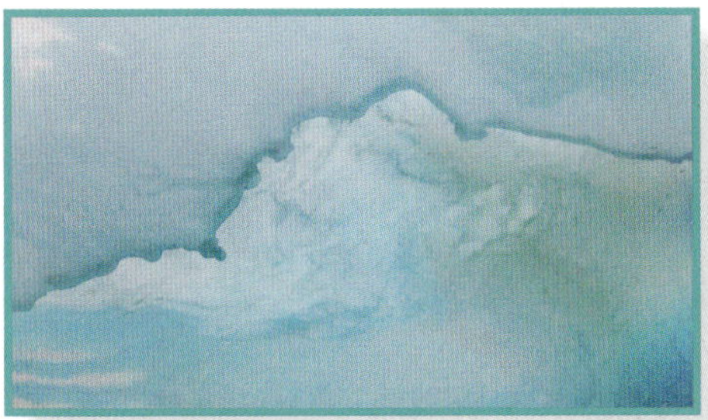

Karen Walker. *Ocean Fantasy.*
Occasionally, the ink flow suggests its own subject. This may be enhanced by brushwork, textures, pens, etc., or simply left alone as in this example.

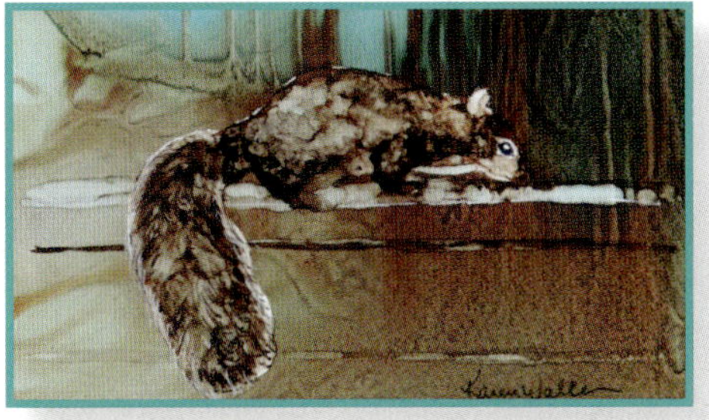

Karen Walker. *Squirrel I.*
Naturalistic colors provide a wooded background for this little squirrel. Only a small amount of lifting and a line of ink are necessary to create the railing.

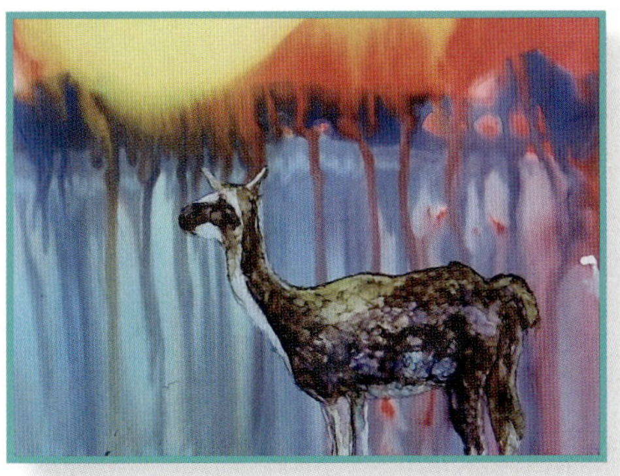

Karen Walker. *Sunrise Llama.*
Ordinary scenes become dramatic with the vivid colors and flow of ink.

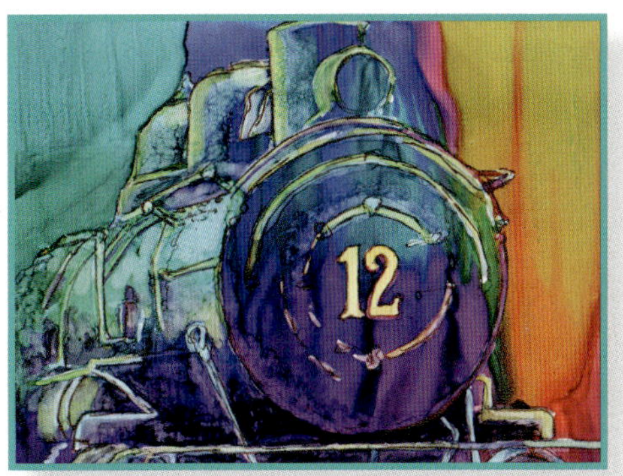

Karen Walker. *The Train.*
The background ink is fully integrated into the subject in this colorful version of Engine No. 12.

Ink Circles

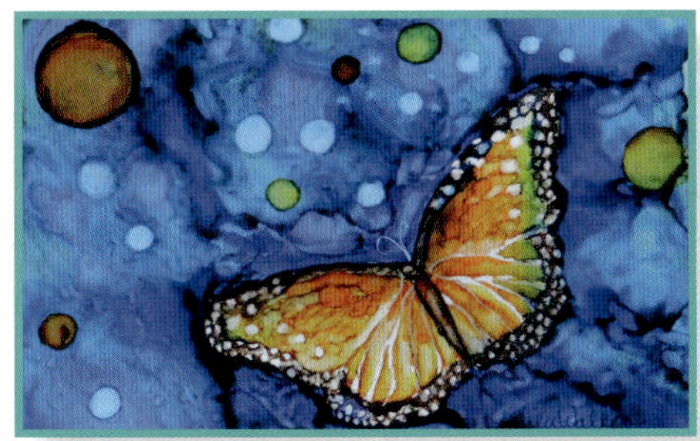

Karen Walker. *Celestial Butterfly.*
Circles of ink and alcohol add a whimsical touch to this butterfly painting. While the ink may be dropped directly onto the dry blue background, the resulting color will be clearer if the circle is lifted with alcohol first.

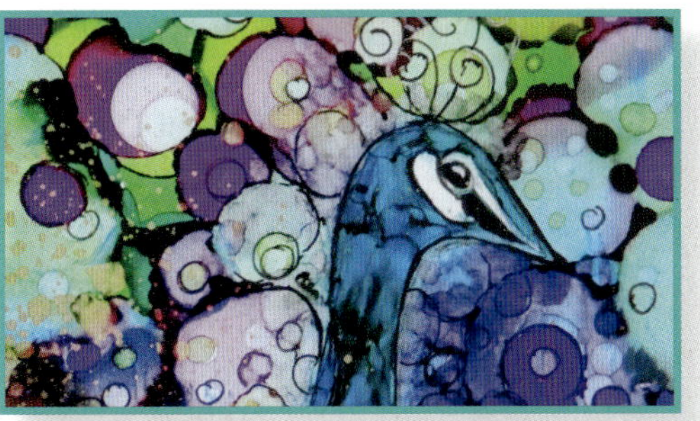

Karen Walker. *Deco Peacock.*
The tail of *Deco Peacock* is formed by a multitude of nested and overlapping circles.

Ink Circles continued...

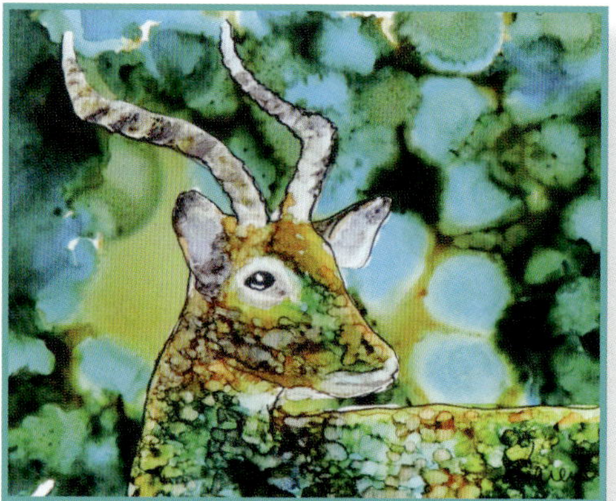

Karen Walker. *African Deer.*
The background of *African Deer* was created by allowing circles of ink to expand into each other, with the paper flat on the work surface.

Textures

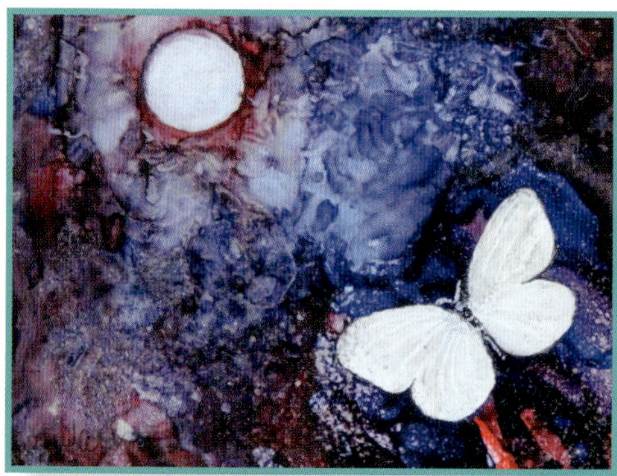

Karen Walker. *White Moth.*
The inky sky of the *White Moth* features a unique texture pattern created by placing plastic wrap over the wet ink.

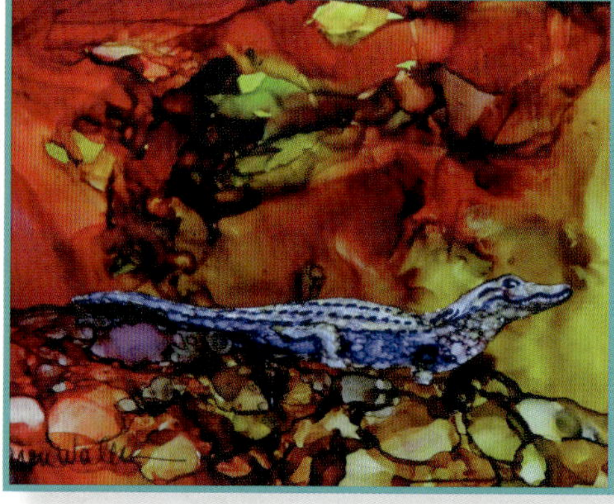

Karen Walker. *Crocodile.*
The textures both of the crocodile and the rocks were created with alcohol. The pattern marks vary in size due to the amount of alcohol used and the thickness of the ink layer. The dark edges formed by the expanding alcohol patterns become the outlines of the rocks.

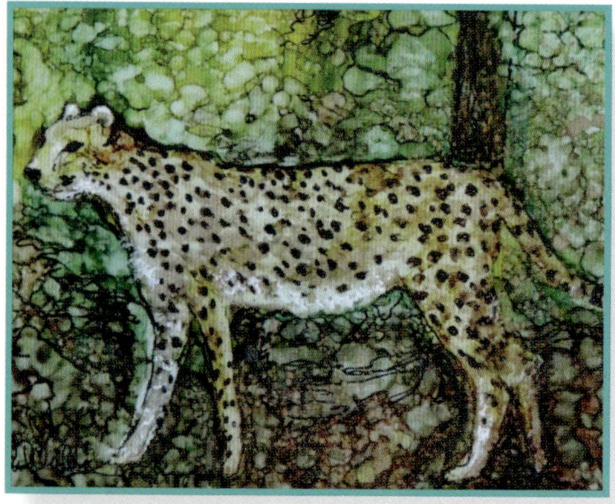

Karen Walker. *Cheetah.*
Felt and cotton balls were used to create the jungle background for this cheetah.

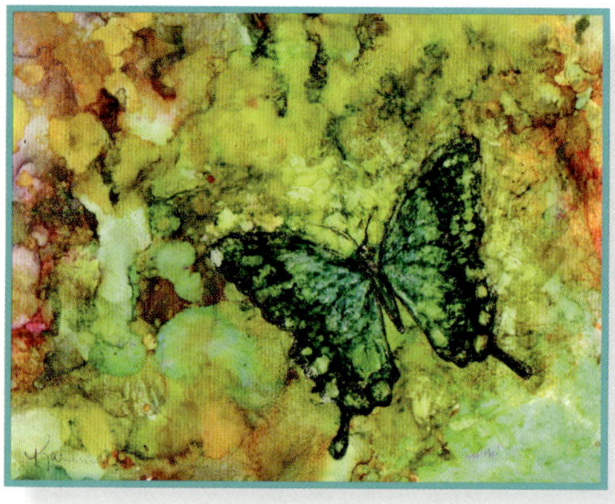

Karen Walker. *Grunge Butterfly.*
In addition to textures created by cotton balls and canned air, the background of *Grunge Butterfly* also has patterns derived from gently folding the paper over on itself.

Air-Blown Effects

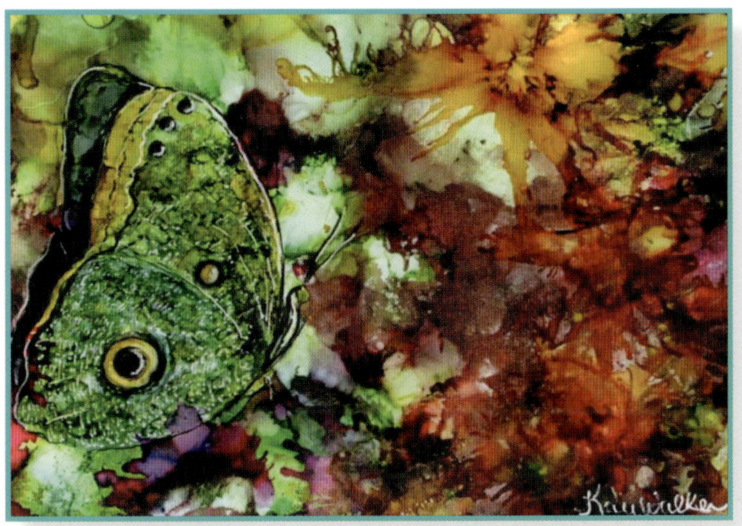

Karen Walker. *Burst into Spring.*
Canned air is used to create air-blown effects. In this instance, the texture was added midway through the painting.

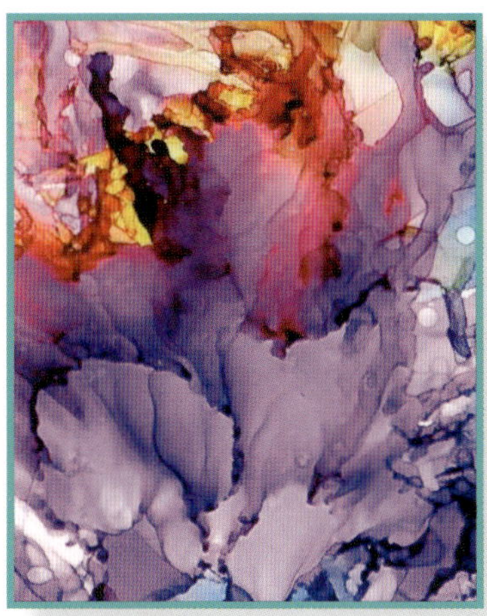

Karen Walker. *Abstract Flower.*
This abstract flower was a nice surprise when creating a background with vibrant, colorful inks.

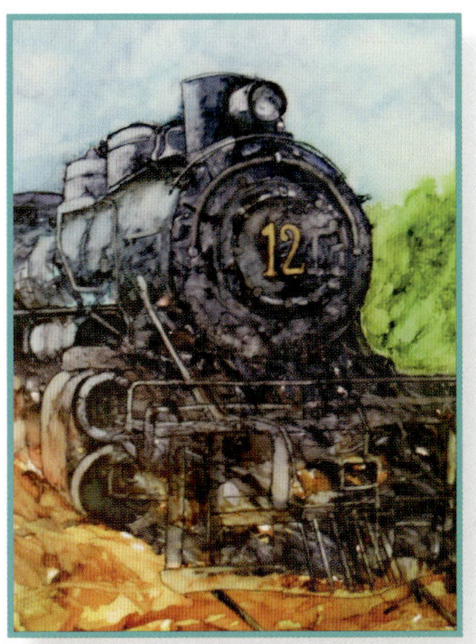

Karen Walker. *No. 12.*
Both the subject and the background contain air-blown elements for a unified appearance.

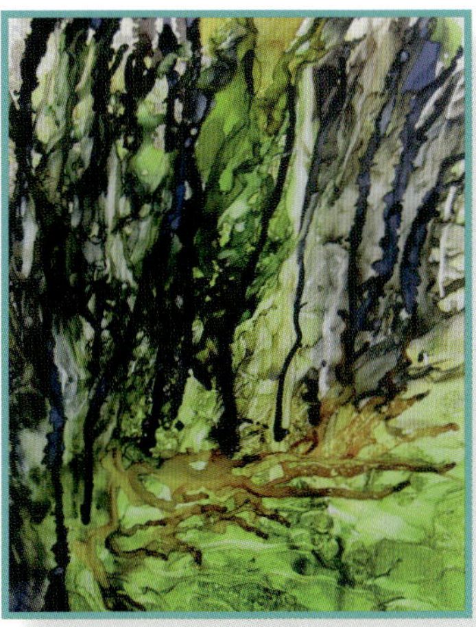

Karen Walker. *Acadian Forest.*
Here, air-blown ink is used to paint an entire piece.

Splattered Alcohol & Ink

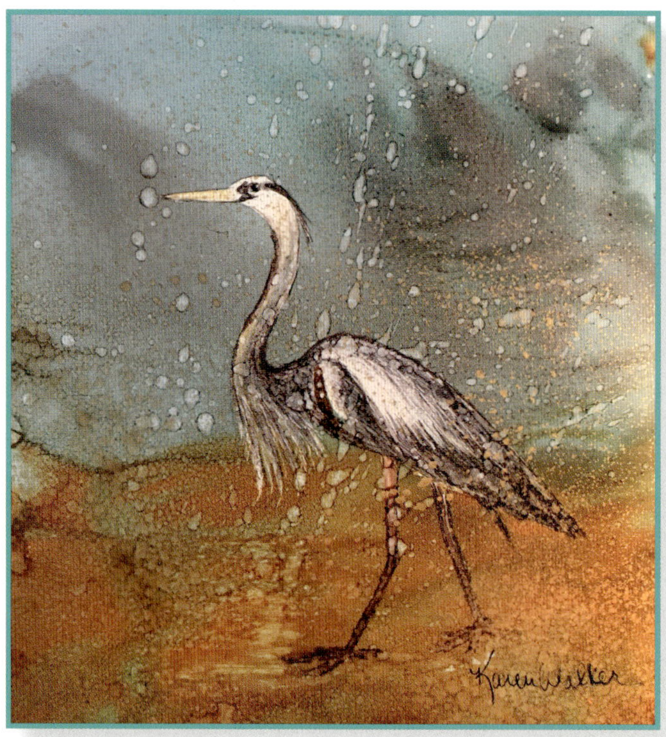

Karen Walker. *Heron Splash.*
The directional alcohol splatter suggests a bird splashing through puddles.

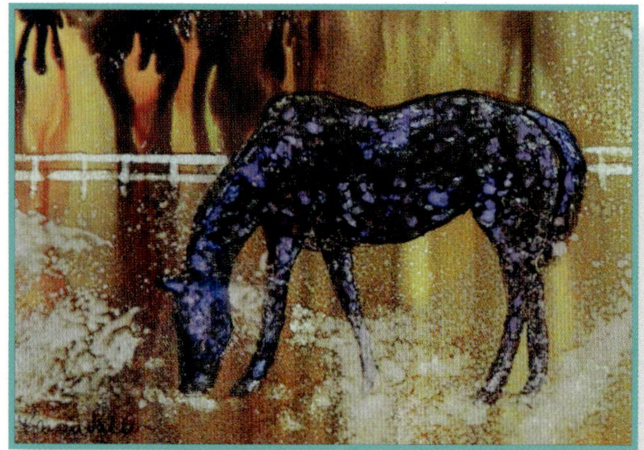

Karen Walker. *Purple Horse.*
Splattered gold ink is used as a decorative element.

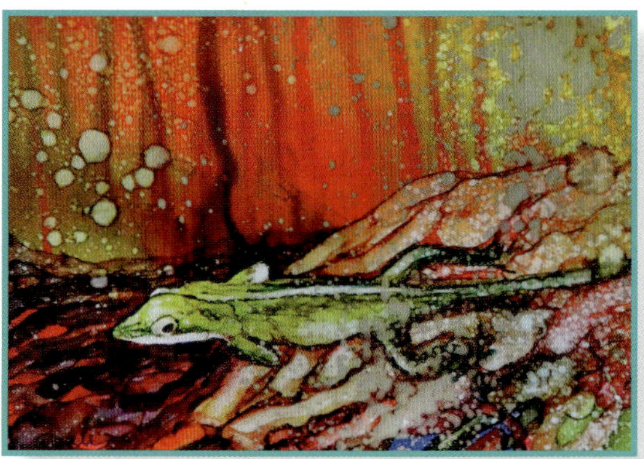

Karen Walker. *Little Lizard.*
Both splattered ink and alcohol form textures throughout this piece.

Masking

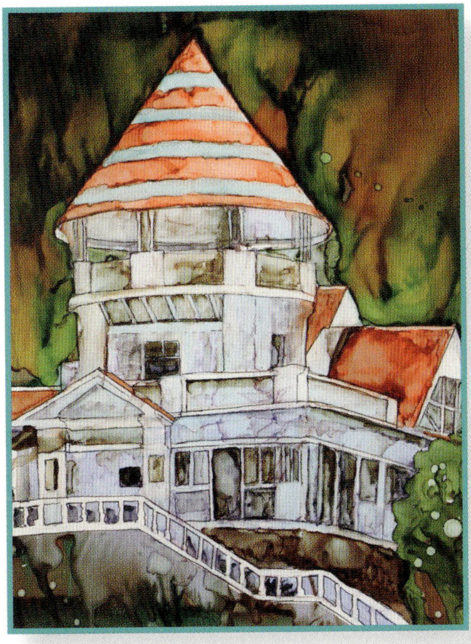

Karen Walker. *Holly Hill House.*
Here, the entire house was masked.

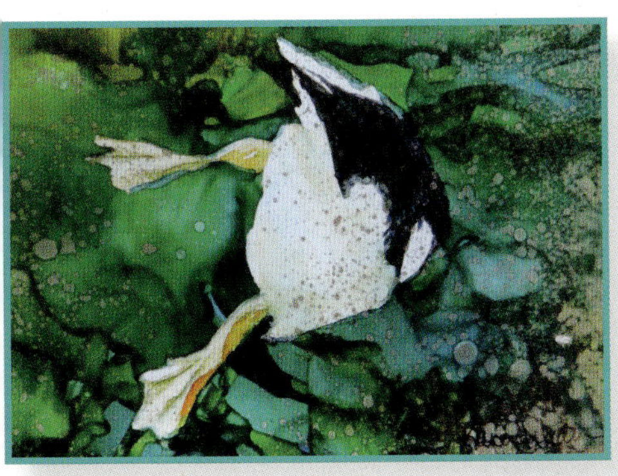

Karen Walker. *Duck!*
The white and detailed areas of the duck are masked prior to inking.

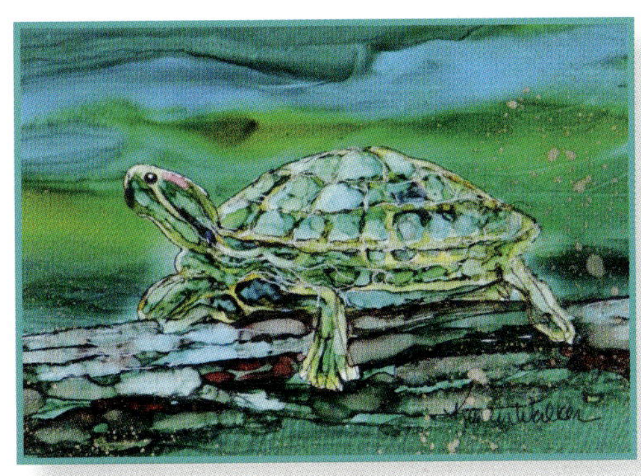

Karen Walker. *Shandisaurus.*
Masking was optional for this piece, but convenient for preserving the outlines.

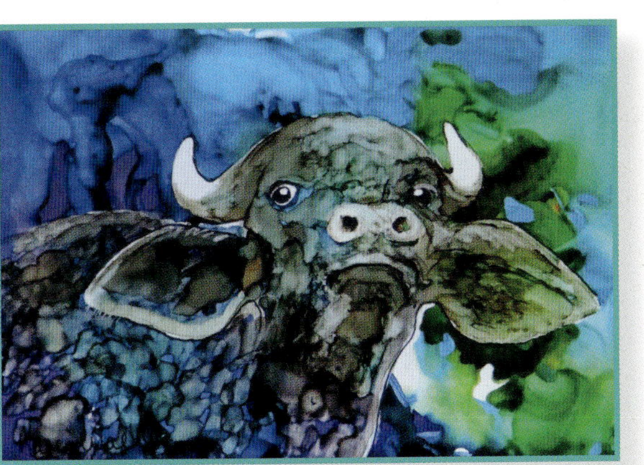

Karen Walker. *Water Buffalo.*
While only the white horns needed be masked, masking was also used for the key lines and facial features.

Lifting

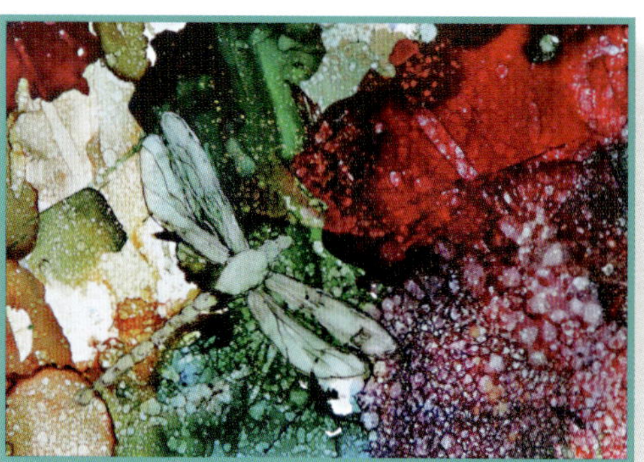

Karen Walker. *Dragonfly.*
A dragonfly is lifted out of a complex inky background.

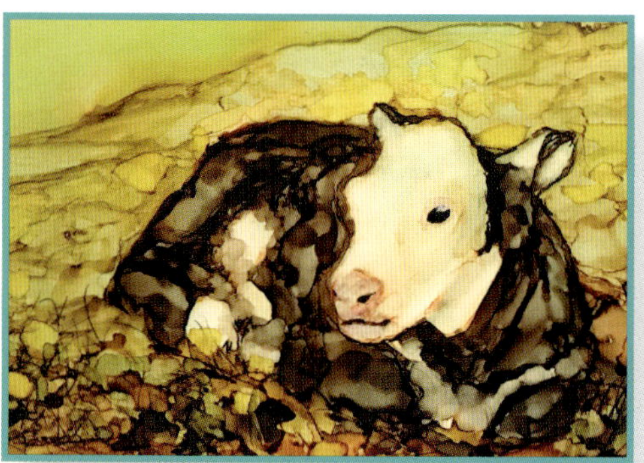

Karen Walker. *Lazy Days.*
The cow is lifted out of the background. The light areas show the warm stain on the paper, while the darker areas are painted in with brown ink.

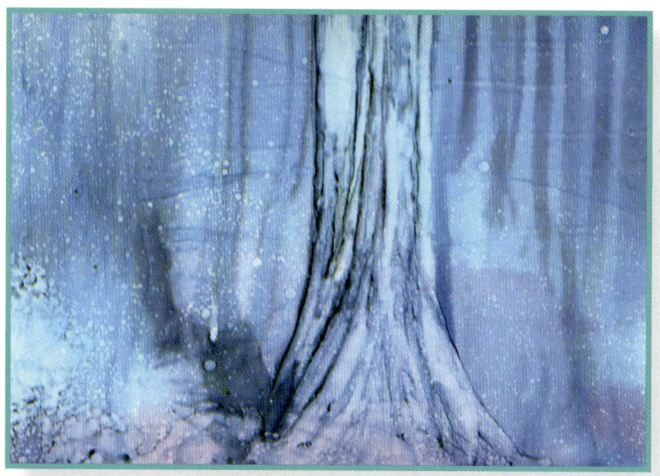

Karen Walker. *Winter Trees.*
The ink flow pattern suggested a wintry landscape, which was enhanced by lifting out the trees with alcohol.

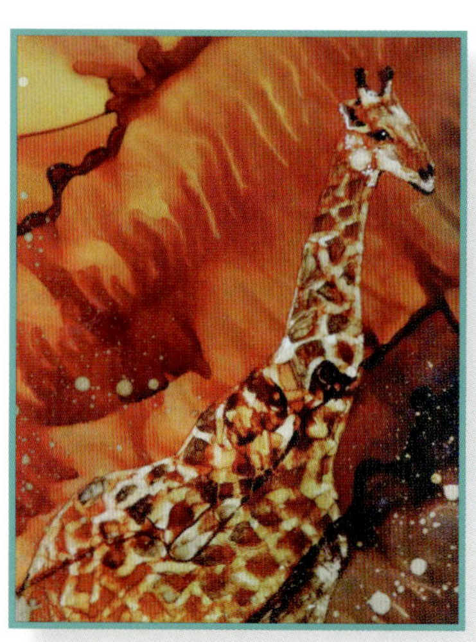

Karen Walker. *Giraffe.*
The giraffe's distinctive pattern was created by lifting out the light lines.

Karen Walker. *Five Blue Irises.*
Lifting is used to create lines and textures in the irises.

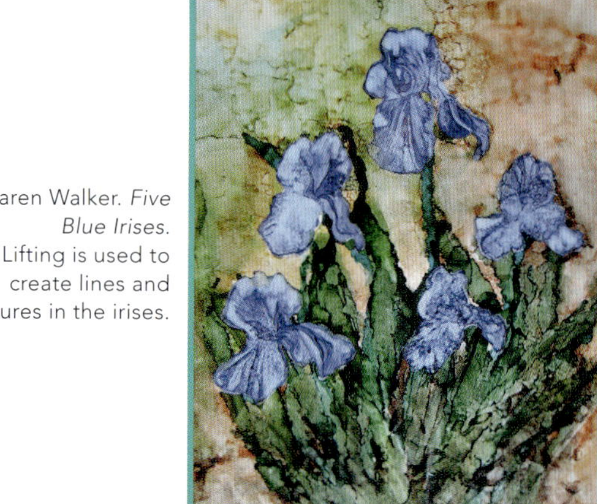

Brushwork

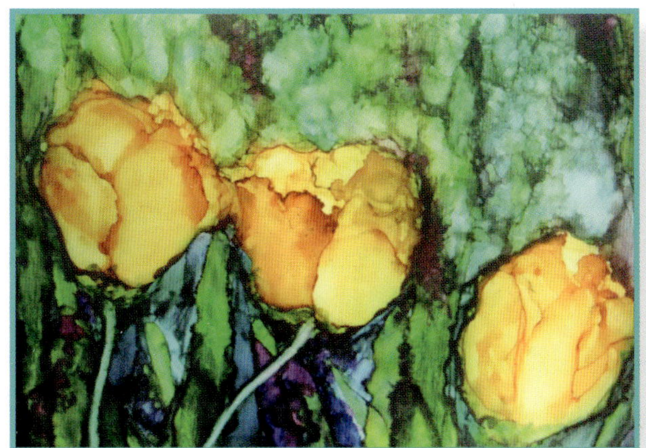

Karen Walker. *Three Yellow Tulips.*
The drop-and-guide method is used to create vibrant, smooth petals for the tulips.

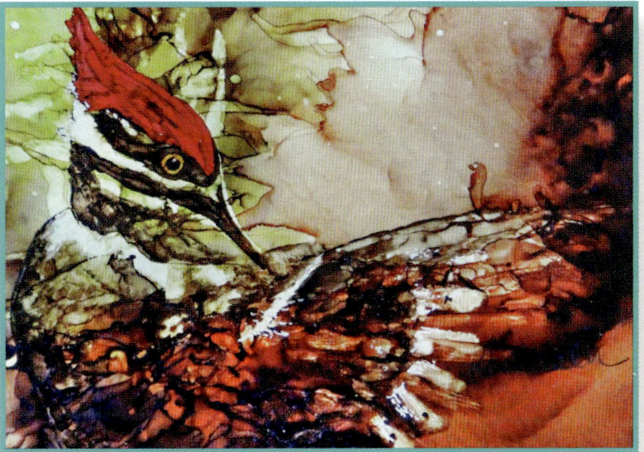

Karen Walker. *Woodpecker II.*
The brush and ink are used to paint in the woodpecker. The background is incorporated as much as possible.

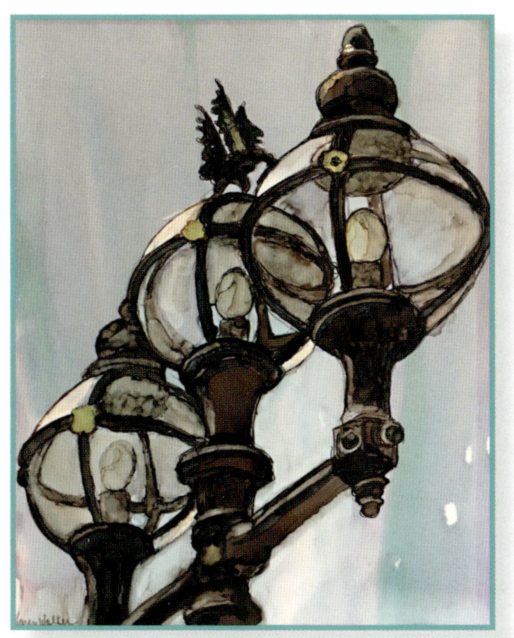

Karen Walker. *Street Lamps.*
Controlled brushwork is required to ink the lamps.

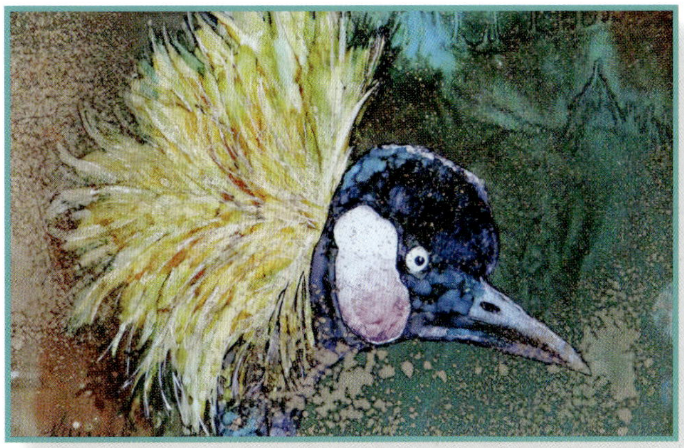

Karen Walker. *Crested Crane.*
The different textures of the crested crane require several styles of brushwork.

Fine-Tipped Pens and Alcohol Ink Markers

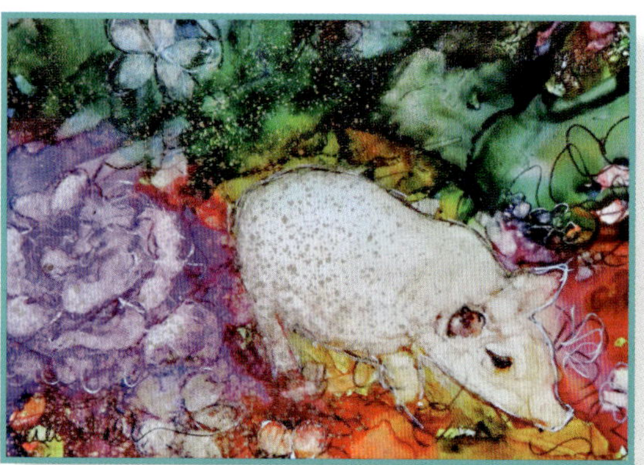

Karen Walker. *Sprightly Spring Piglet.*
Both white and black pens were used for decorative patterning.

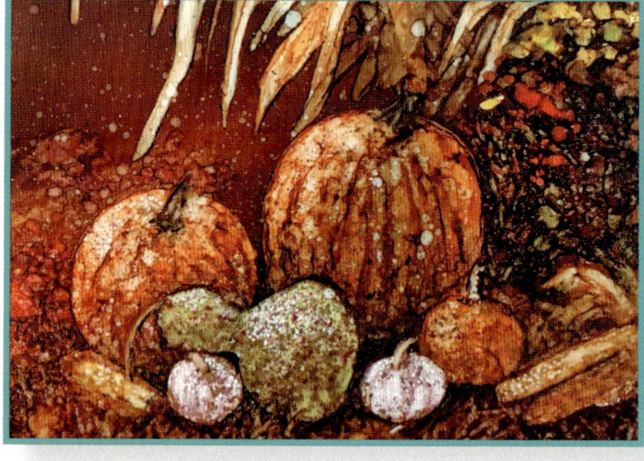

Karen Walker. *Autumn Scene.*
Alcohol ink markers are used to lift the strands of straw and to add controlled color throughout the piece.

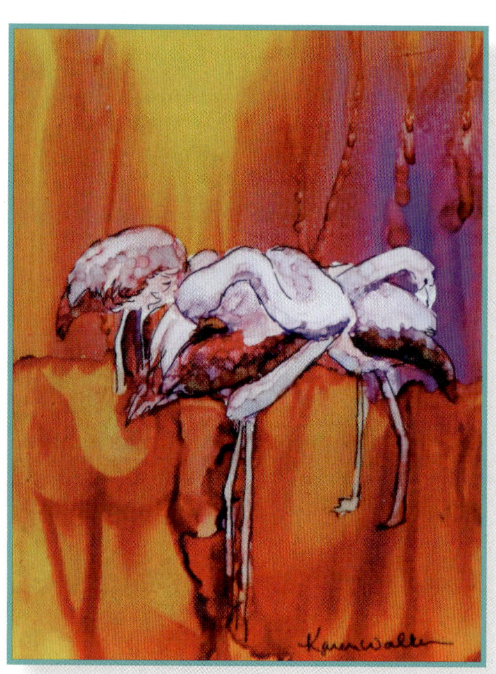

Karen Walker. *Red Hot Flamingos.*
The black pen is used to define the outlines of the birds.

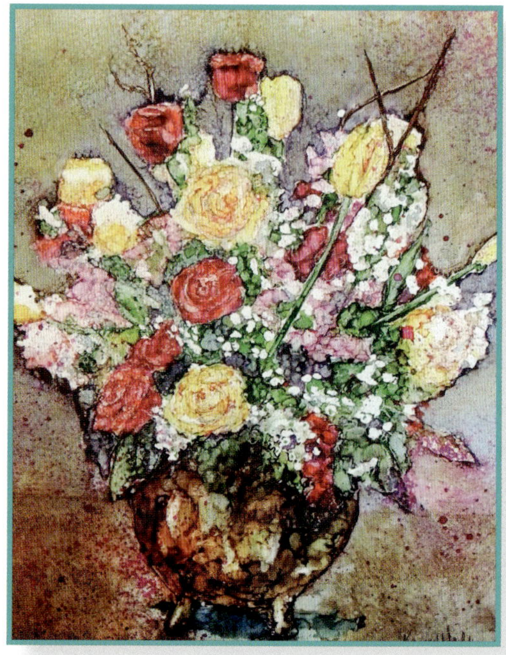

Karen Walker. *Formal Arrangement.*
The initial layers of color in the flowers are added with markers. They are later intensified with the ink applied by the brush.

Fine-Tipped Pens and Alcohol Ink Markers Continued...

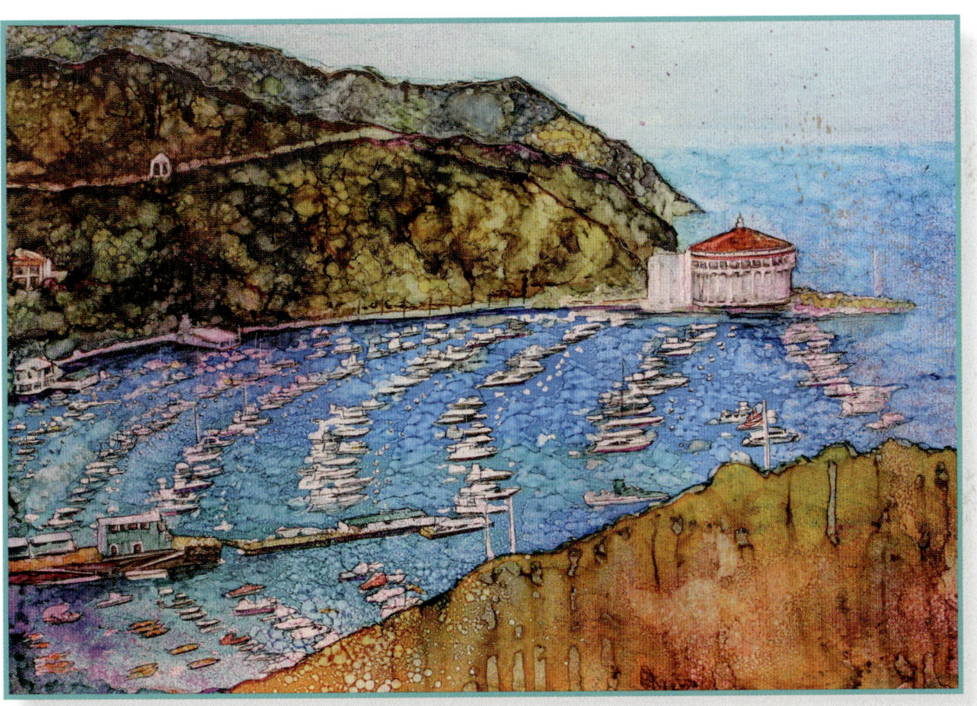

Karen Walker. *Avalon Bay.*
The boats and buildings are drawn in with pen in this large painting of Avalon Bay.

3 Florals

From single blossoms and flowering plants to gardens and bouquets, florals are wonderful subjects for alcohol ink painting. These five projects offer a variety of backgrounds and techniques.

Dogwoods: Inky background with masking

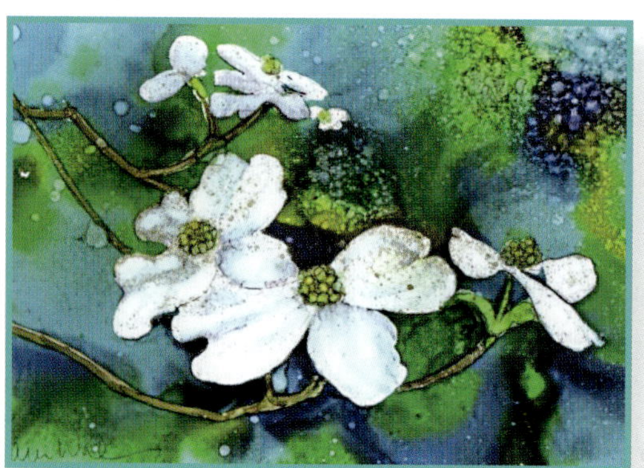

Hibiscus: White background with direct painting

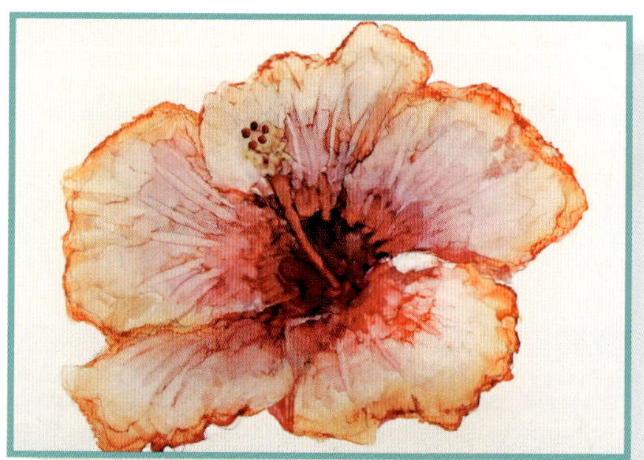

Blue Iris: Solid black background with a double-masking technique

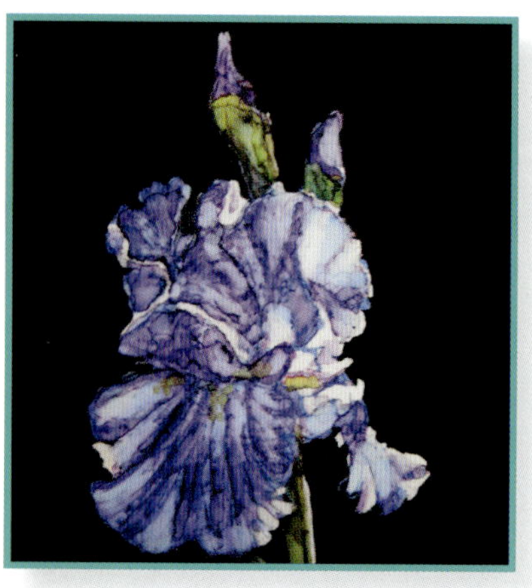

Cottage Garden: Inky background with lifting and a small amount of masking

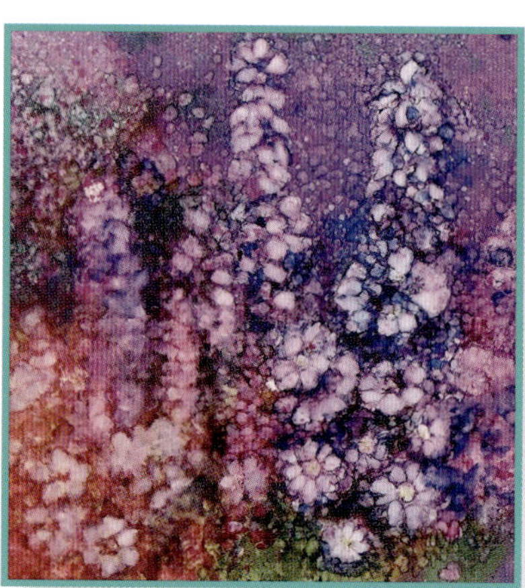

Bird of Paradise: Inky background with lifting

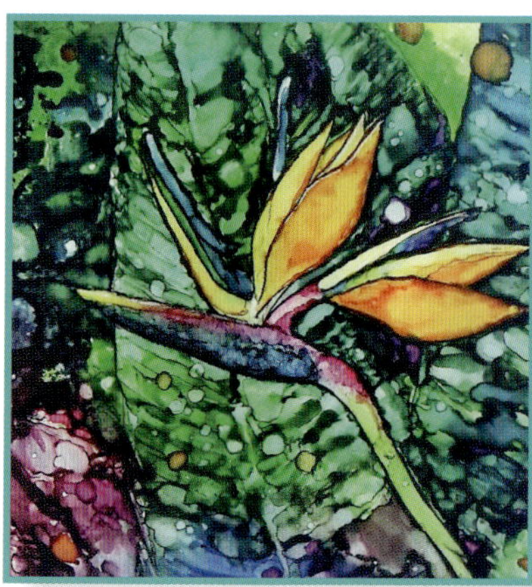

Project 3 - Dogwoods

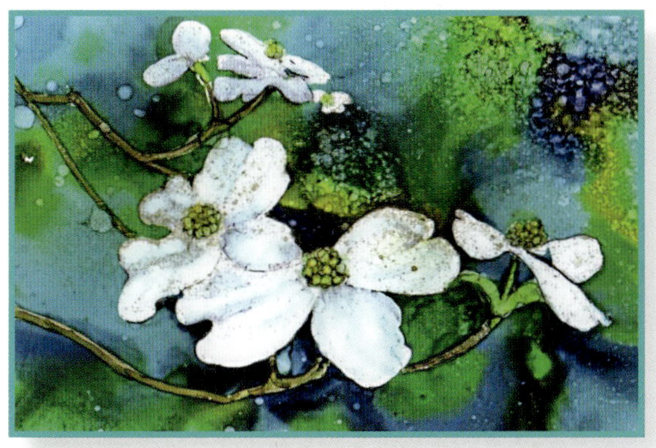

Karen Walker. *Dogwoods.*

As a North Carolinian, I love painting dogwoods, our state flower. In this project, the blossoms and branches are masked entirely. The background ink layer is loosely added, and the flowers are painted in.

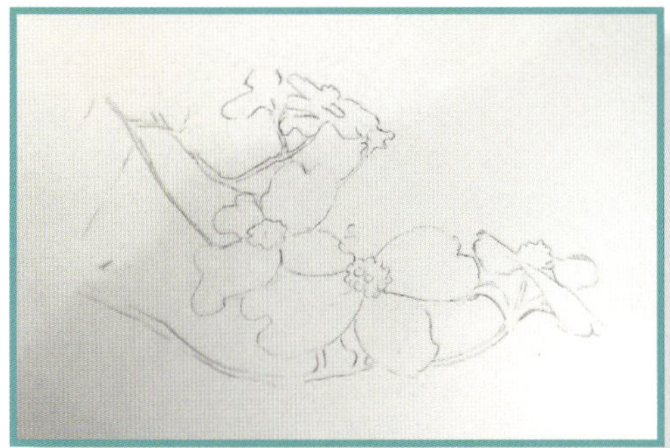

1. Lightly sketch the outline of the dogwood blossoms and branches in pencil.

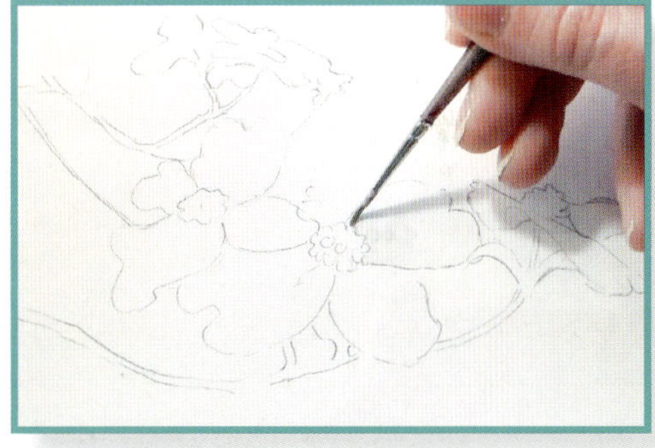

2. Apply masking fluid by using a small brush to the blossoms and the branches. Let dry.

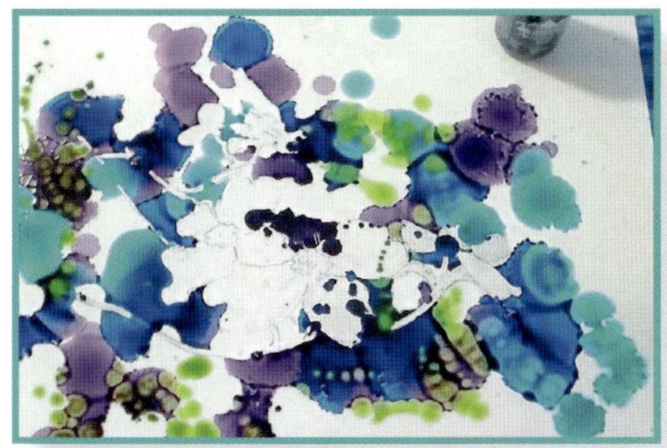

3. Add the background by dropping various colors of ink.

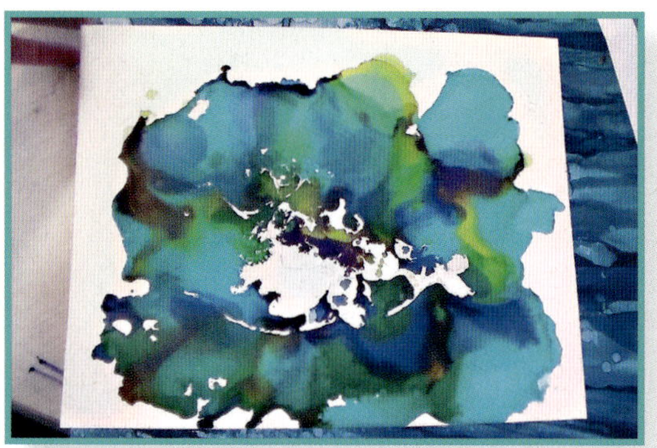

4. After inking, use the small brush to fill in any small gaps. Allow to fully dry.

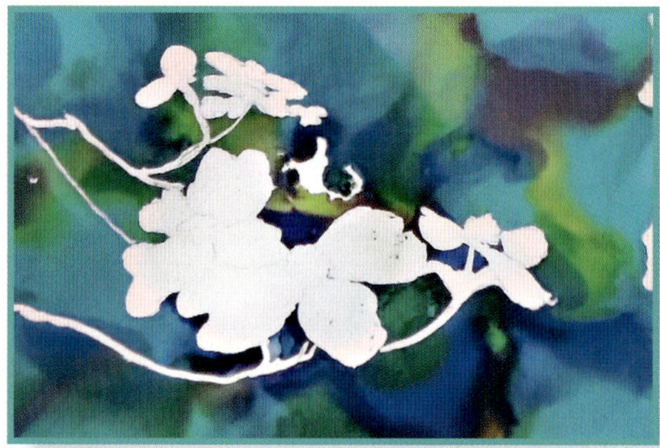

5. Remove the masking fluid.

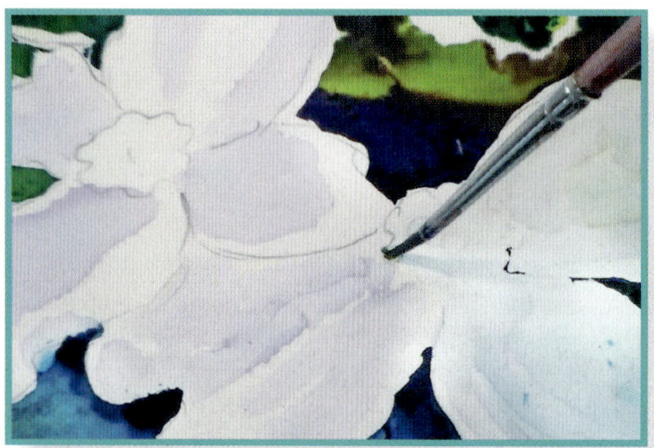

6. Using the brush and ink dispensed in the welled palette, tone the white flowers. Add a first layer of color to the center of the blossom.

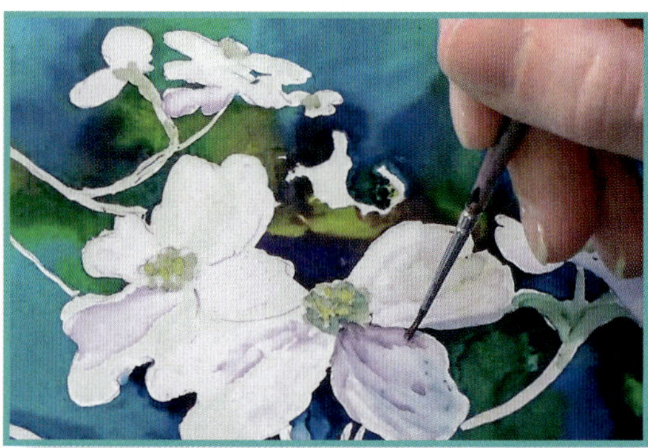

7. Slowly build up color and soften any unwanted hard edges by using the brush and alcohol.

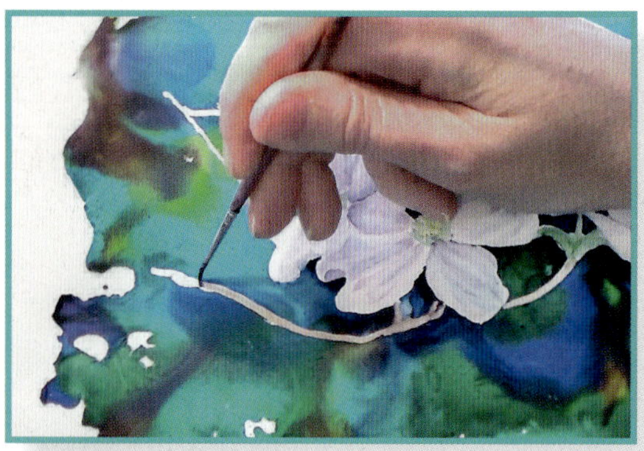

8. Brush in the branches and dark areas in the blossoms.

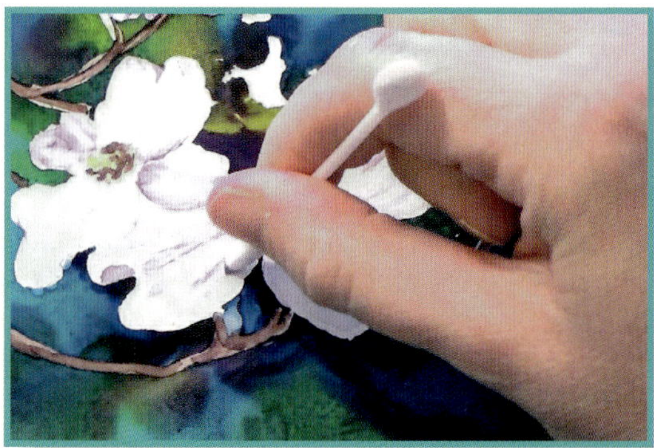

9. Add highlights by lifting ink, using the cotton swab and alcohol.

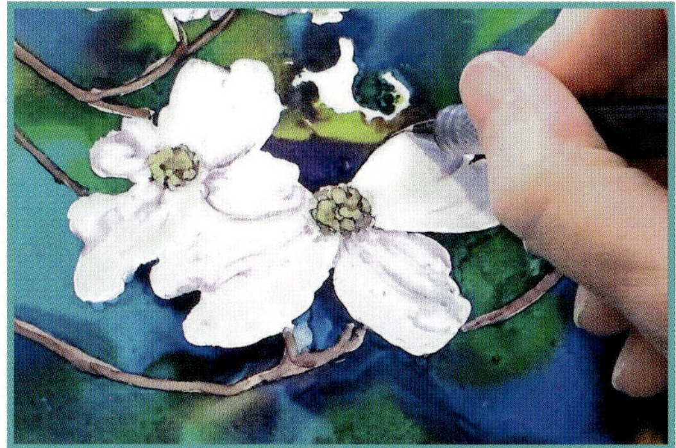

10. Define the edges and details with the fine-tipped pen.

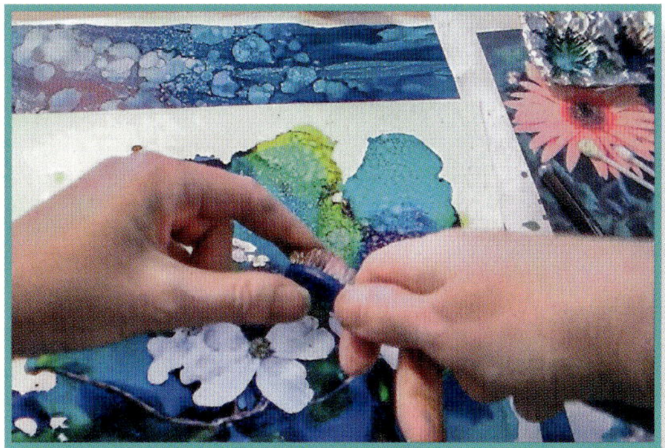

11. Fill in gaps in the background and add texture by dabbing with the cotton ball and splattering ink and alcohol using a toothbrush selectively across the painting.

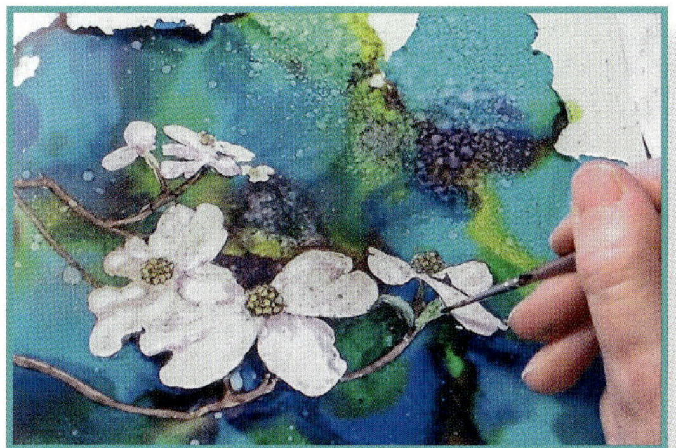

12. Make final adjustments with the brush and pens.

Variation: Spring Blossoms

Karen Walker. *Spring Blossoms.* The steps presented for the *Dogwoods* may be used to paint any tree with pale blossoms. Here the color palette is switched to pinks and purples.

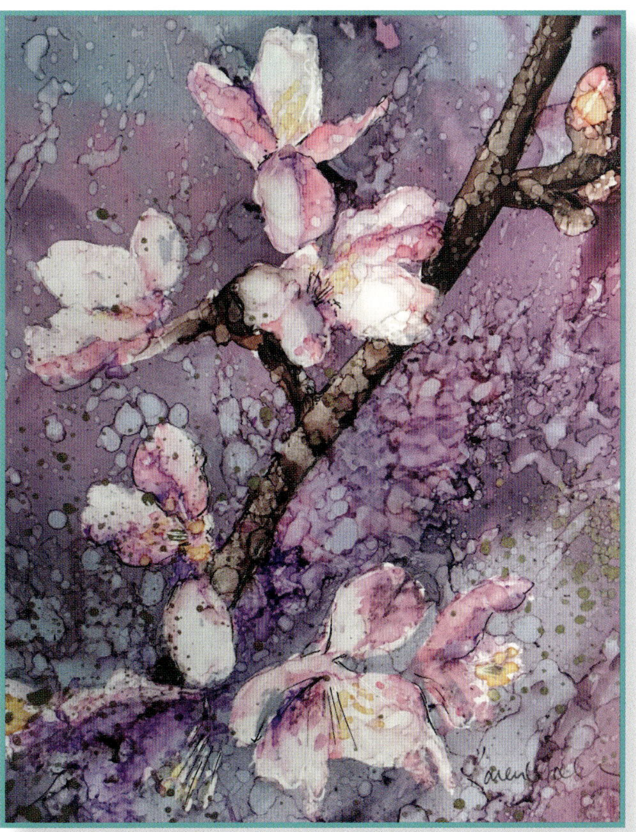

Project 4 - Bird of Paradise

Karen Walker. *Bird of Paradise*.

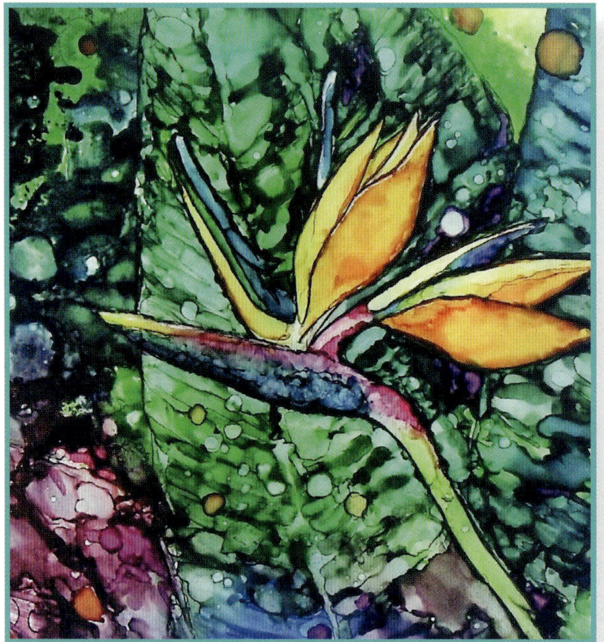

Bird of Paradise was created by lifting the flower from an inky abstract background. This is one of my favorite techniques for highlighting both the inkiness of the alcohol inks and the subjects, which seamlessly emerge from the background.

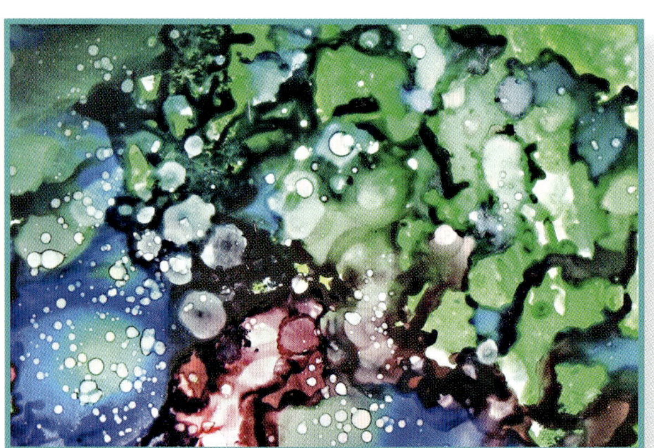

1. Create an inky jungle background.

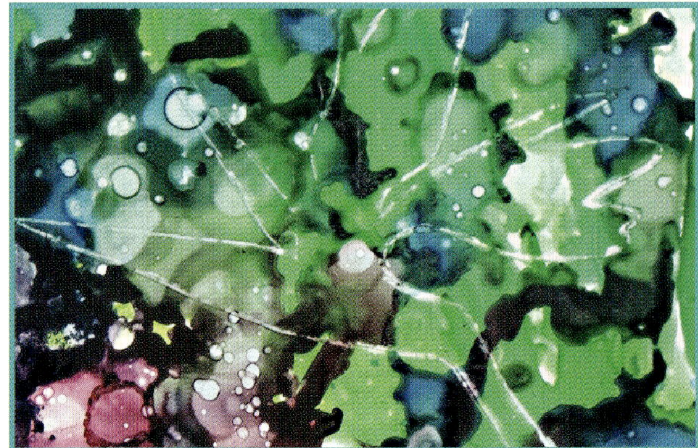

2. Use the brush or marker to sketch out the area to be lifted.

3. Using alcohol, lift the background ink with the cotton swab and the brush. Leave some of the background ink in the dark areas of the subject to create unity.

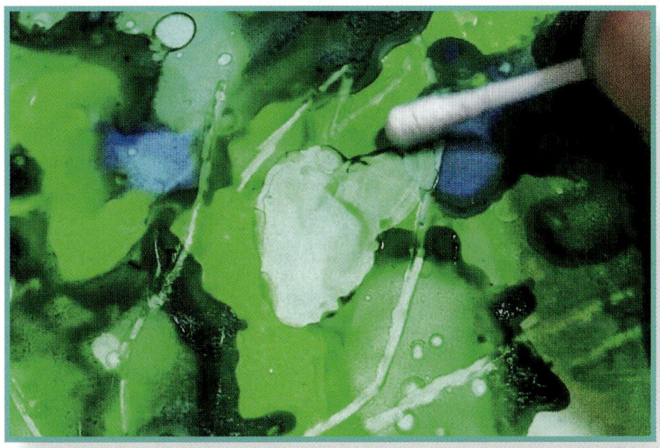

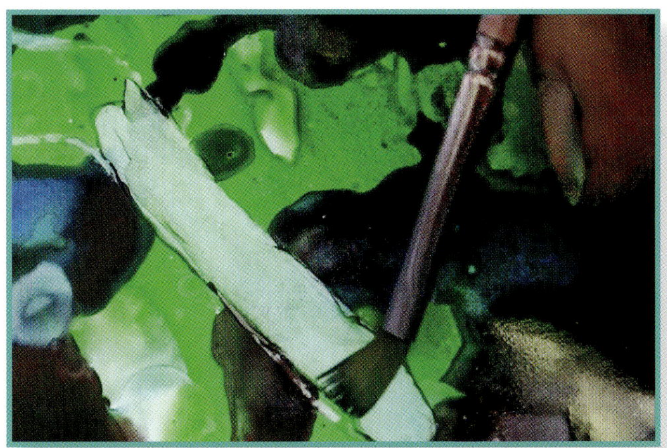

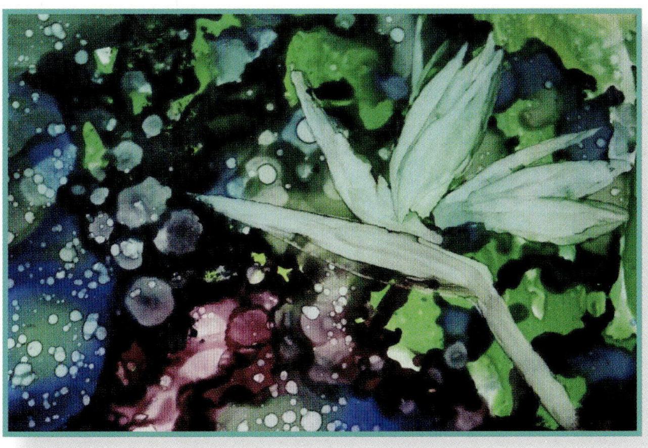

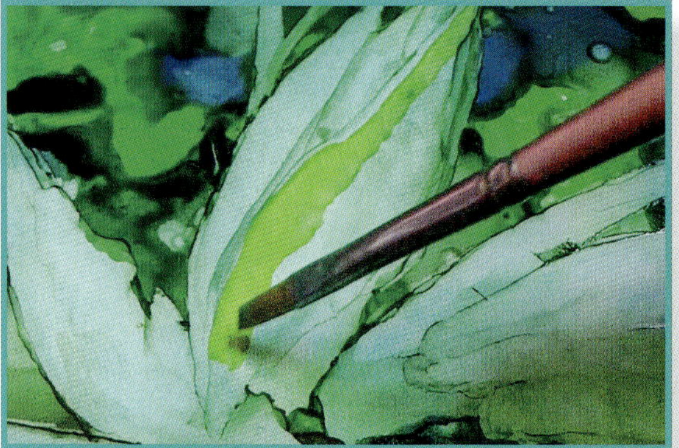

4. Once as much ink has been lifted as possible, add in yellow ink with the brush.

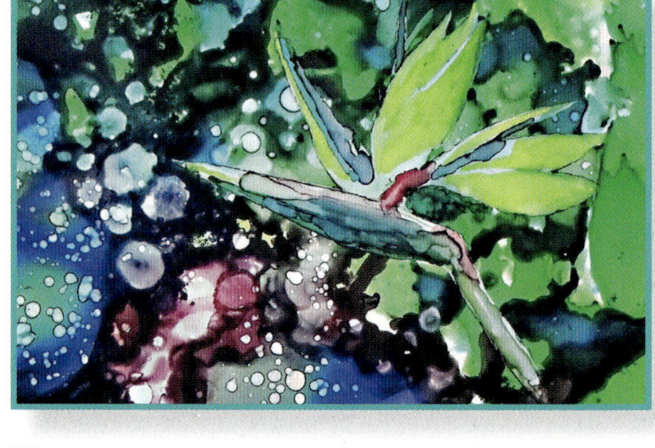

5. Continue adding ink with the brush.

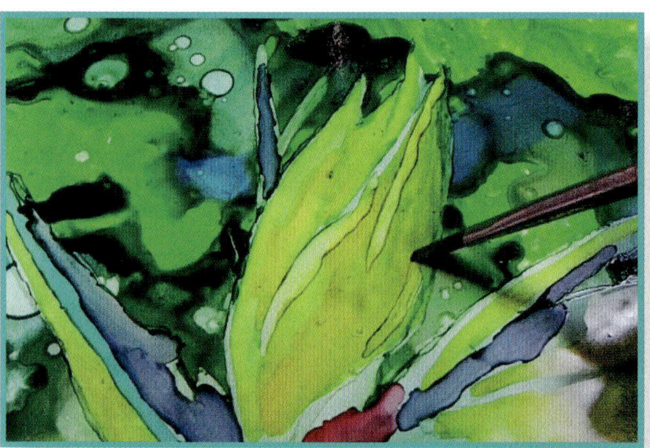

6. Create highlights by lifting ink with alcohol and the brush.

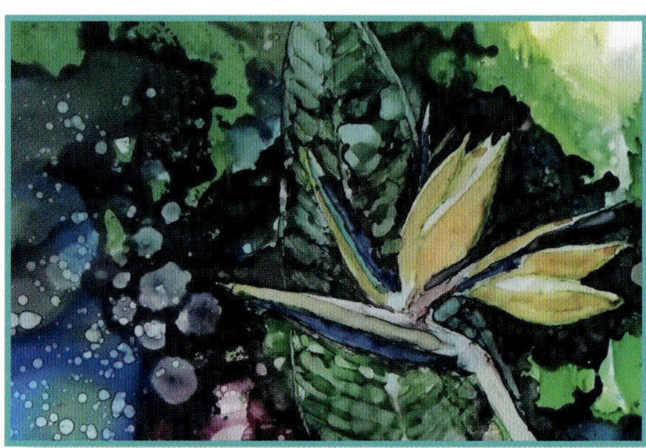

7. Lift out the leaf in the background by using the brush and alcohol.

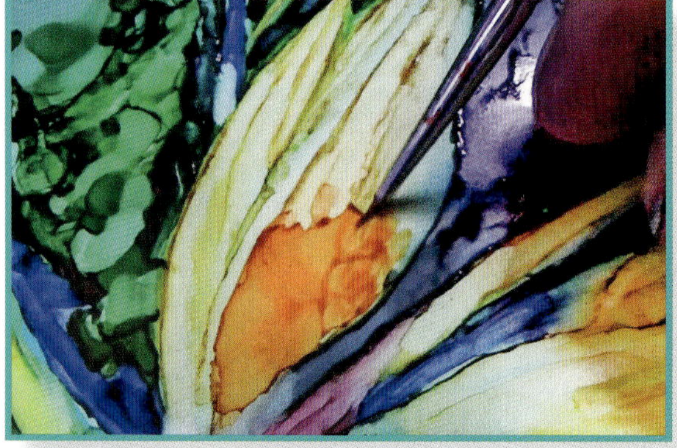

8. Intensify the ink. To create smooth areas of ink, use the drop-and-guide method by dropping the ink from the bottle and directing the edges with the brush while the ink is still wet.

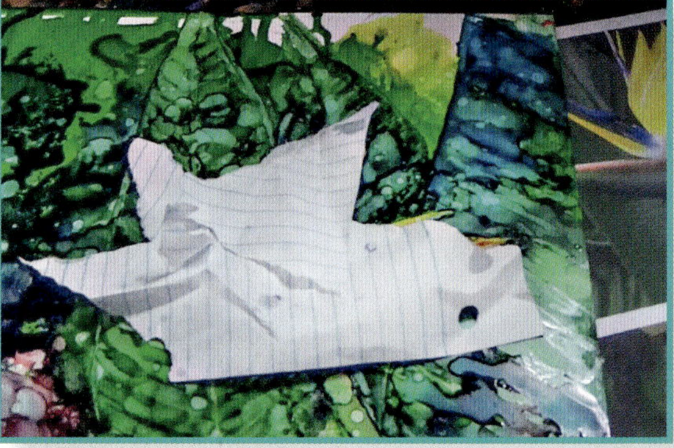

9. Splatter blending solution or alcohol over the painting. Lay irregular pieces of paper over the blossom to protect it from the splattering.

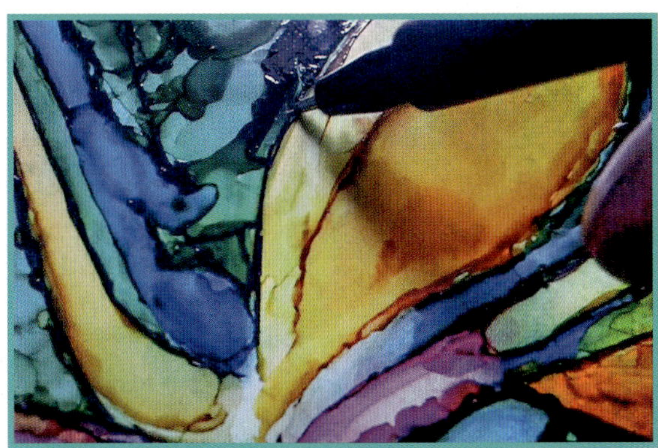

10. Add definition with the fine-tipped pen.

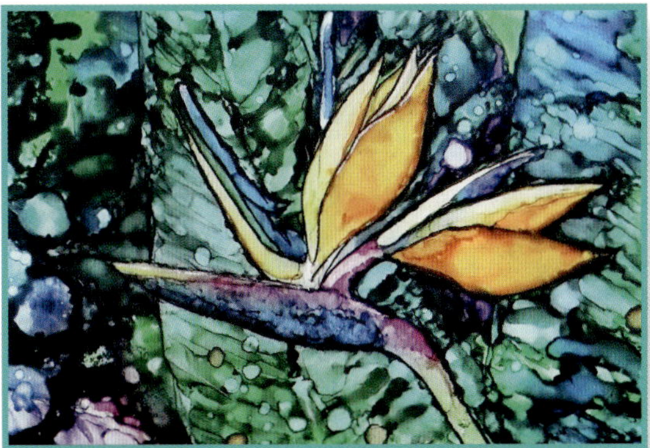

11. Finalize by adding dots of color into the background and making last adjustments.

Variation: Wisteria

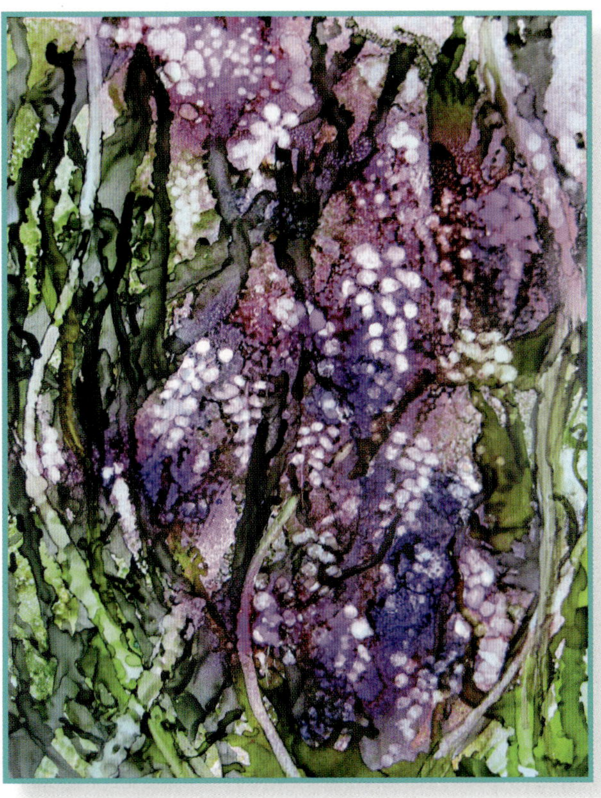

Karen Walker. *Wisteria*.
While the *Bird of Paradise* was entirely lifted, a few lines and highlights of Wisteria were masked. The resulting paintings are similarly inky and emergent from the background.

Project 5 - Hibiscus

Karen Walker. *Hibiscus*.

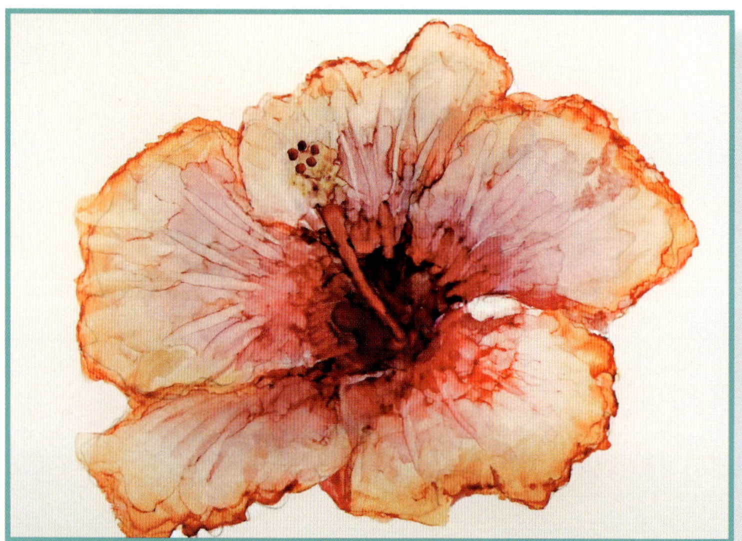

For me, directly painting on Yupo® and leaving a white background is very difficult. The challenge is to keep the paper clean and the ink under control, while still painting loosely. For a painterly feel, blend inks wet-in-wet.

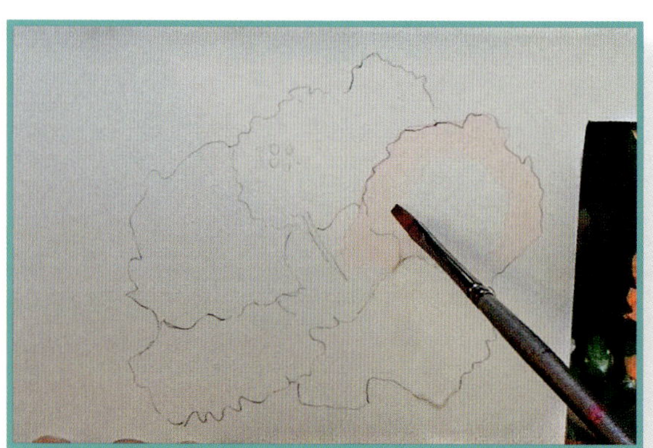

1. Beginning with a very lightly sketched outline, add the first layer of pale ink with the brush.

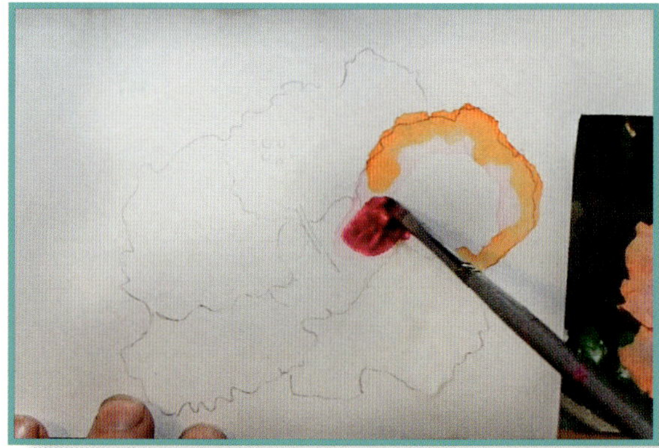

2. Add in several more colors, allowing them to blend while the inks are still wet.

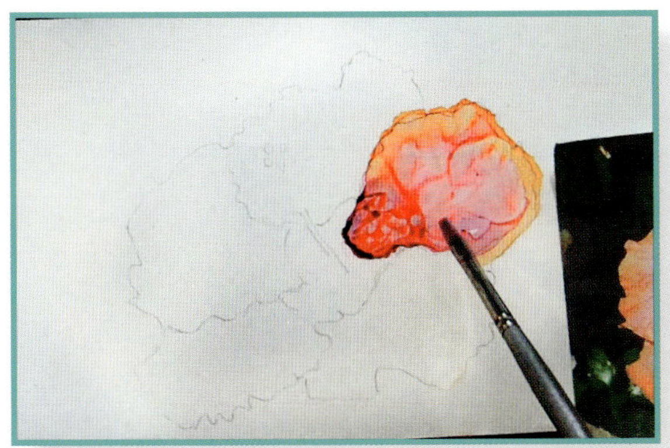

3. Brush in a small amount of alcohol to lighten, blend, and add inky textures to the petal.

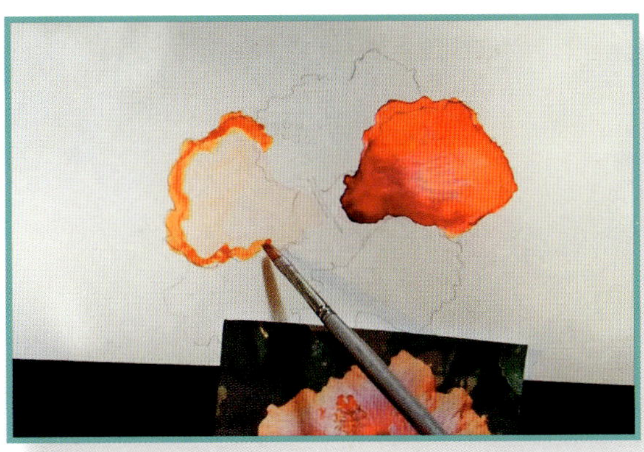

4. Repeat for the other four petals.

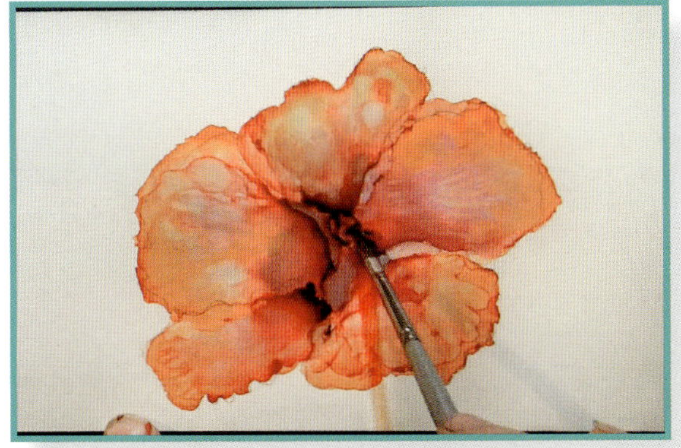

5. Create the center of the flower by adding in dark ink with the brush.

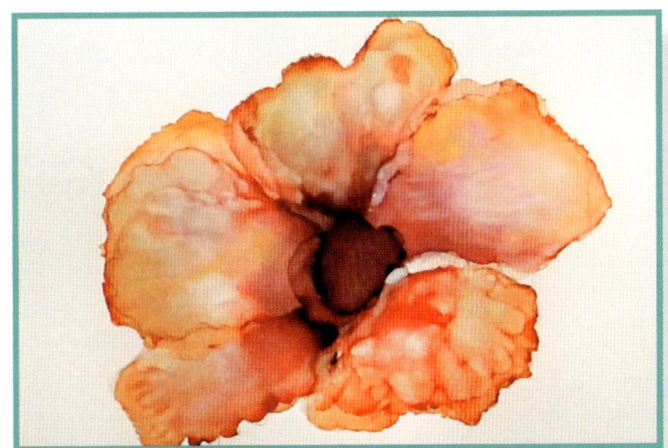

Hibiscus in progress...

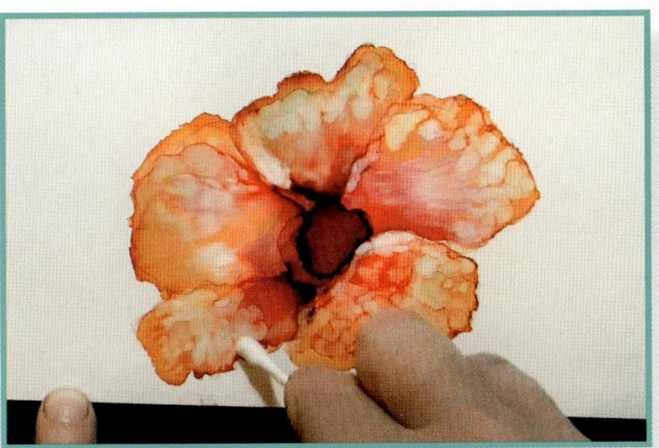

6. Use the cotton swab to lift ink to lighten, add texture, and create dimensionality.

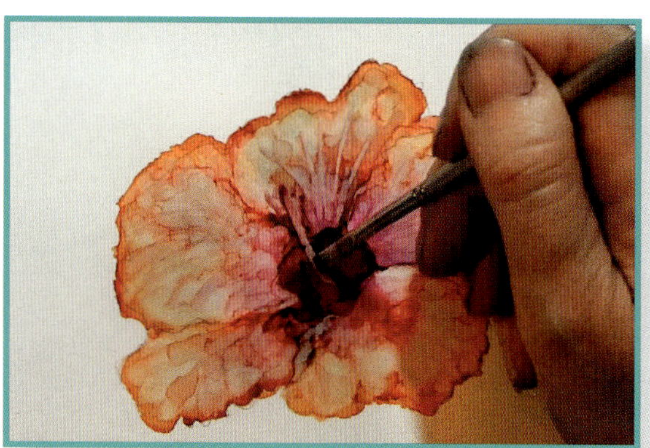

7. Use the brush to lift and add in the pistil.

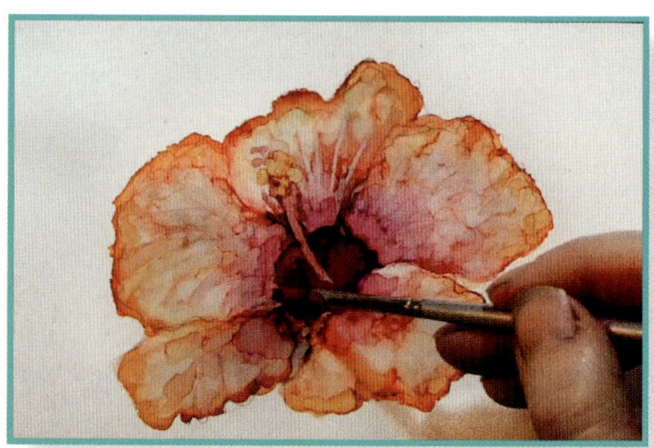

8. Paint in additional details with the small brush.

Variation: We Three Penguins

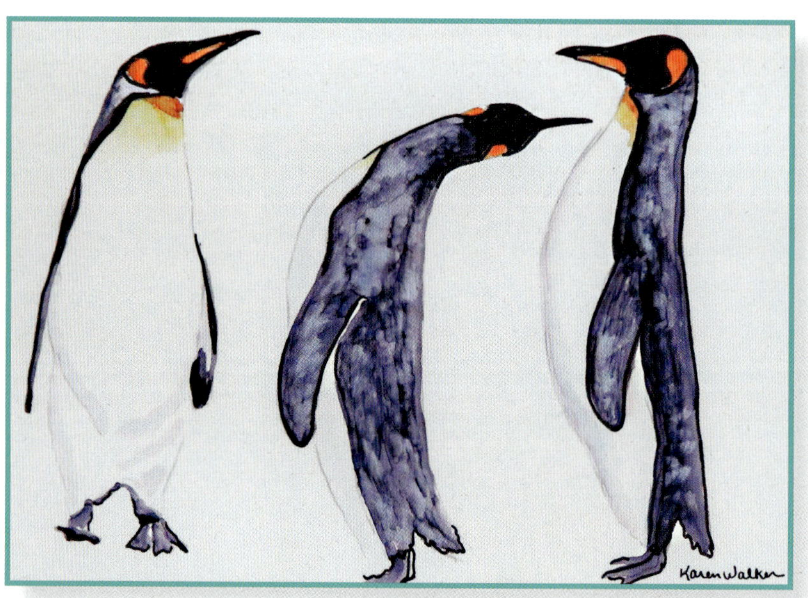

Karen Walker. *We Three Penguins.*
We Three Penguins also features a white background. Here, the brushwork was more straightforward but no less challenging to maintain the white paper.

Project 6 - Cottage Garden

Karen Walker. *Cottage Garden.*

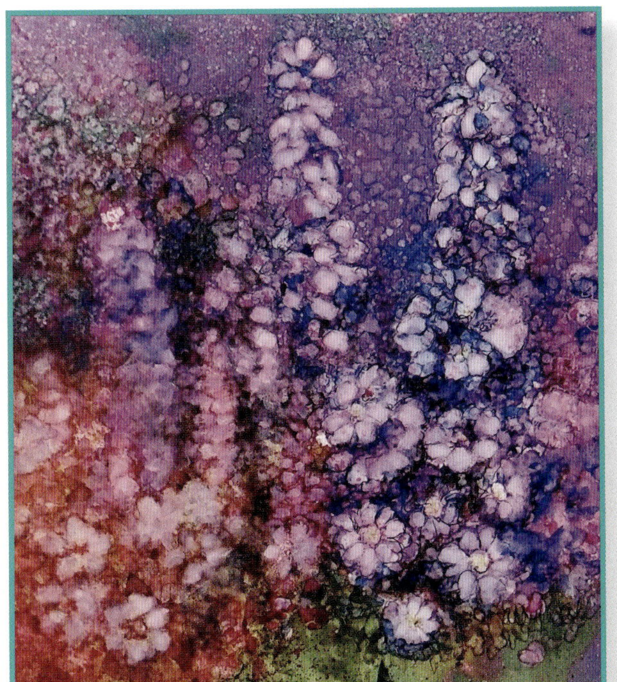

To capture the rambling feel of a cottage garden, small highlights of the flowers are masked, leaving the majority of the painting to be lifted out of the randomly colored background.

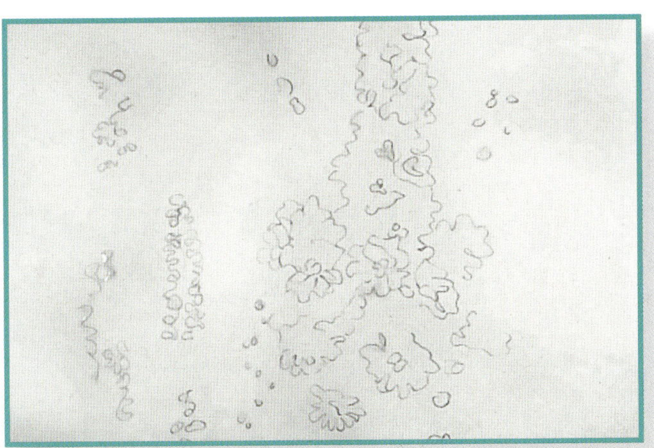

1. Lightly draw and partially mask the light areas of the flowers.

2. Create the background by splattering multiple colors of ink and using the cotton ball to blend.

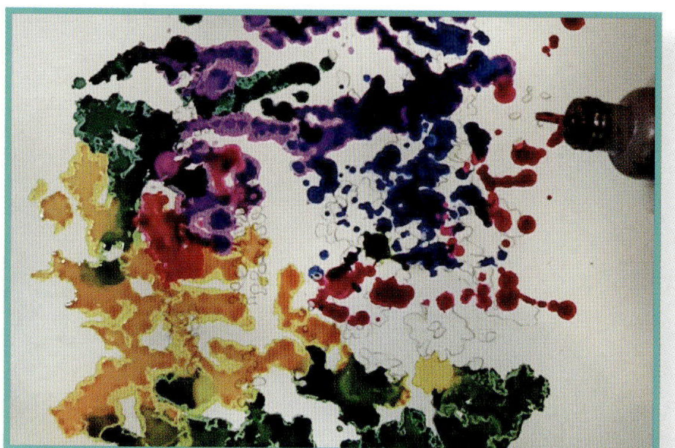

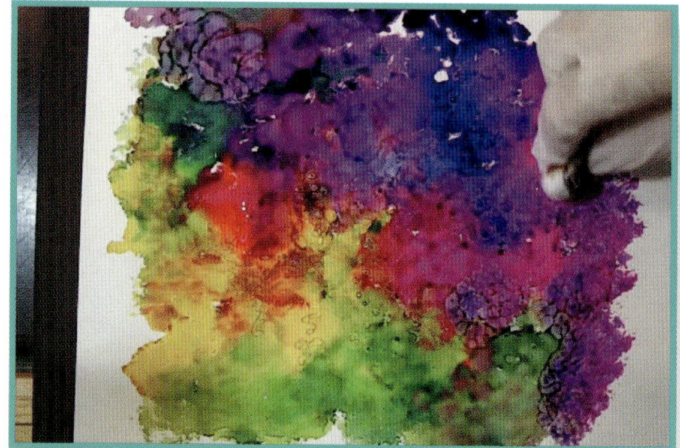

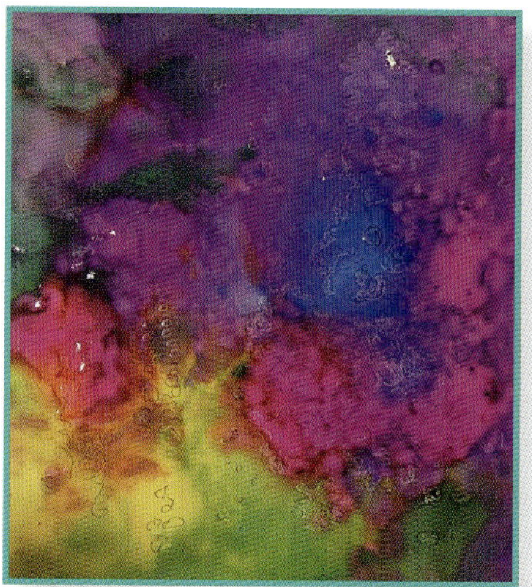

3. Let dry.

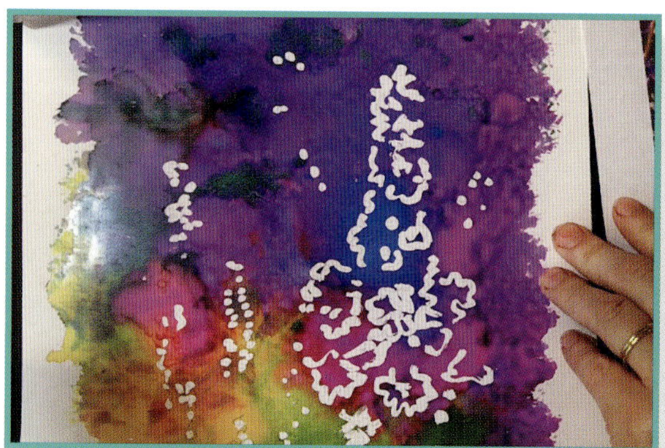

4. Remove the masking fluid.

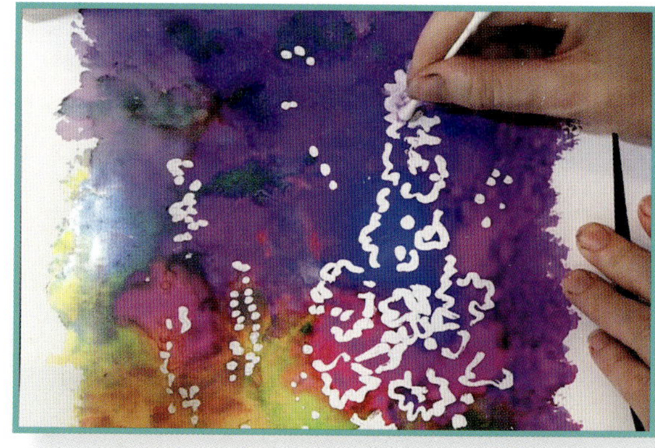

5. Use the cotton swab and alcohol to lift, blend, and create flowers.

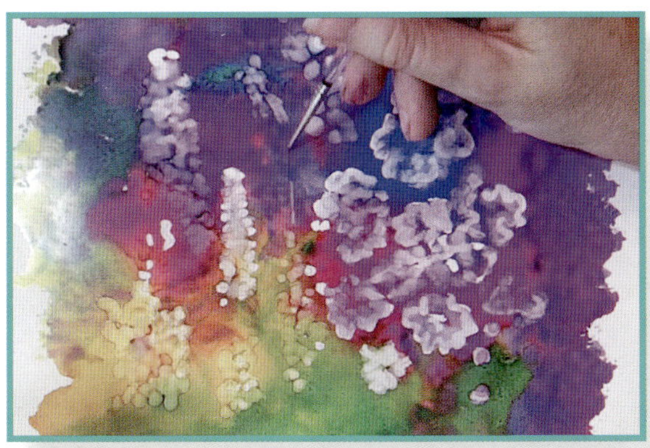

6. Use the brush and alcohol for finer lines.

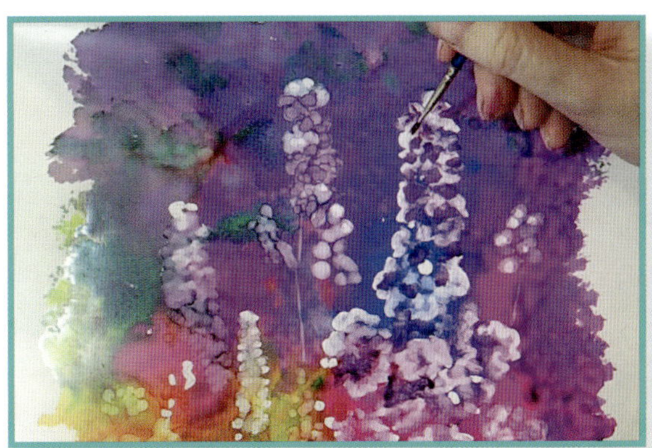

7. Add darks with the brush and purple ink.

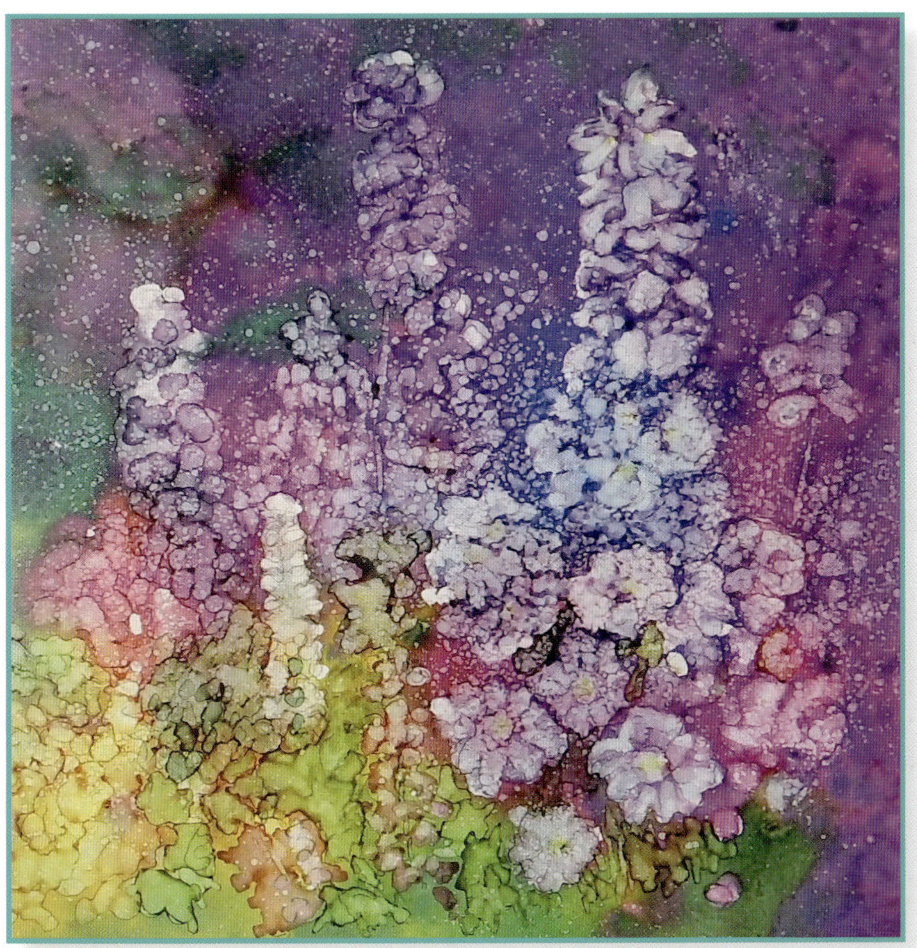

8. Splatter with alcohol.

Close-ups of Detail Work

9. Finish the painting by adding details and adjusting values.

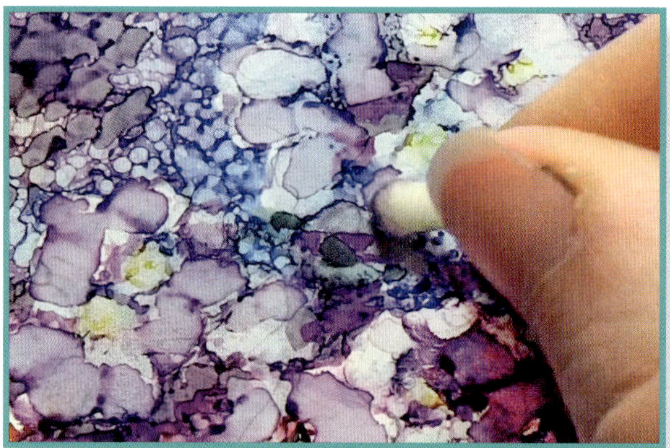

Lifting with the cotton swab

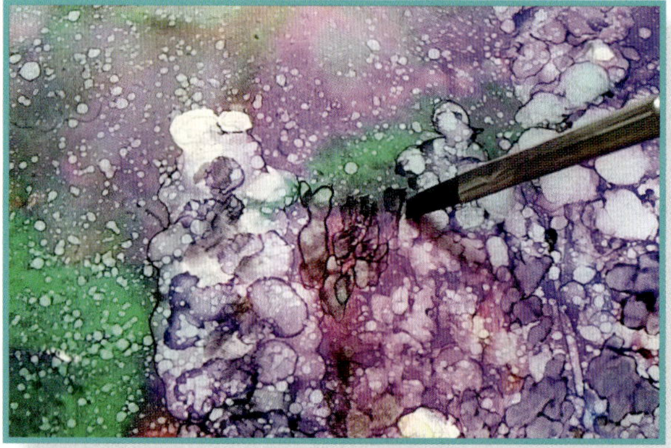

Adding darks with the brush

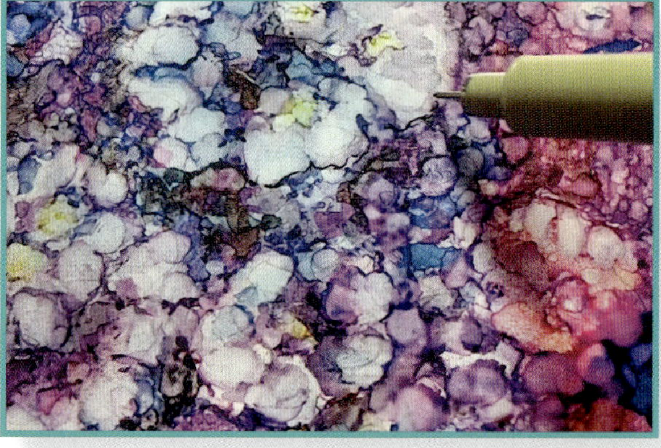

Fine lines with the black pen

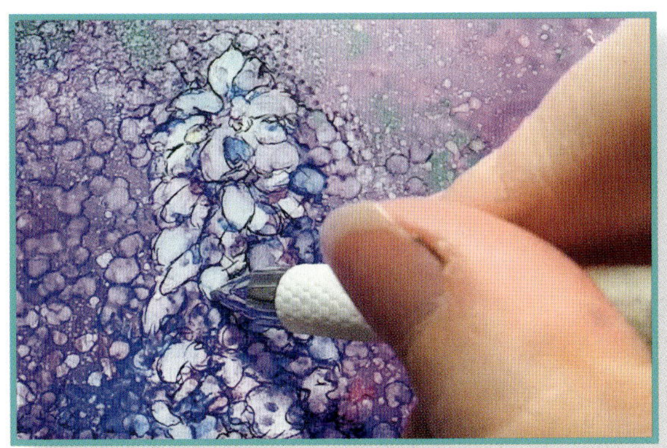

Fine Highlights with the white pen

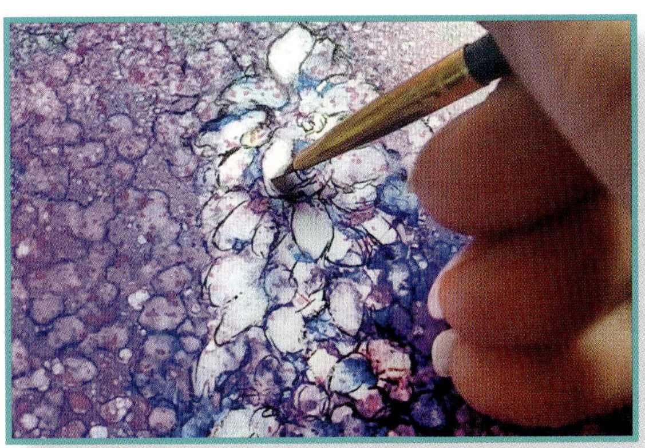

Intensifying the whites with opaque white ink

Variation: Two Euros

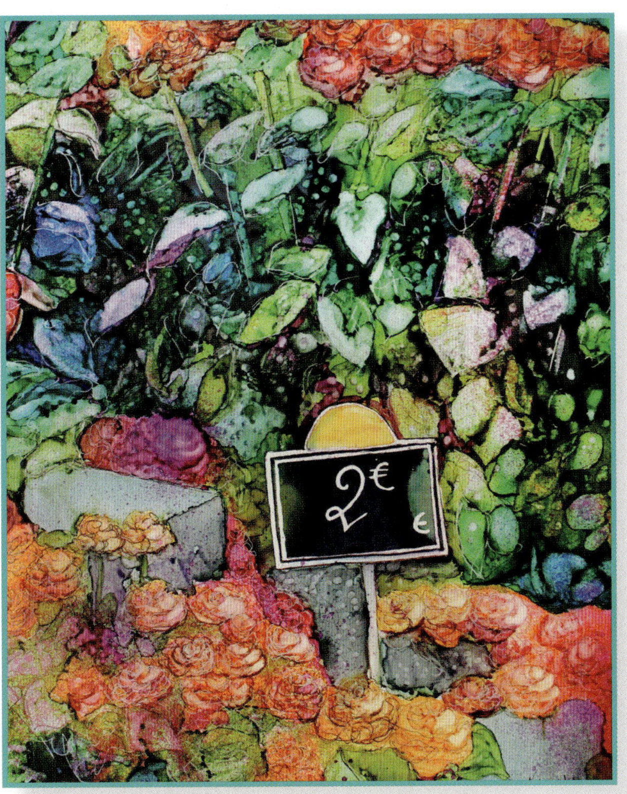

Karen Walker. *Two Euros*
The flower market at La Madeleine was the subject for *Two Euros*. Like *Cottage Garden*, the challenge was to create distinctive blossoms and a mass of flowers simultaneously.

Project 7 - Blue Iris

Karen Walker. *Blue Iris.*

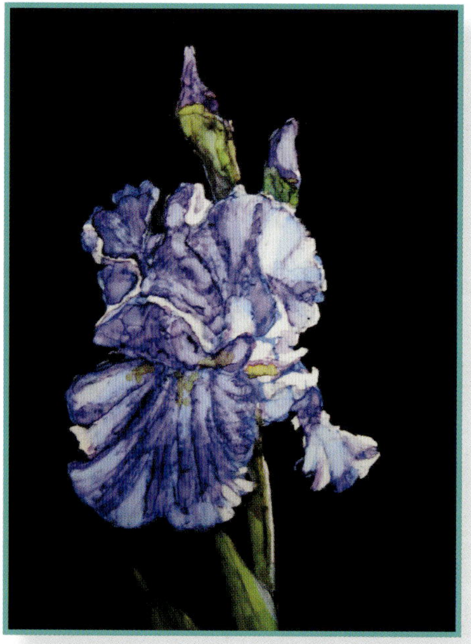

This project uses a technique of masking twice—once to preserve the whites, and a second time to preserve the pale blue under the black. While the black background is particularly dramatic, this same process would apply to any background you might choose.

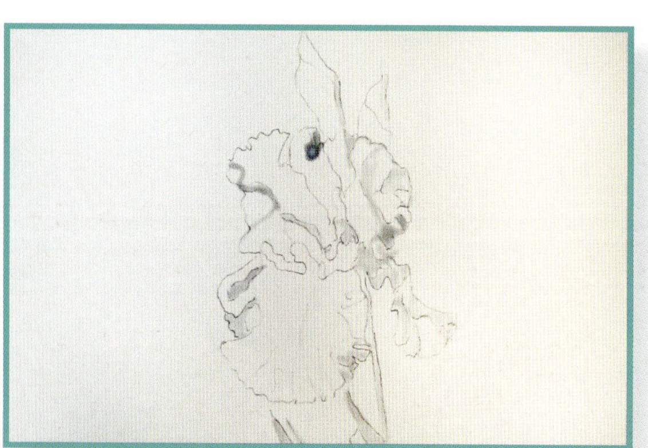

1. Lightly sketch the iris and mask the areas that are to remain white.

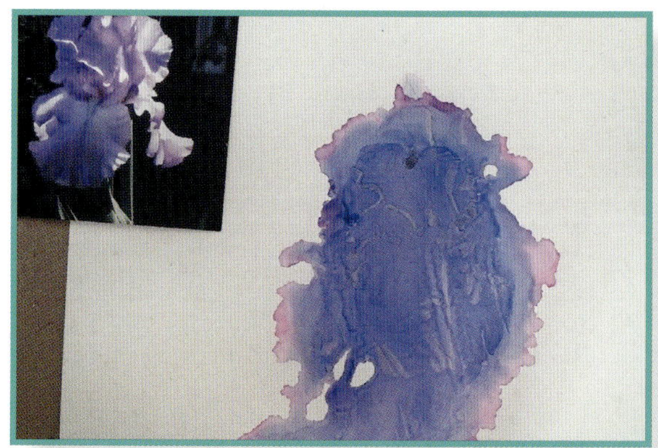

2. When the masking fluid is dry, cover the flower area with blue and purple ink.

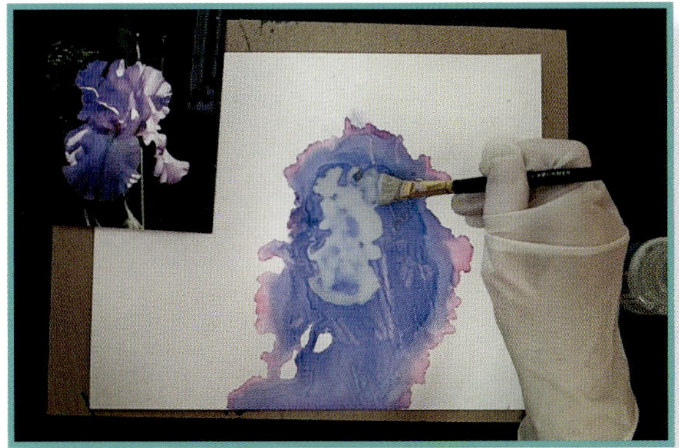

3. When the ink is completely dry, mask the entire iris with a thick layer of masking fluid.

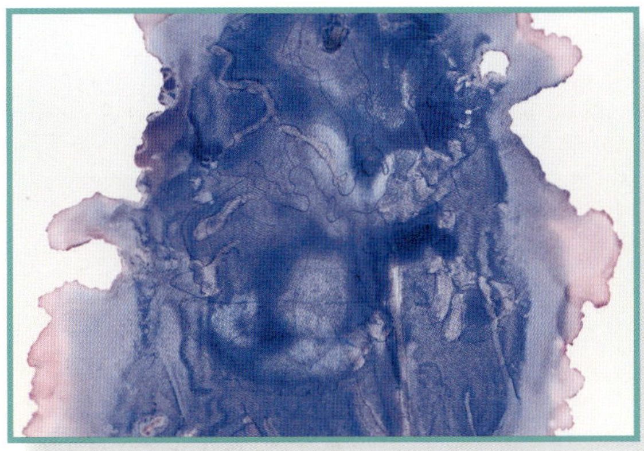

4. Let dry.

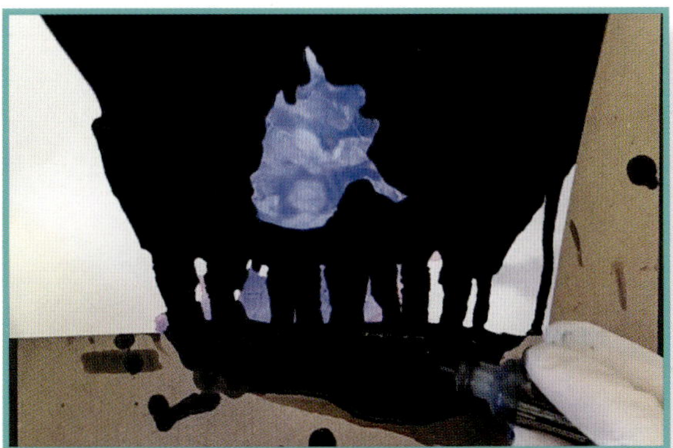

5. Cover the entire background with a thick, solid layer of black ink. While the masking fluid should protect the flower, it is still wiser to minimize inking over it.

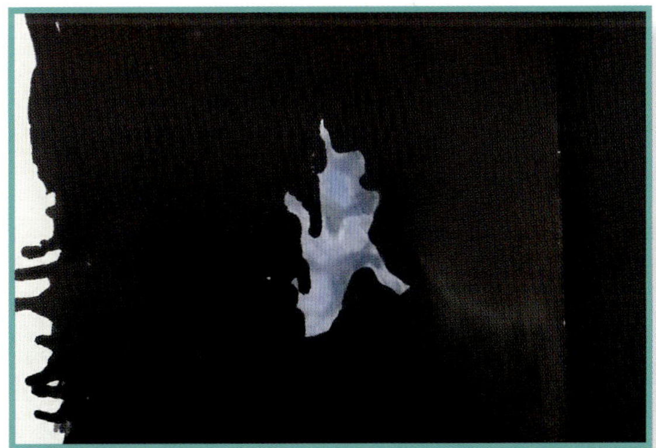

6. Let dry.

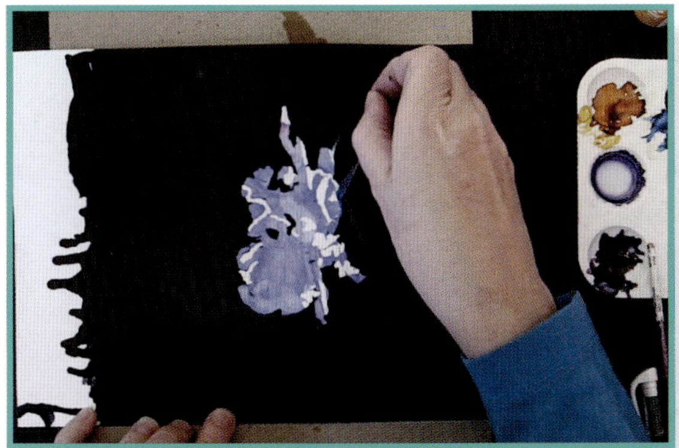

7. Carefully remove the masking fluid, trying not to get fingerprints on the black background.

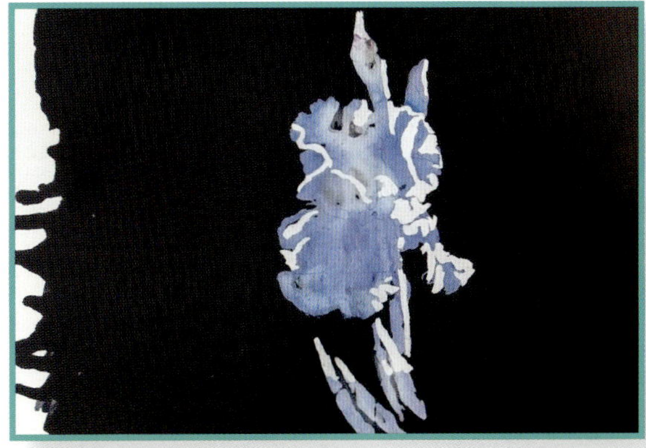

Blue Iris - In progress...

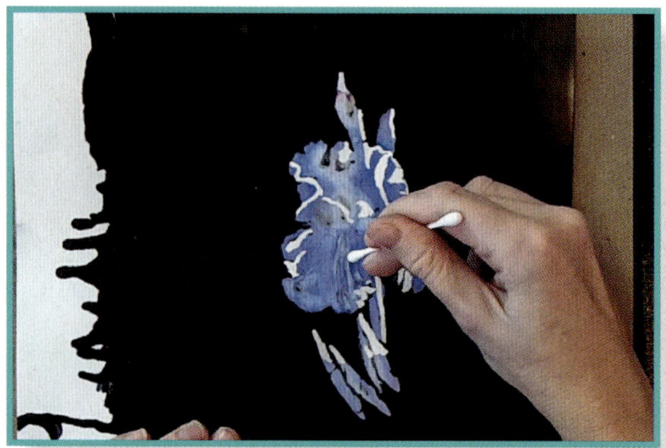

8. Use the cotton swab and alcohol to lift the ink to create folds and texture in the petals.

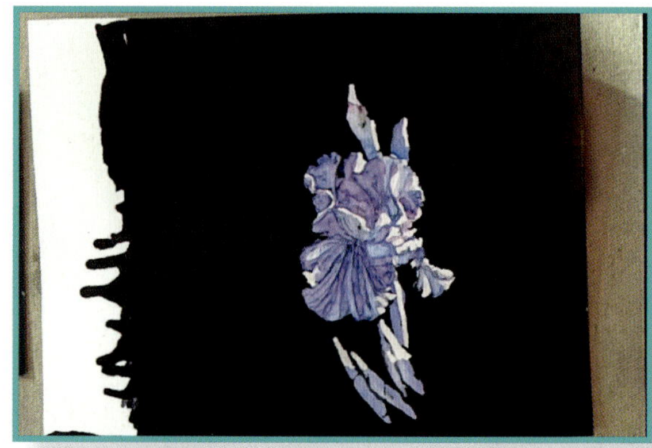

9. Add darks with the brush and purple ink.

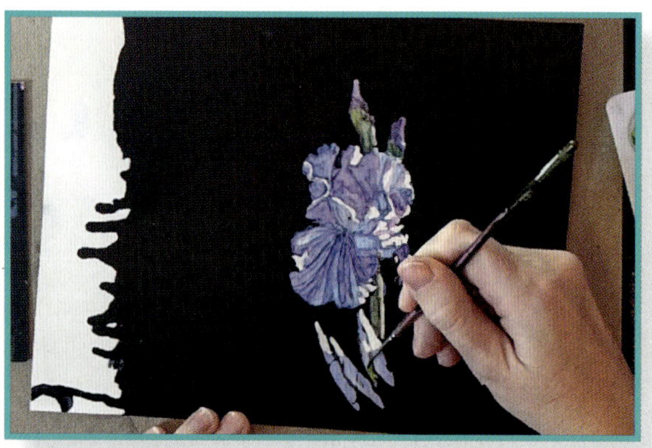

10. Add green ink to the leaves.

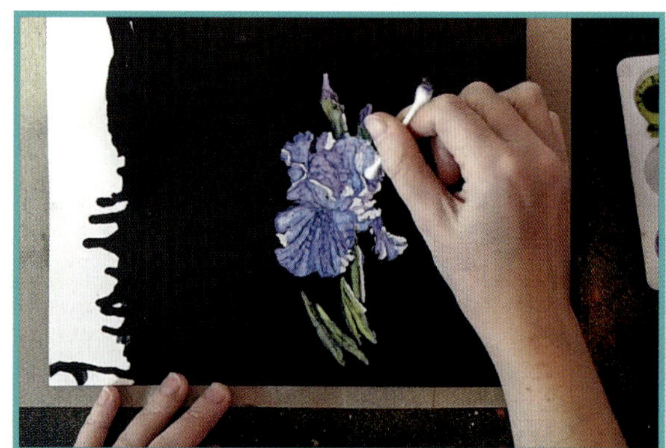

11. Use the cotton swab and alcohol to create texture.

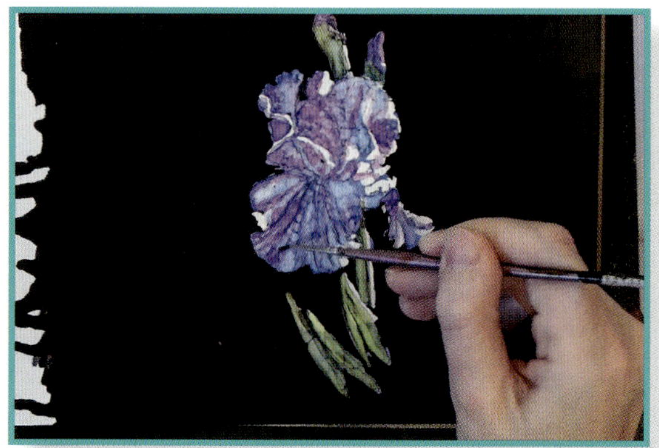

12. Add more darks with the brush and ink.

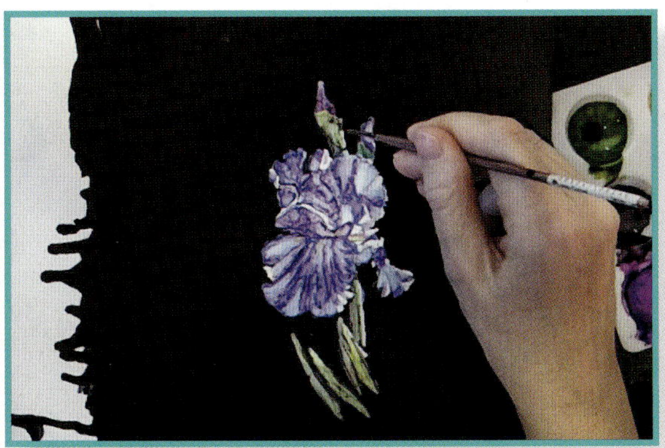

13. Add a hint of yellow to the greens and for the beard.

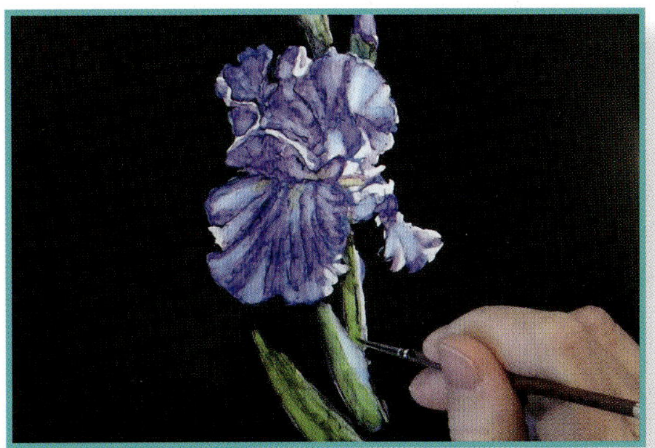

14. Make final touches, including filling in the leaves.

Variation: Iris Garden

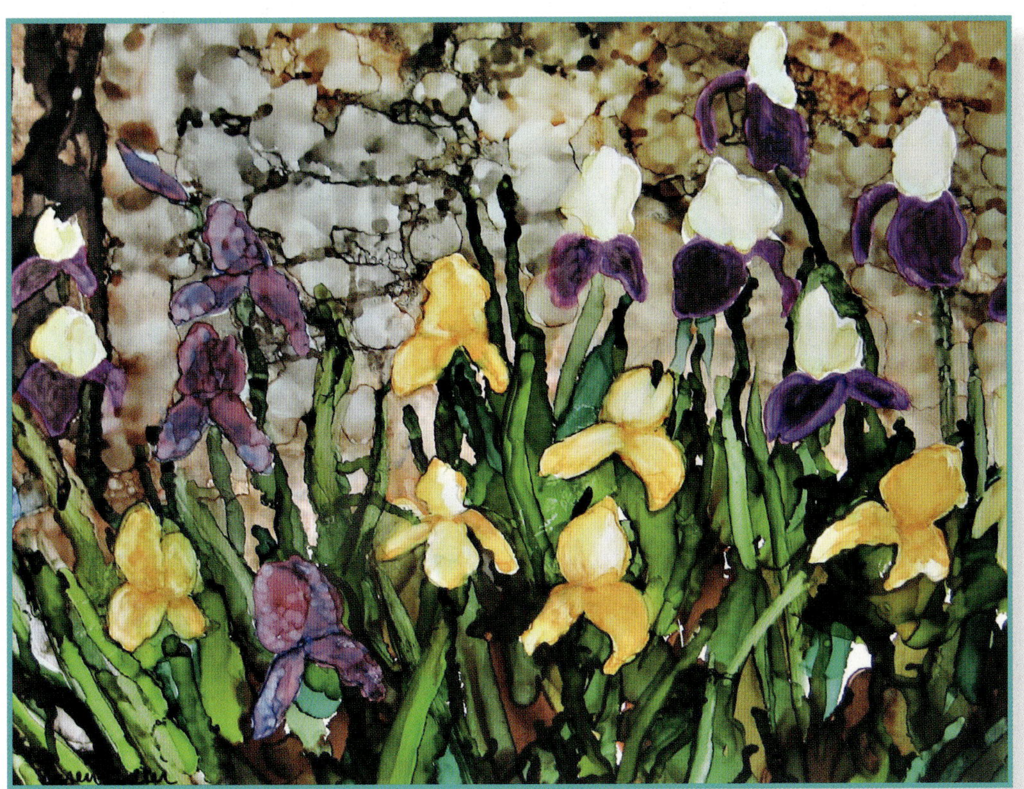

Karen Walker. *Iris Garden.*
Iris Garden takes an opposite approach to the *Blue Iris*. Here, the blooms are stylized with the drop-and-guide technique, and much attention is paid to the textured background.

4 Animals

Wild animals, especially birds, are probably my favorite subject for alcohol inks. Wildlife offers opportunities for detail, while the surroundings can be as inky and colorful as desired. Many of my animal paintings incorporate the background into the subject—painterly camouflage!

Confetti Peacock: Vivid inky background incorporating the tail and lifting

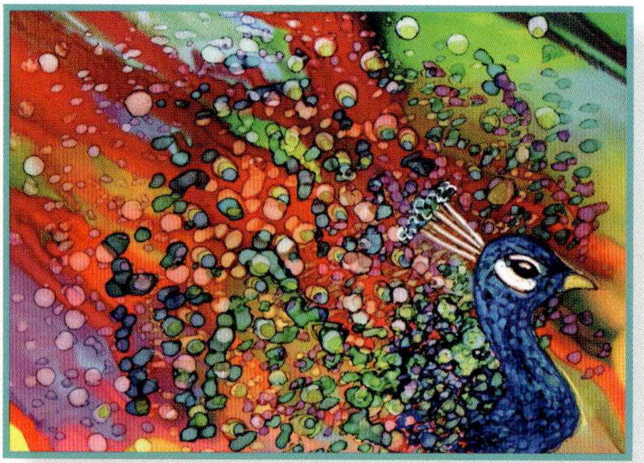

Little Kitten: White background with direct painting

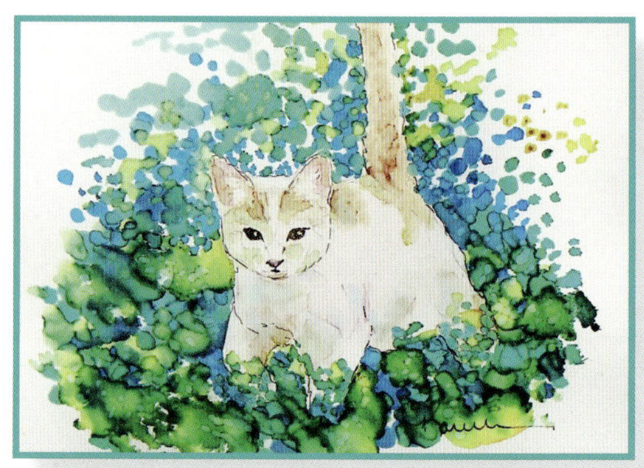

Dancing Koi: Inky background with lifting

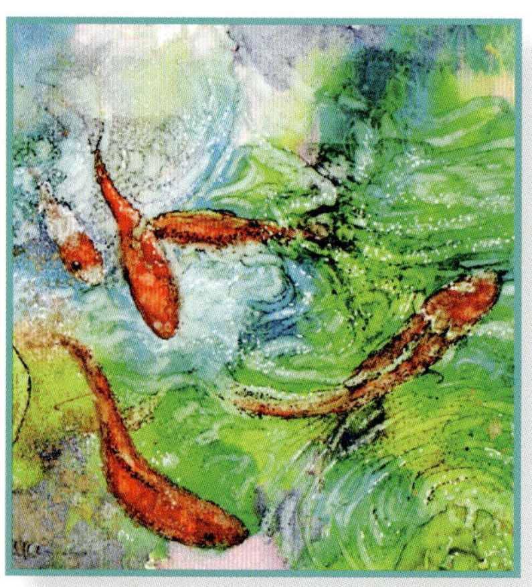

Lion: Inky background with masking and brush/penwork for the fur

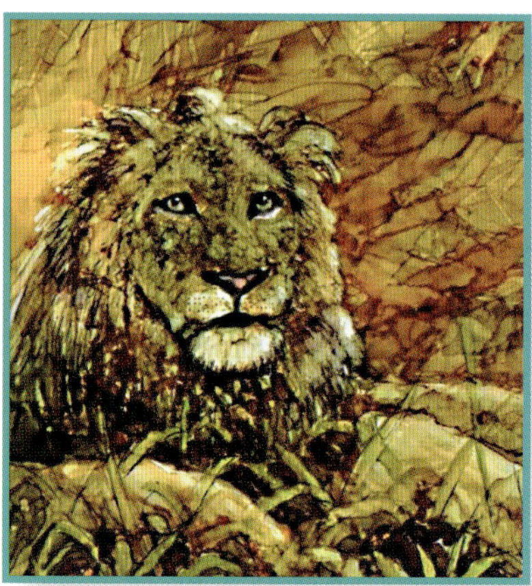

Hidden Zebra: Inky background with masking

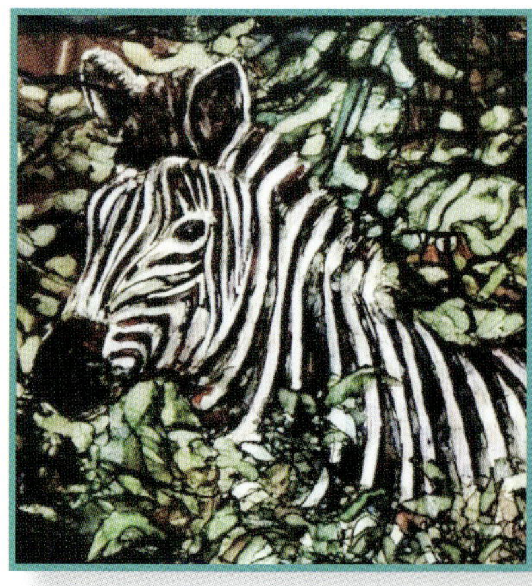

Project 8 - Confetti Peacock

Karen Walker. *Confetti Peacock.*

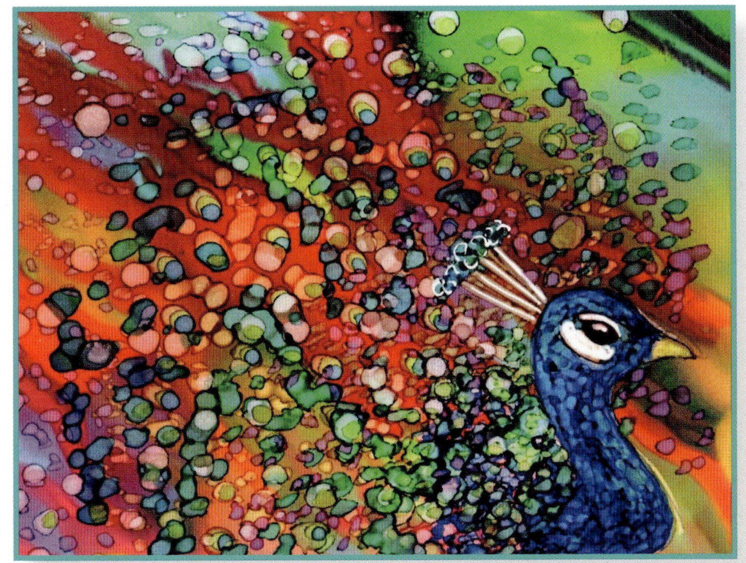

This fun and colorful piece features dynamic ink flow for the background, lifting for the head and body, and dotted color via the brush for the tail. The dabbing technique for the tail would also work well for trees!

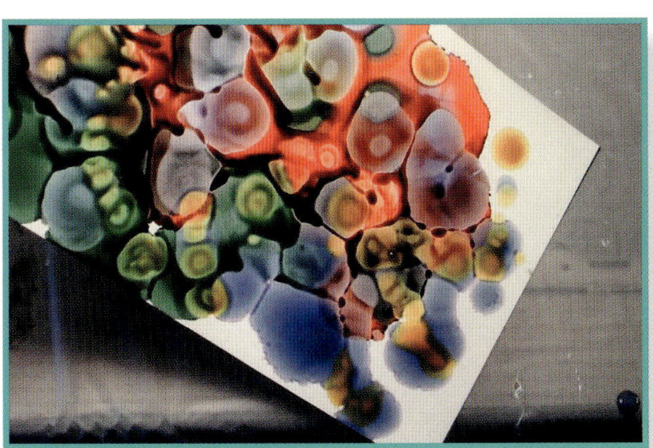

1. Create a colorful inky background by dropping ink on the flat paper. For the diagonal pattern, lift the paper and hold vertically at an angle.

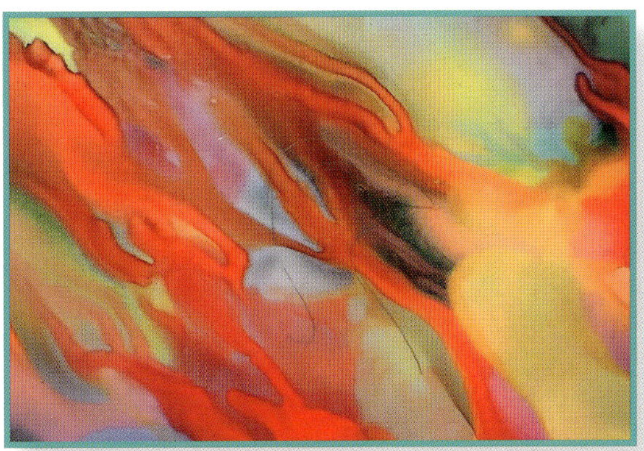

2. After the ink is dry, make a light sketch in pencil.

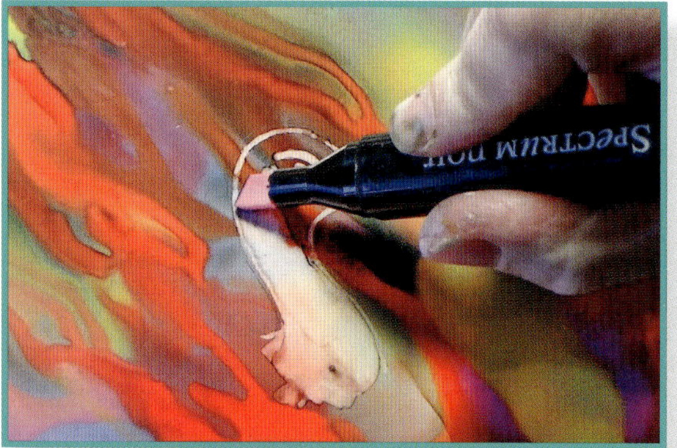

3. Lift out the peacock shape by using a pale alcohol ink marker, taking advantage both of the fine- and chisel-tipped ends.

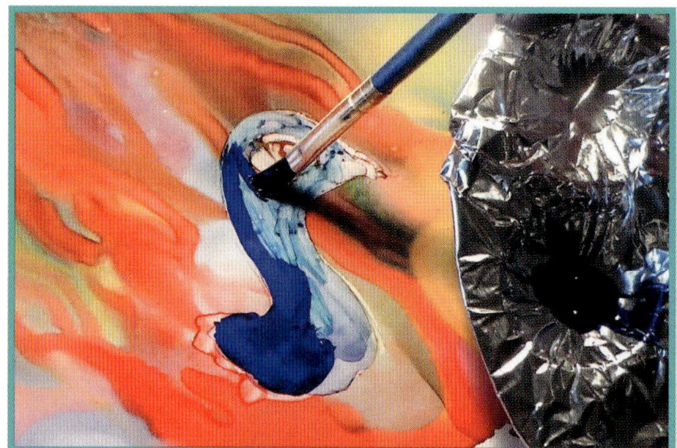

4. Fill in the blue head and neck area with several layers of ink. Use the brush and ink from the welled palette, the markers, or both.

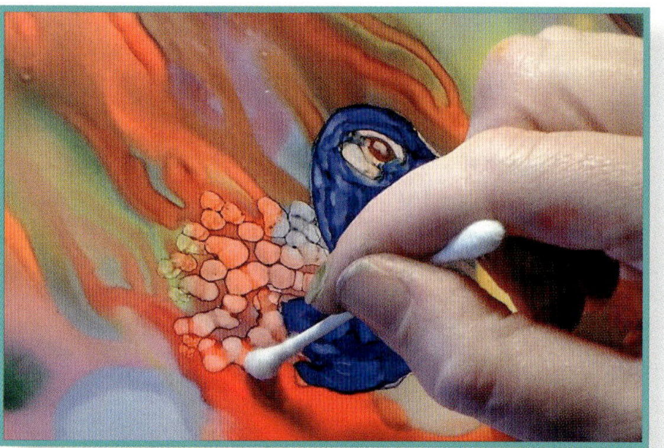

5. Use alcohol and the cotton swab or brush to lift ink for the tail and texture the bird.

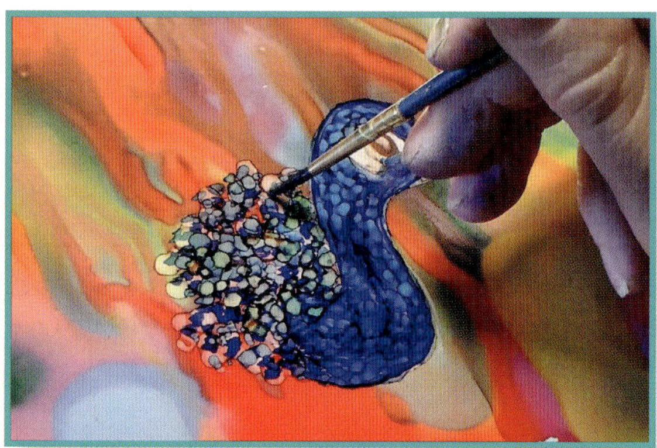

6. Dab multiple colors of ink with the brush to create the tail.

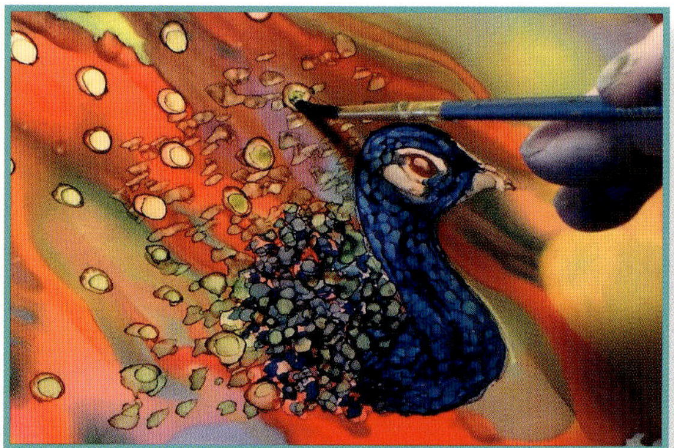

7. Extend the tail outward by repeating the pattern of lifting out the shapes with alcohol and adding in new colors of ink.

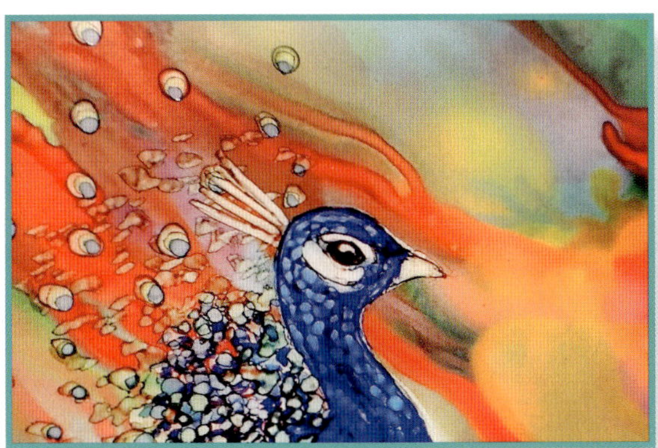

8. Define the face by using pens, markers, and the brush.

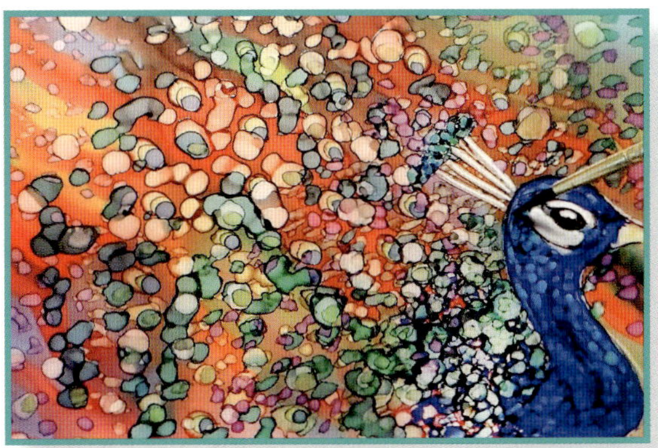

9. Add more ink to the tail and a few finishing touches.

Variation: Snowshira

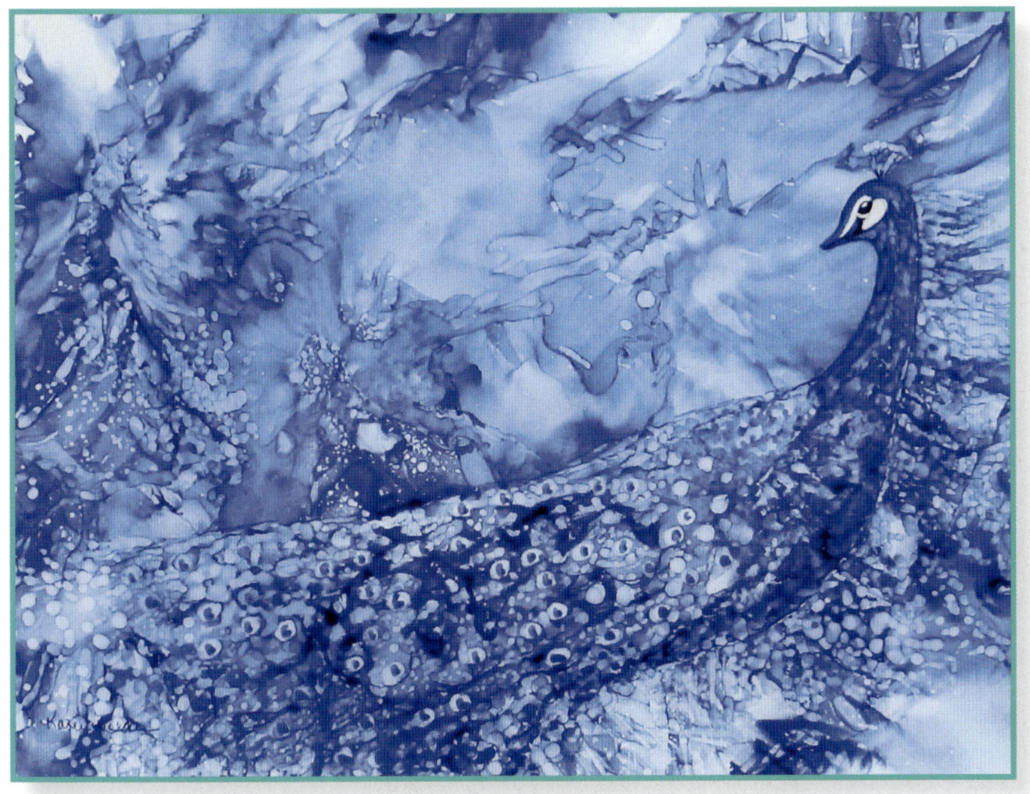

Karen Walker. *Snowshira.*
Peacocks are one of my favorite subjects to paint. While most of my peacocks are intensely colored, such as *Confetti Peacock, Snowshira* presents a monochrome approach.

Project 9 - Little Kitten

Karen Walker. *Little Kitten.*

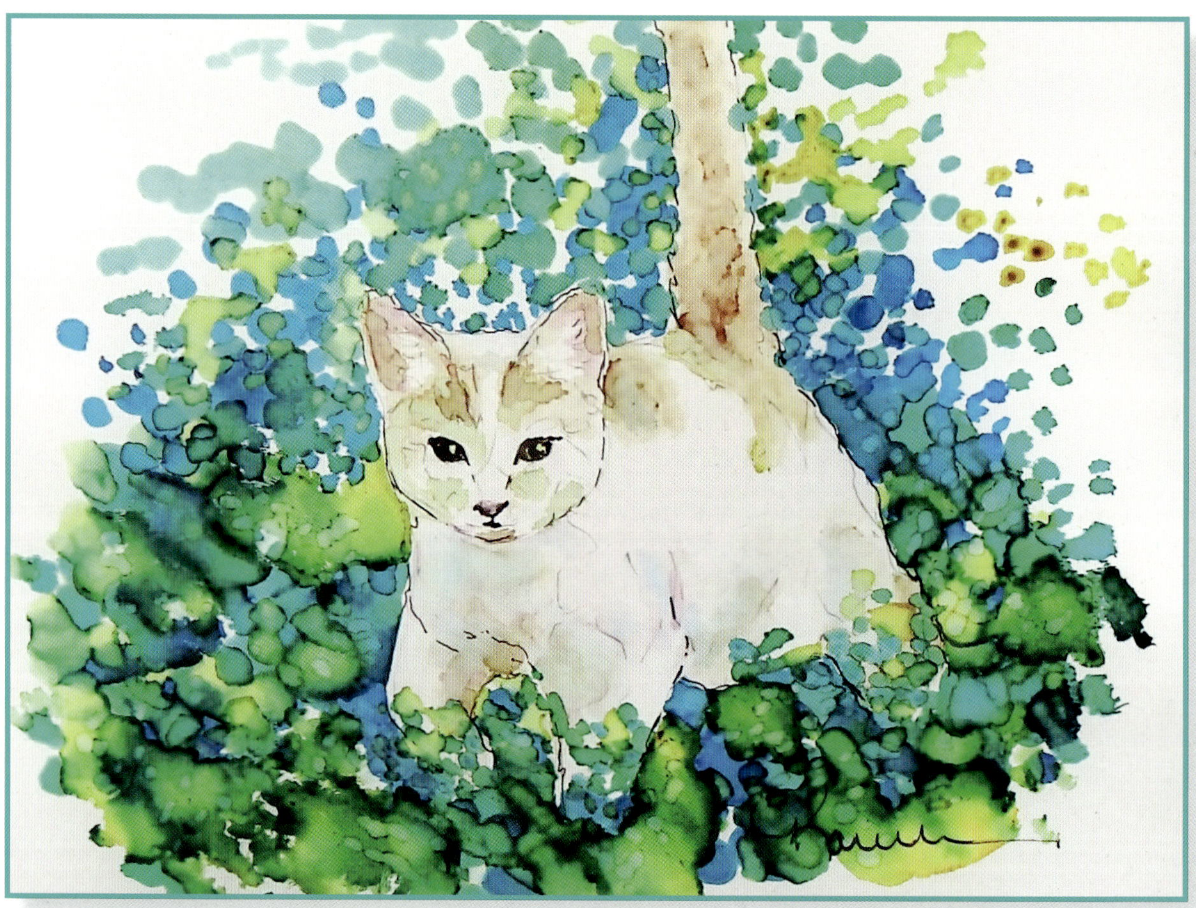

Little Kitten is another example of direct painting on Yupo®. Here, masking is used as a convenience to protect the white of his fur from any accidental drops of ink.

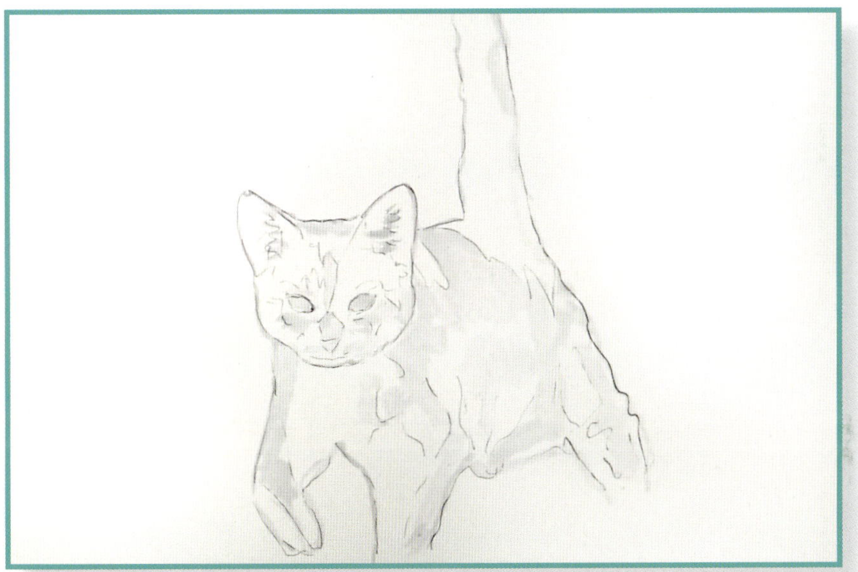

1. Lightly sketch and partially mask the drawing.

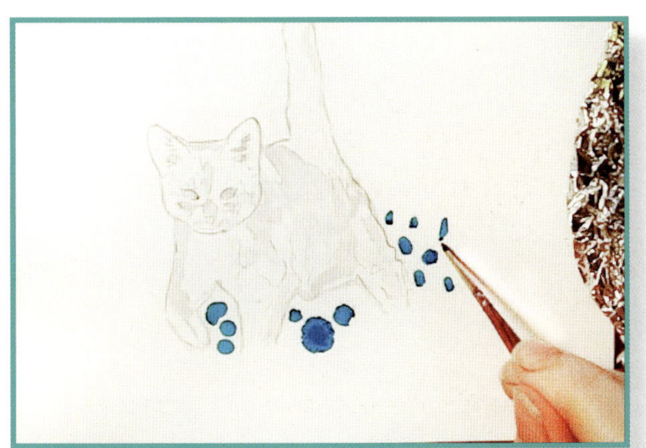

2. Using the brush and ink dispensed into the welled palette, begin to dab in the background.

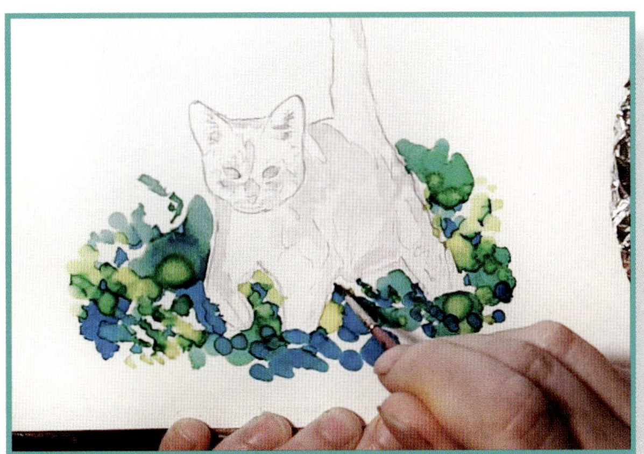

3. Continue adding ink and alcohol to create the grassy background.

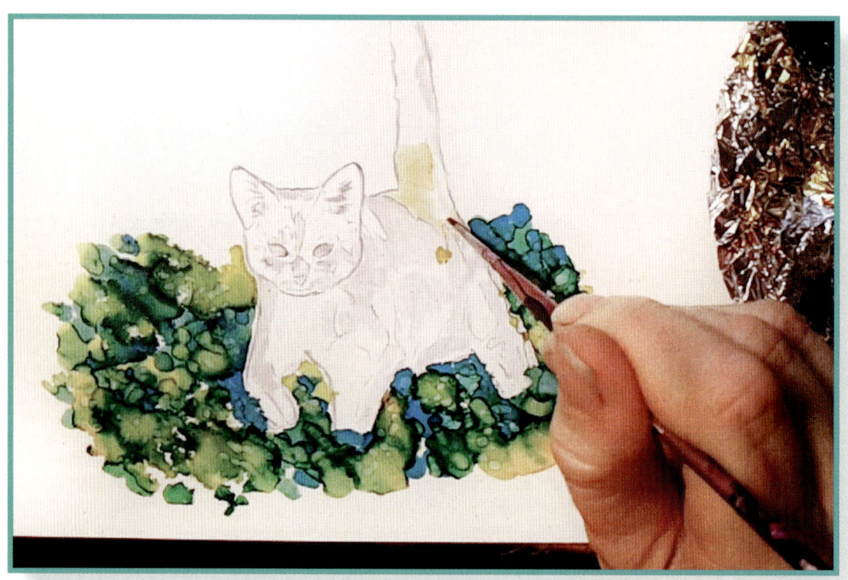

4. Use the brush to paint in the cat—pale purple is used to tone the white fur. Light shades of ink may be created by diluting ink with alcohol in the welled palette.

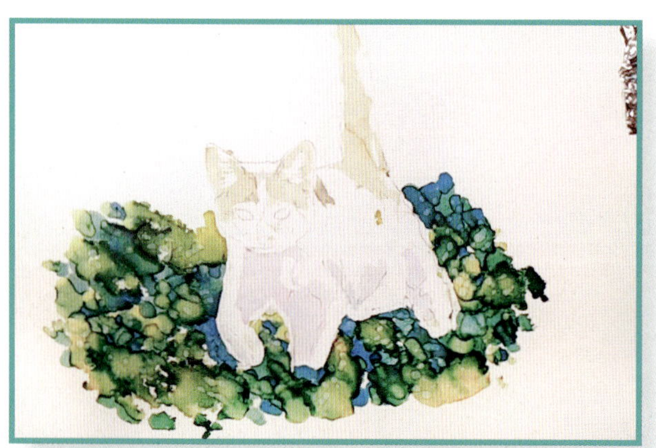

5. Remove the masking fluid.

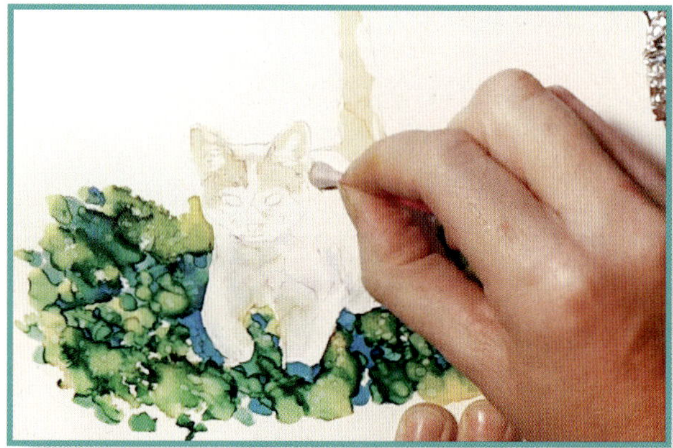

6. Use the cotton swab and alcohol to soften edges and blend in the masked areas.

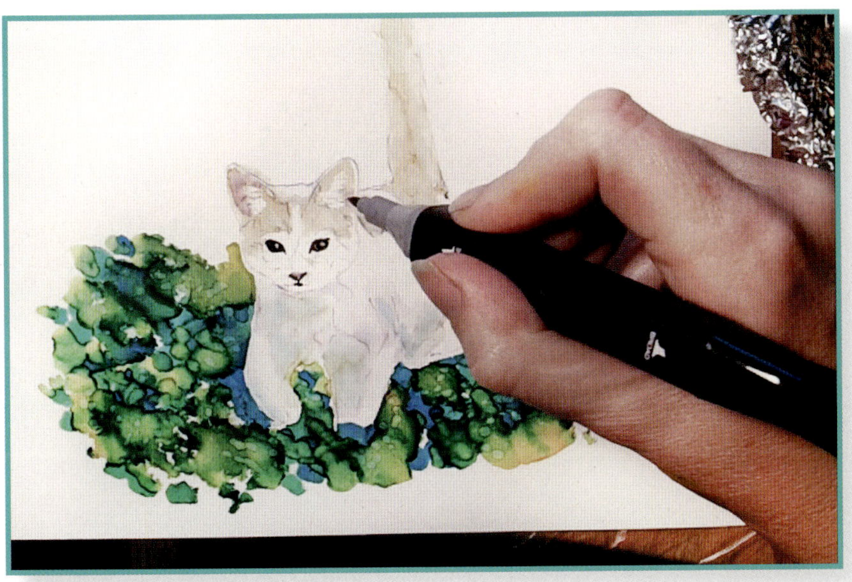

7. Add details using the fine-tipped black pen for the eyes and pink marker for the ears and nose.

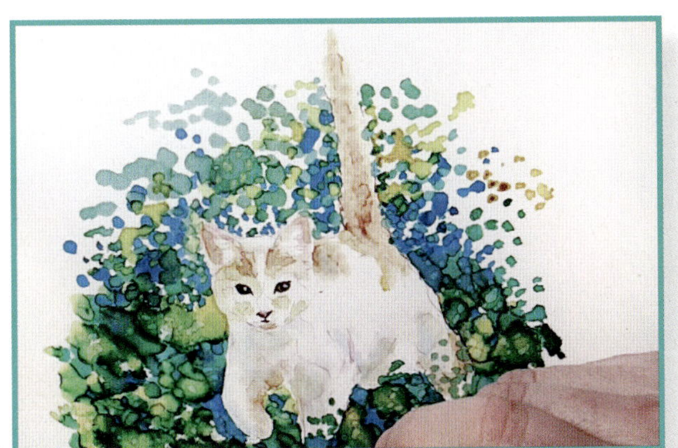

8. Add darker values in the fur and continue working on the background.

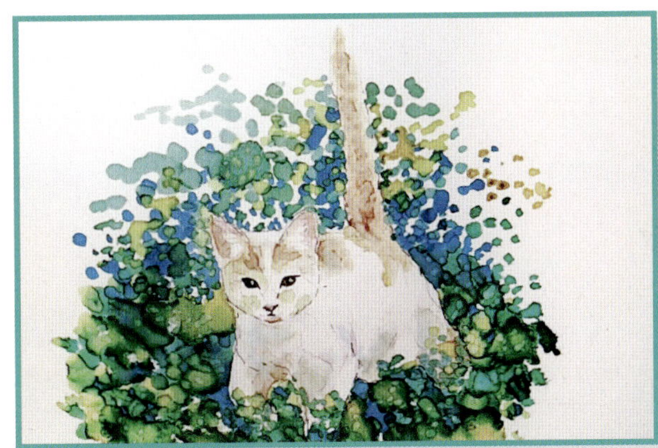

9. Finish by softening hard edges, integrating the cat into the background, and adding a few defining lines.

Variation: Inkatoo

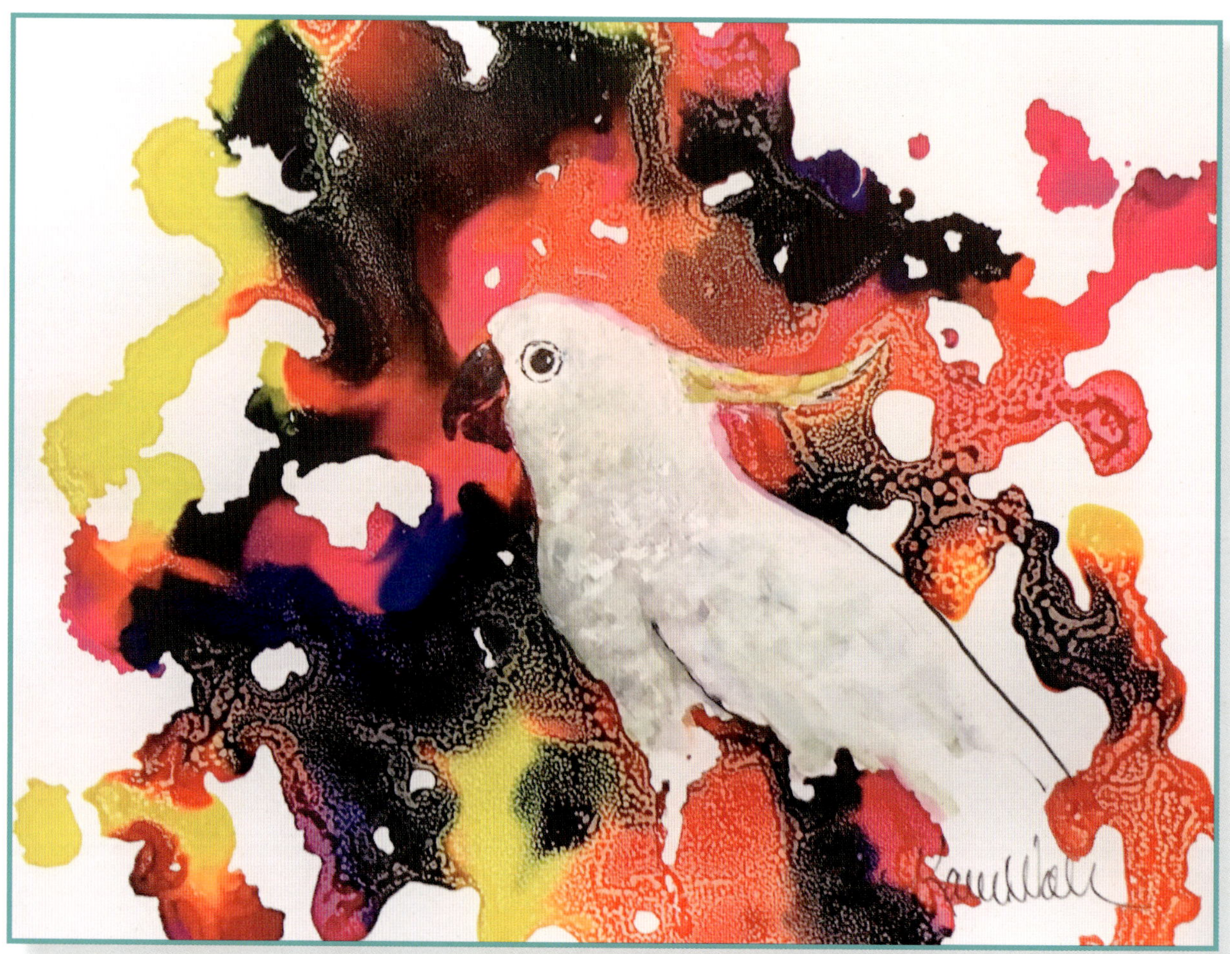

Karen Walker. *Inkatoo.*
Like *Little Kitten, Inkatoo* is a white subject against an inky backdrop. However, the two paintings diverge in *Inkatoo's* less controlled, ink-splattered background.

Project 10 - Dancing Koi

Karen Walker. *Dancing Koi.*

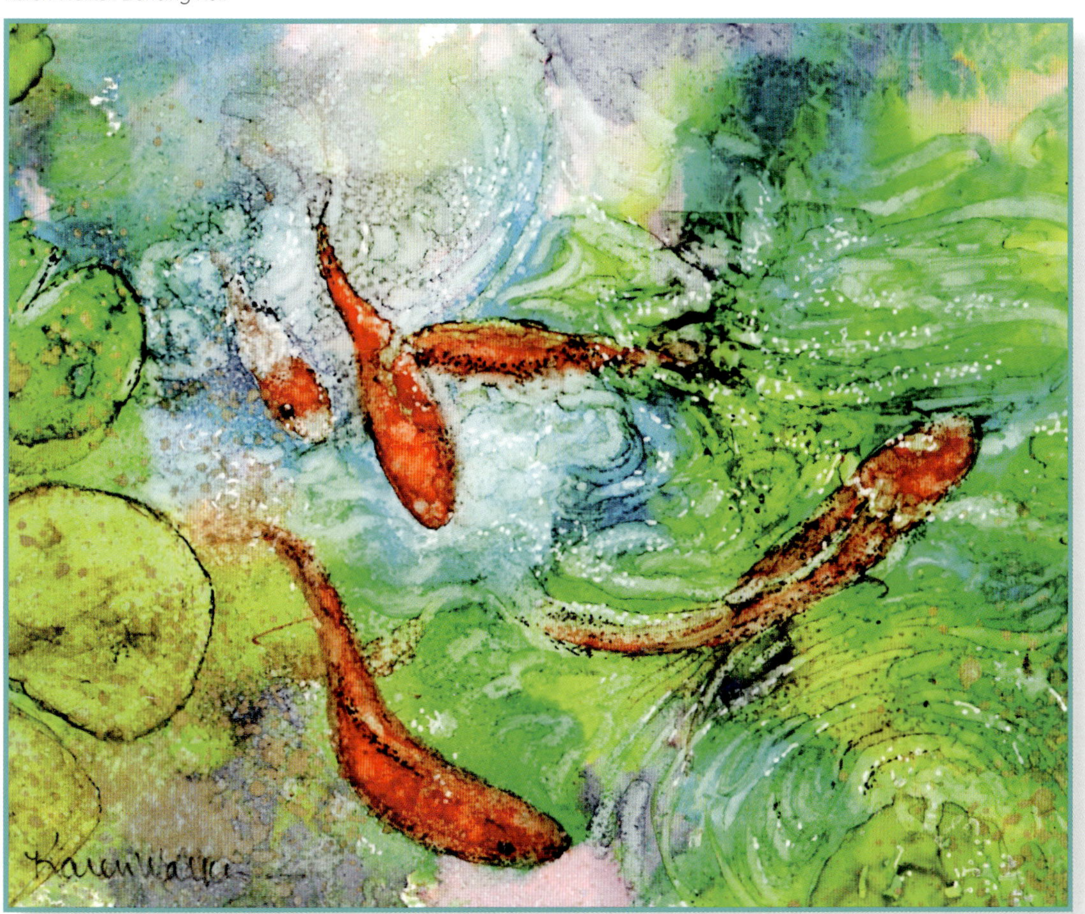

Dancing Koi is a painting that uses two of the three main techniques—dropping ink (via bottle and brush) and lifting. This is a wonderful subject for those favoring a loose ink style, since there is no masking!

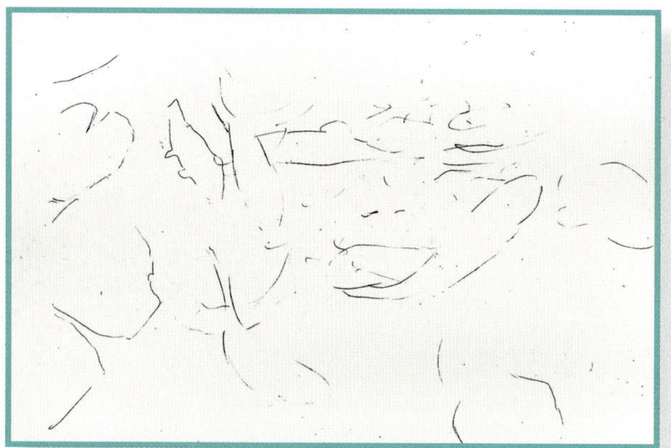

1. Lightly sketch the overall design of the painting in pencil on Yupo® paper.

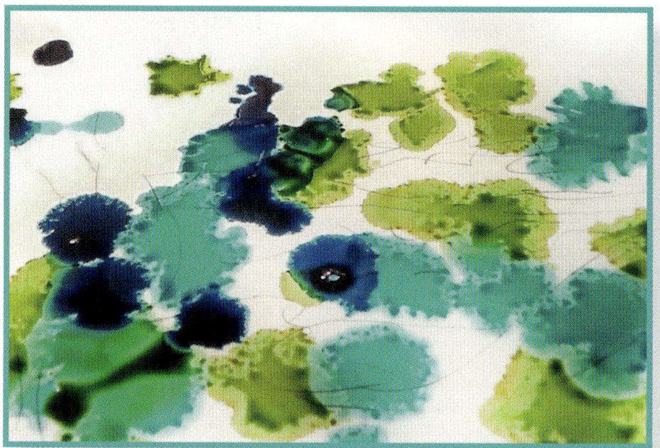

2. Add several drops of each of the background alcohol ink colors in a random pattern until the paper is nearly covered.

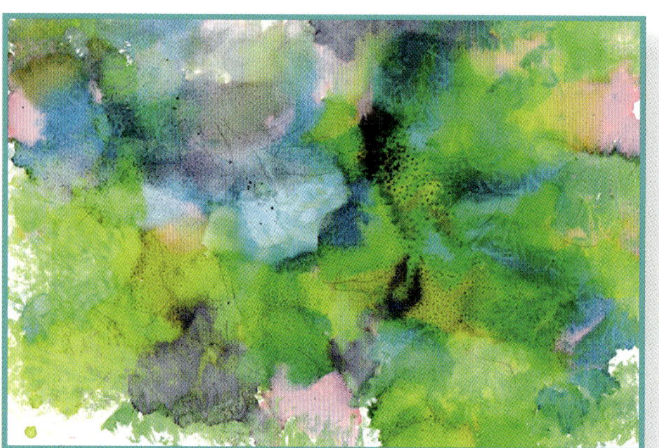

3. Blot the excess ink with a paper towel and dab to fill in all of the white space. Under a thin layer of ink, the drawing should still be visible.

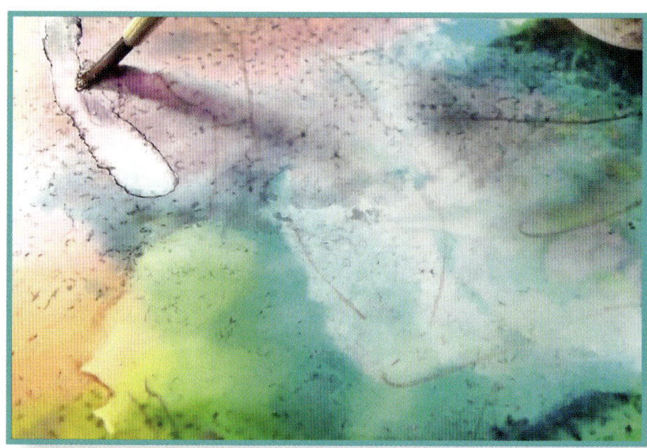

4. Using alcohol and the small brush, lift out koi shapes.

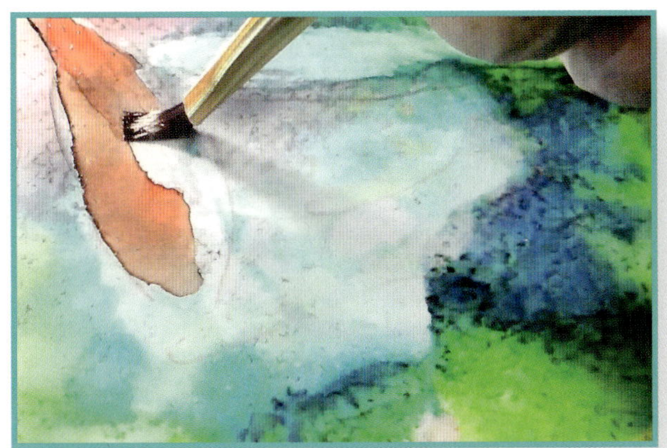

5. Fill in the koi with orange ink, using the brush and ink dispensed into the welled palette or alcohol ink markers.

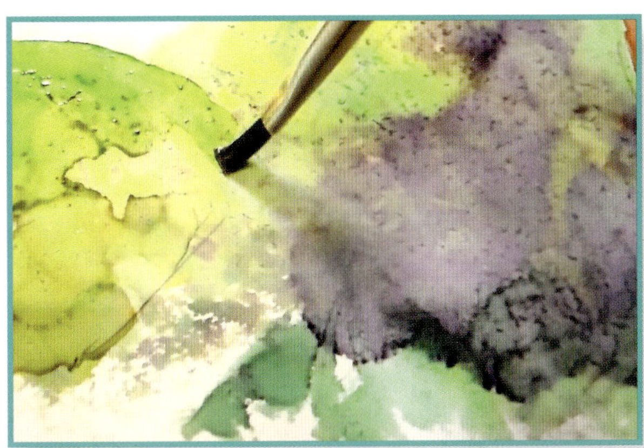

6. Define the water lilies with the brush and green ink.

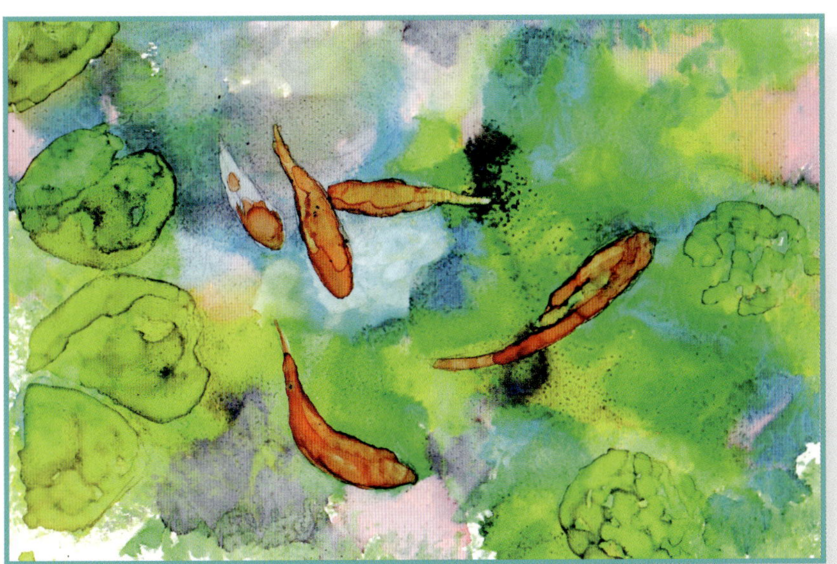

Dancing Koi - In progress...

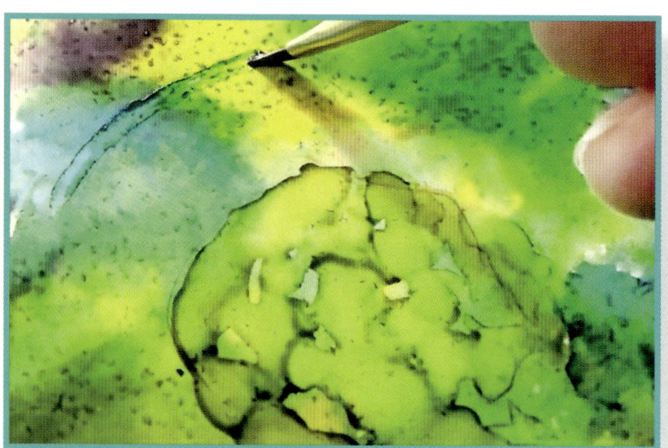

7. Create water lines by lifting the ink using the brush and alcohol.

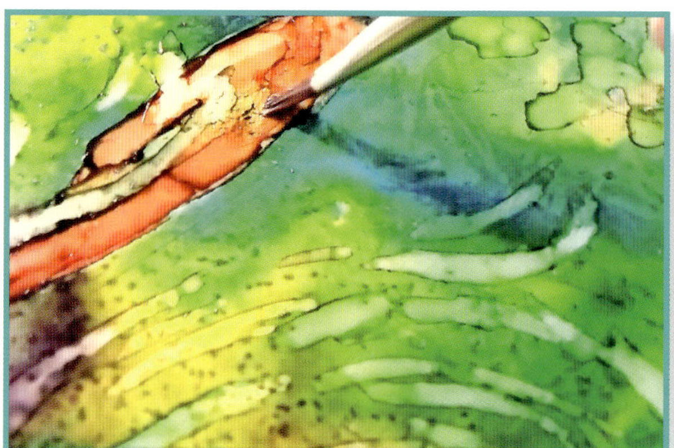

8. Redefine key elements of the painting by adding more ink, as necessary, to the koi and water lilies.

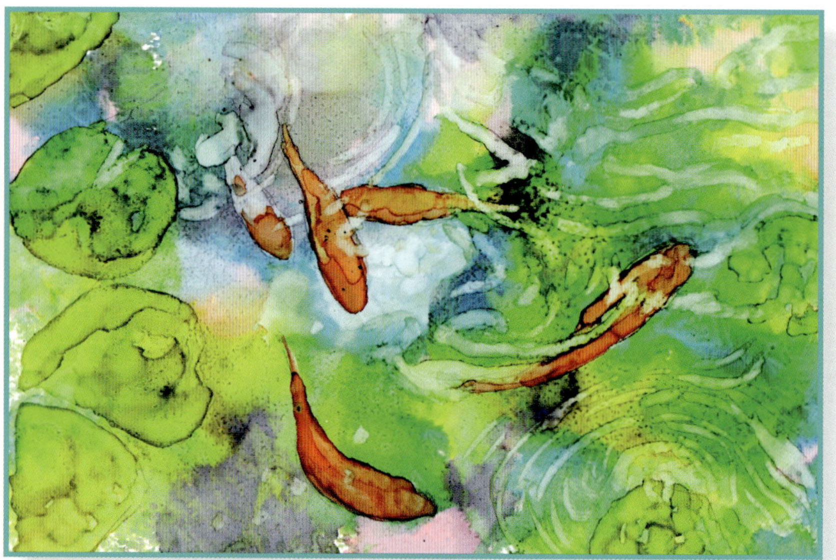

Dancing Koi - In progress...

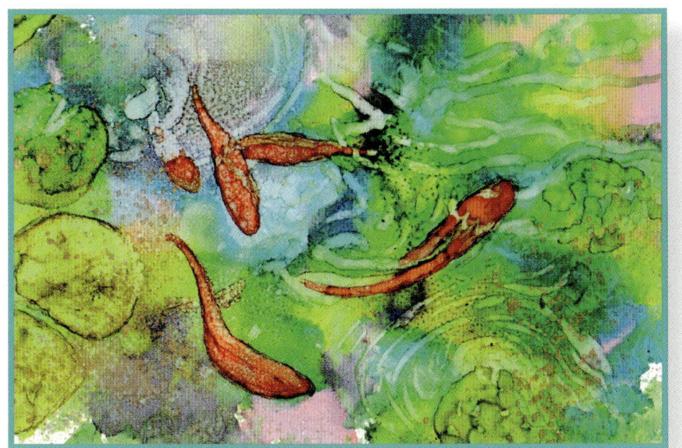

9. Add watery effects by lightly splattering the painting with alcohol and gold ink.

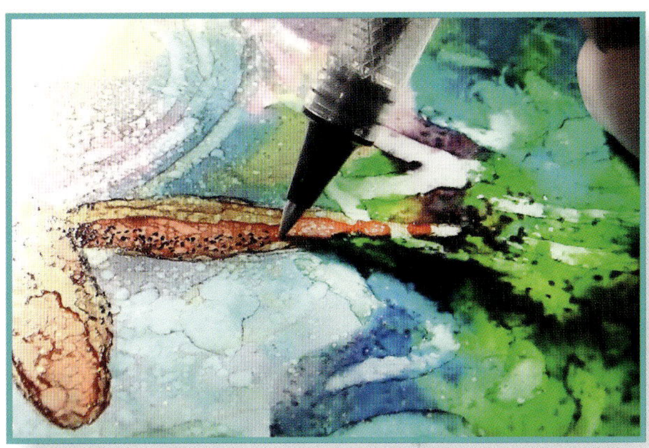

10. Add details with the black and white fine-tipped pens.

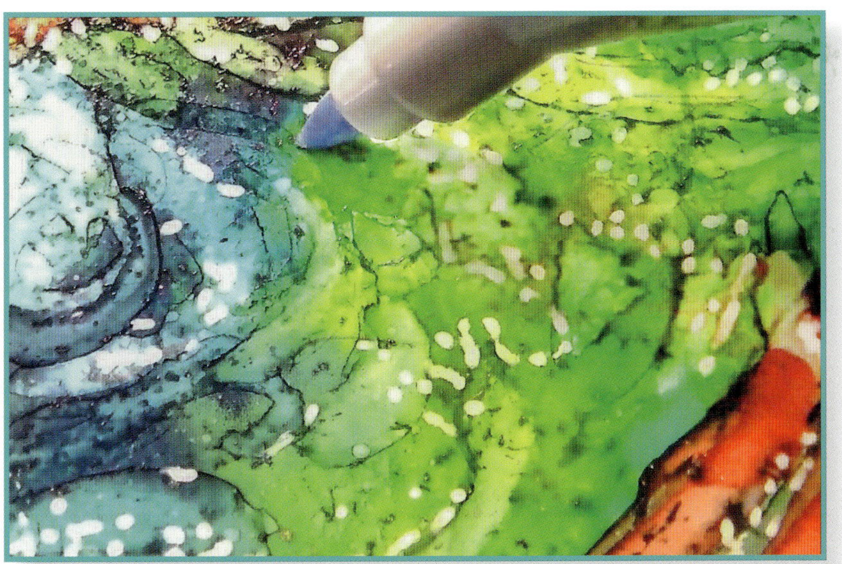

11. Review the painting and make final adjustments using the brush, pens, and markers as needed.

Variation: Koi

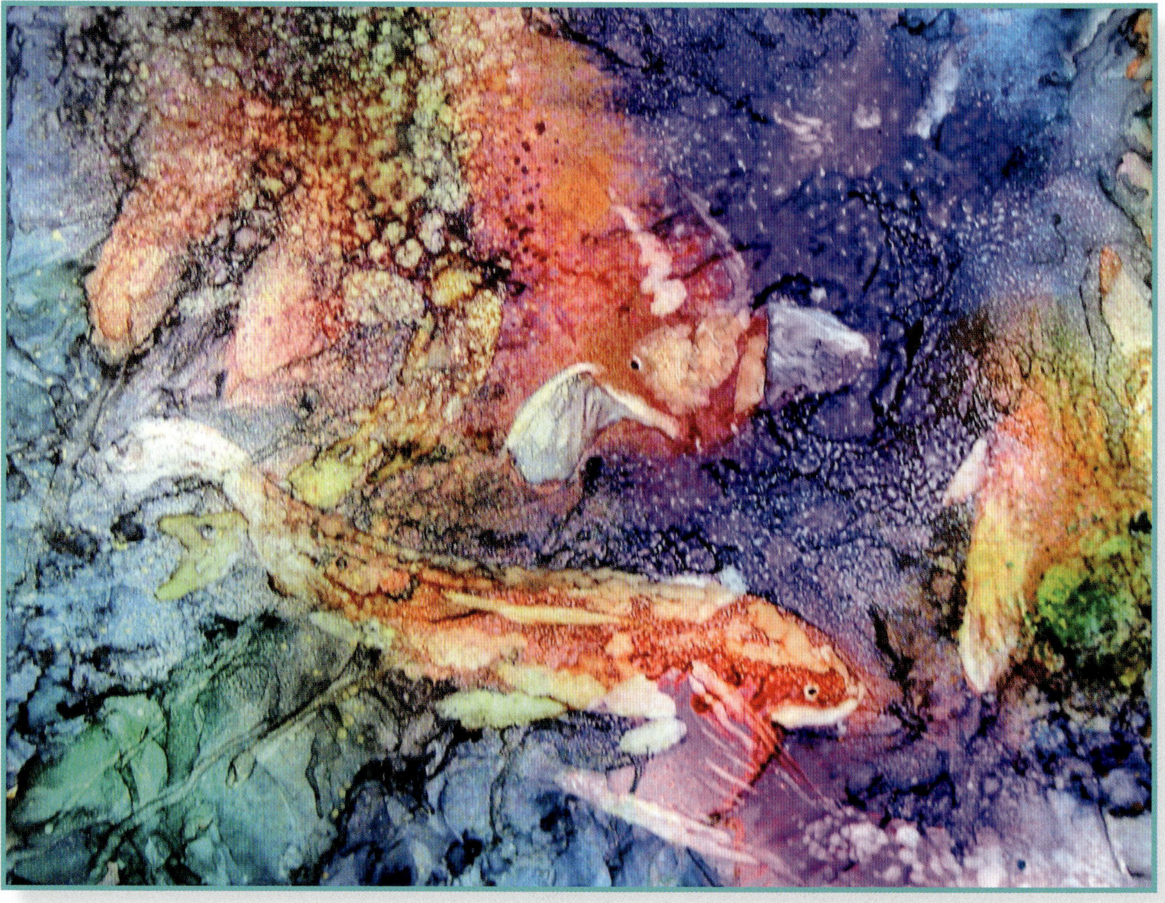

Karen Walker. *Koi*.
Water-related subjects such as *Koi* are natural fits for ink painting. This colorful rendition of koi began with a few masked areas but largely took advantage of the natural patterns of the ink.

Project 11 - Lion

Karen Walker. *Lion.*

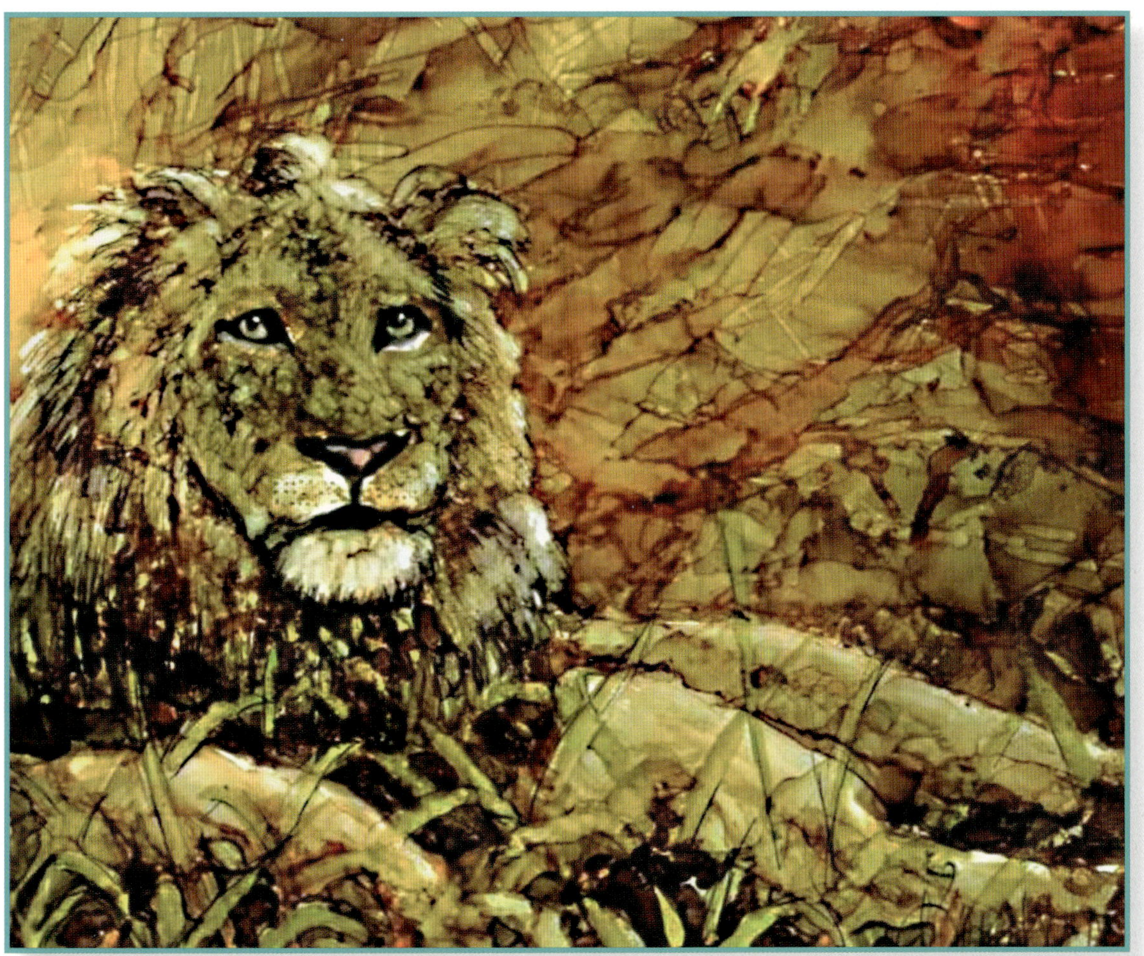

Lion is all about fur and textures. This project uses four techniques for fur: brush and alcohol, brush and ink, markers, and fine-tipped pens. The trick is integrating the precision of fur with the inkiness of the remainder of the piece.

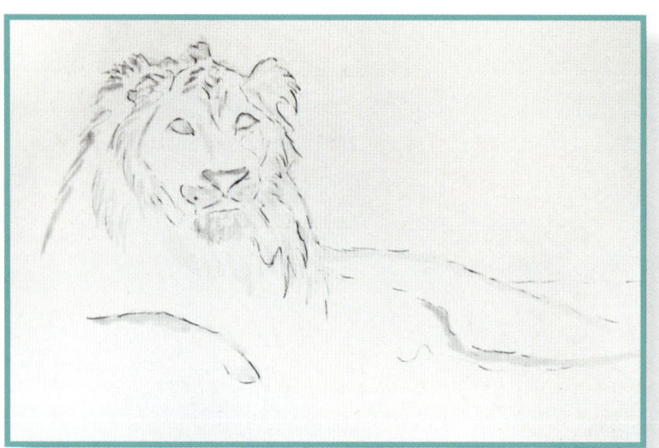

1. Lightly sketch and mask the drawing so that the design is visible after the inking.

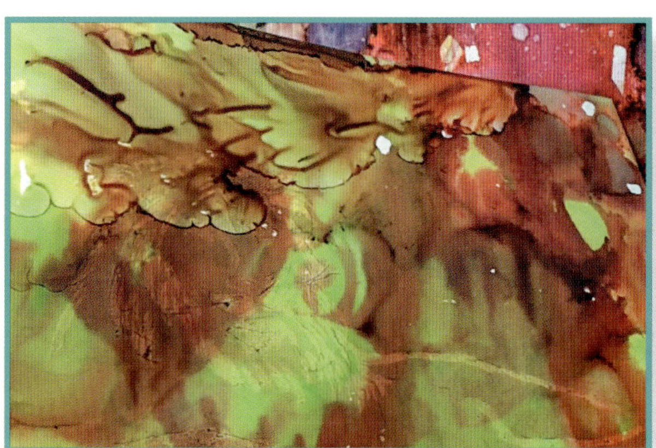

2. Create an inky background by dropping ink and alcohol.

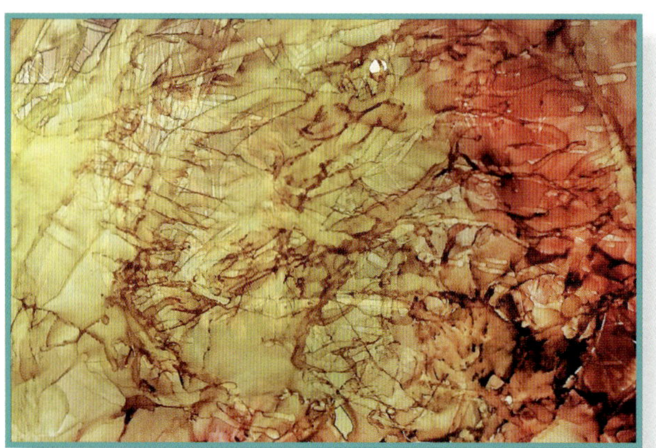

3. Create air-blown effects throughout the background.

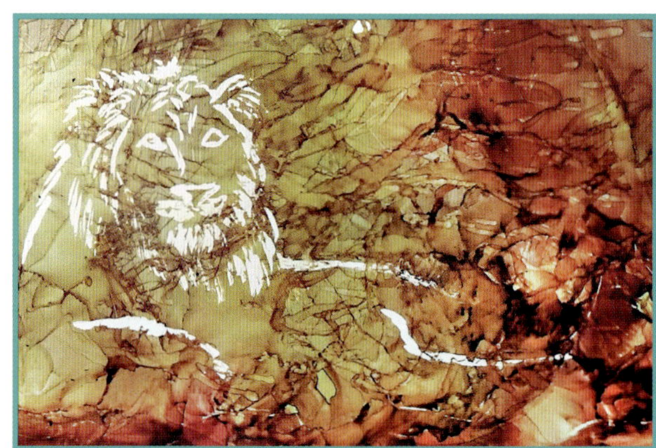

4. Remove the masking fluid.

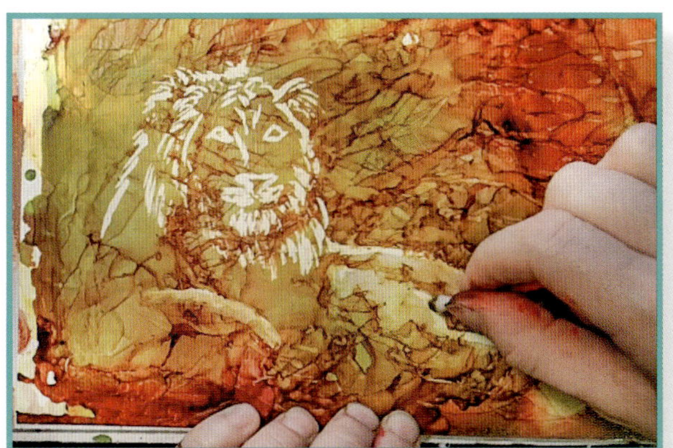

5. Lift and blend areas with alcohol and the cotton swab.

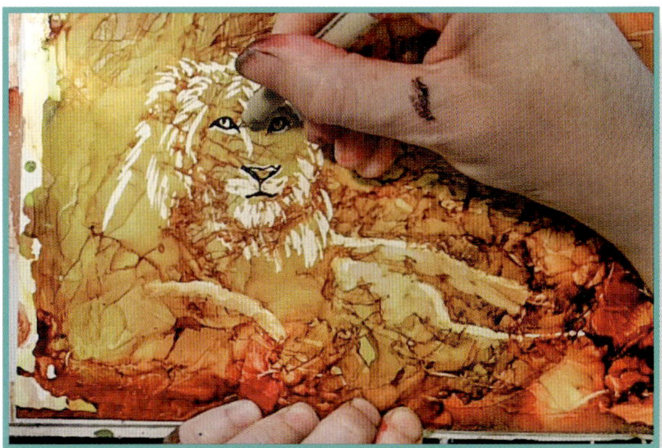

6. Define the facial features with the fine-tipped black pen.

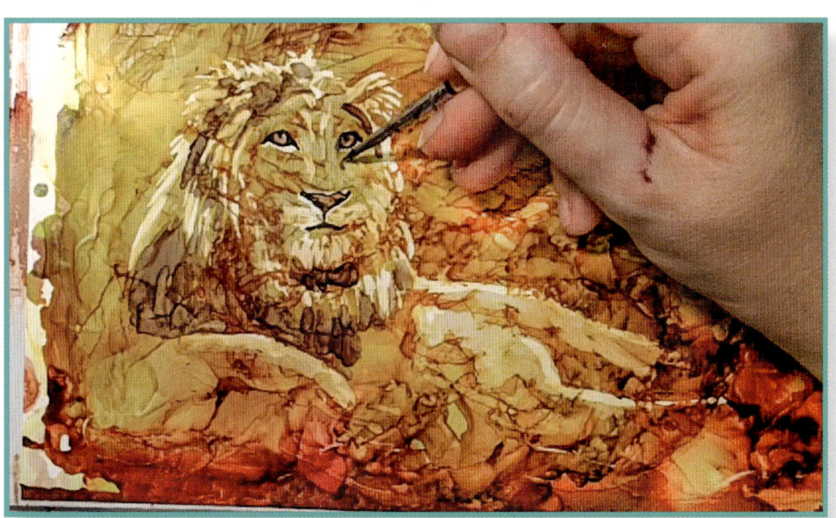

7. Use the brush and ink to paint in darks.

Four Techniques for Fur

8. Create a variety of textures for the lion's fur.

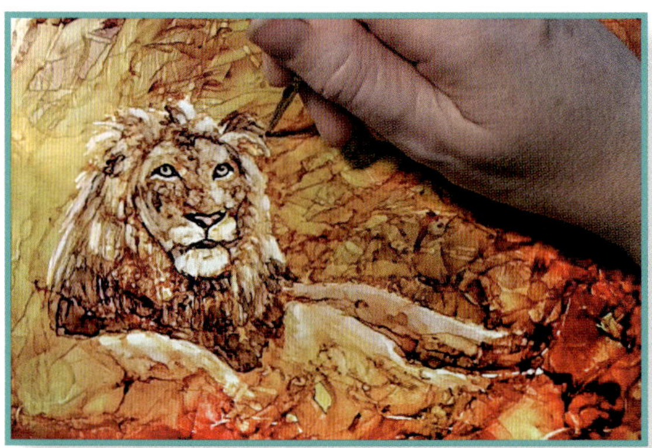

Brush and alcohol or ink

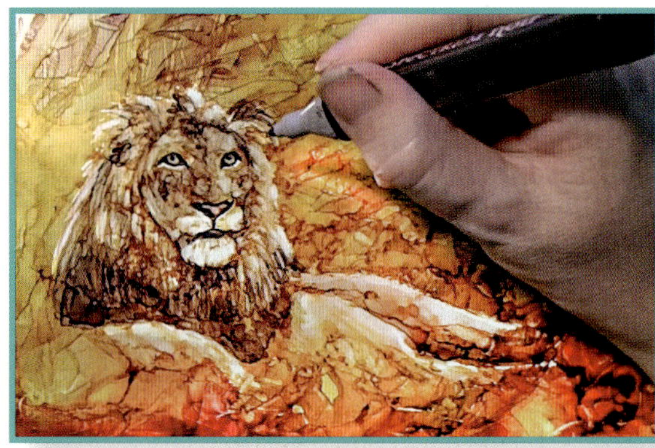

Alcohol ink marker

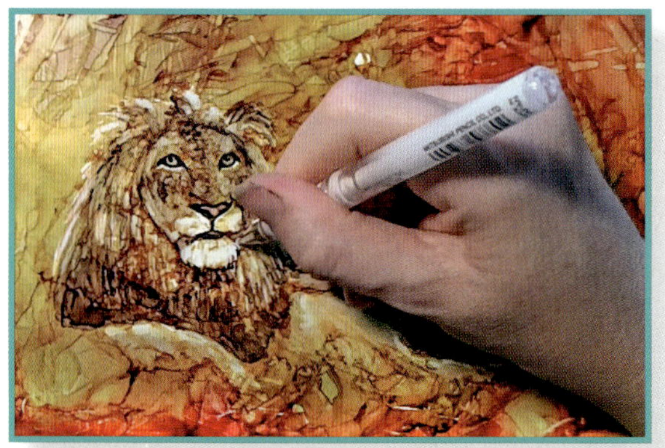

White pen

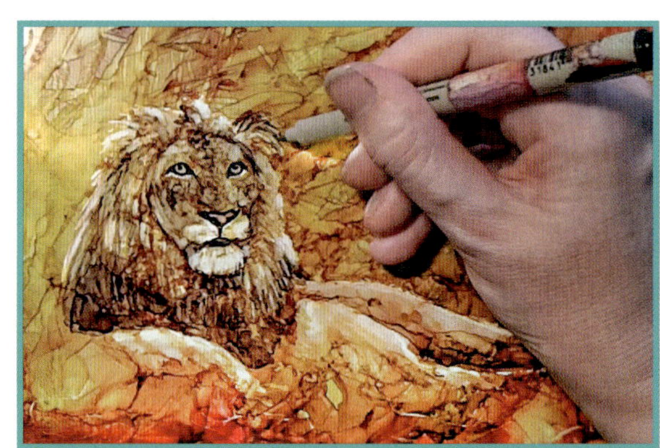

Black pen

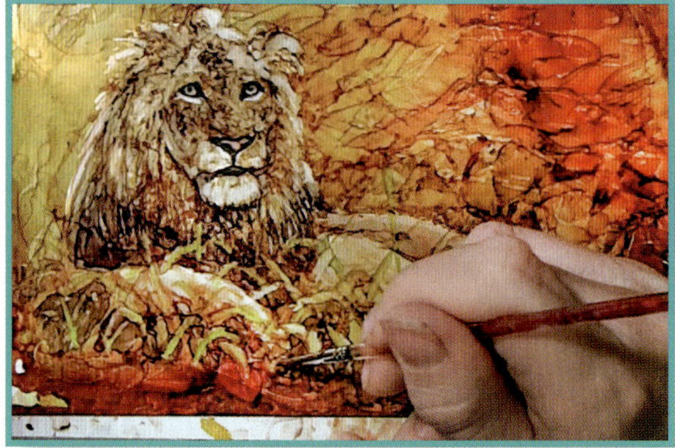

9. Add grasses and integrate the subject into the background. Review the painting and make finishing touches.

Variation: Cool Lion

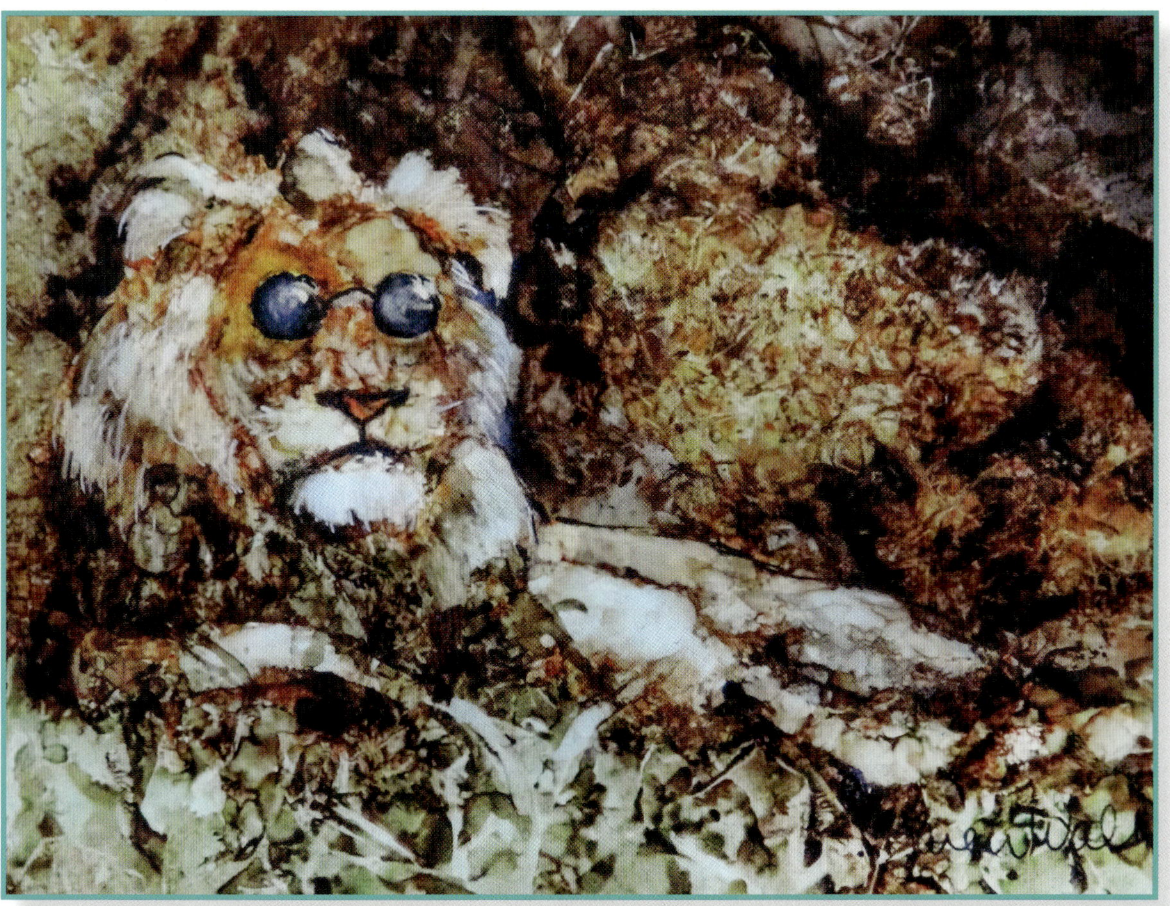

Karen Walker. *Cool Lion.*
Cool Lion is the much hipper cousin of our demonstration lion. The pose and techniques are largely the same; however, there were some difficulties in painting the eyes of the *Cool Lion.* A pair of sunglasses, and problem solved!

Project 12 - Hidden Zebra

Karen Walker. *Hidden Zebra.*

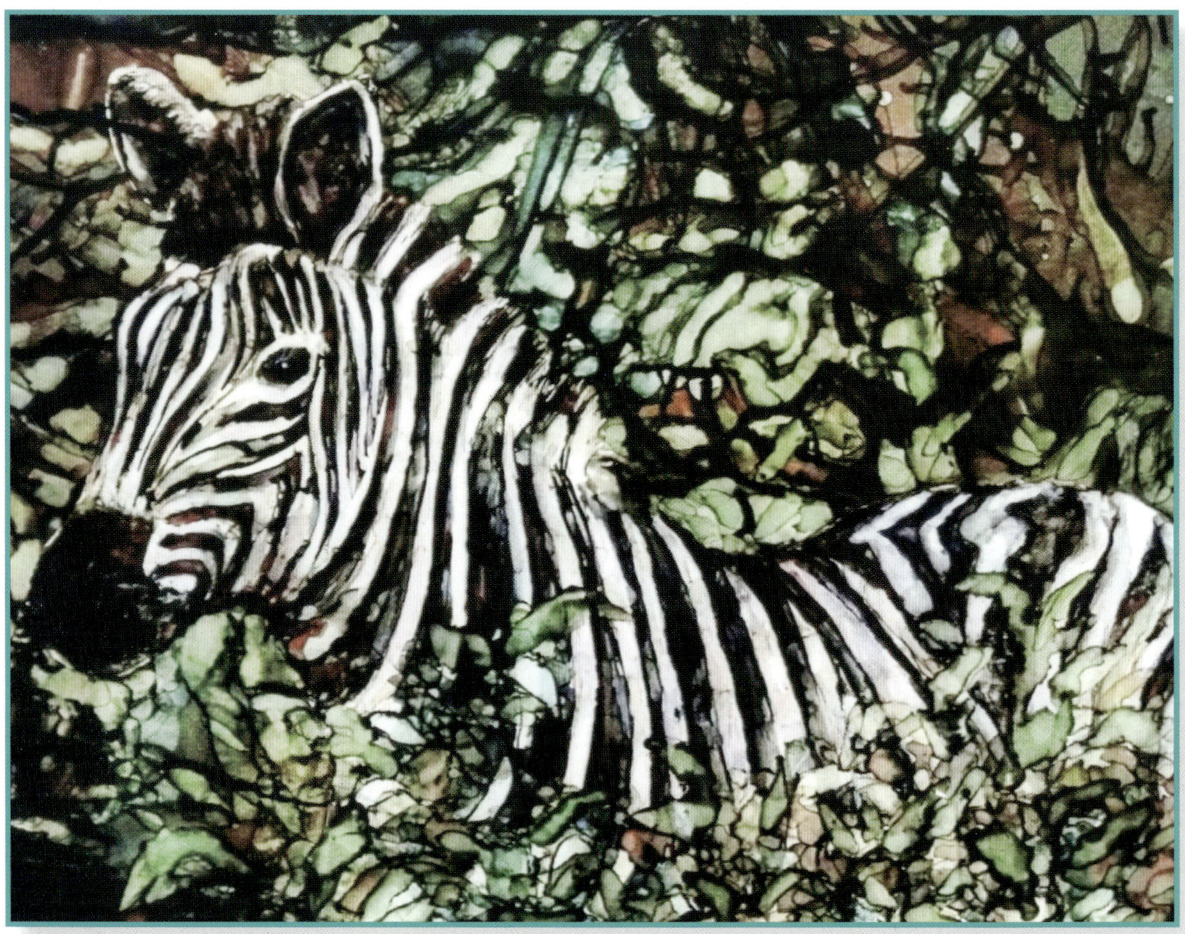

While zebras are perfect projects for practicing masking, remembering which stripes are light and which are dark when masking can be surprisingly challenging. In painting the zebra, I used a fair amount of color—black and white animals are anything but black and white.

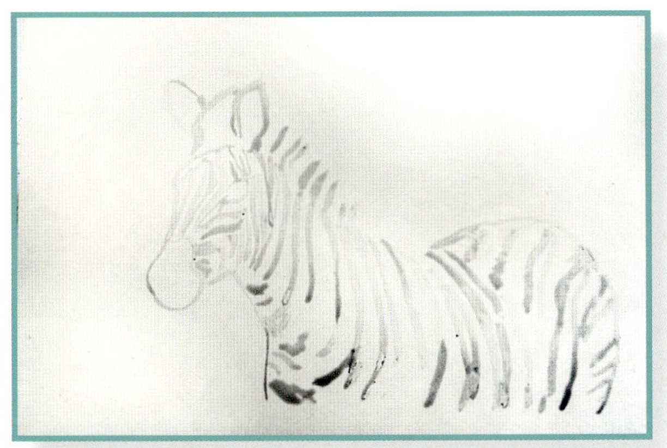

1. Begin with a masked drawing.

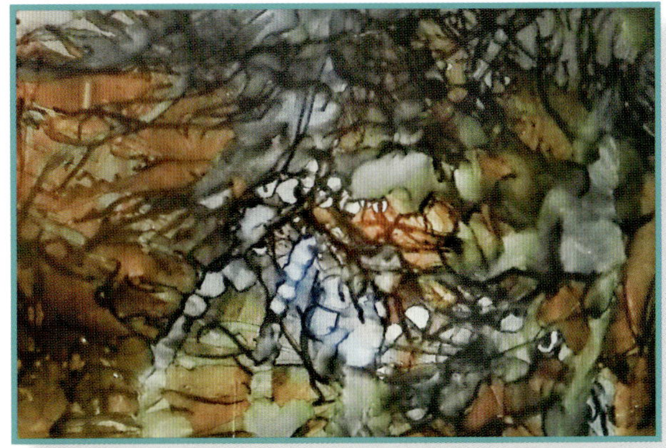

2. Create an inky forest background with blown-air effects.

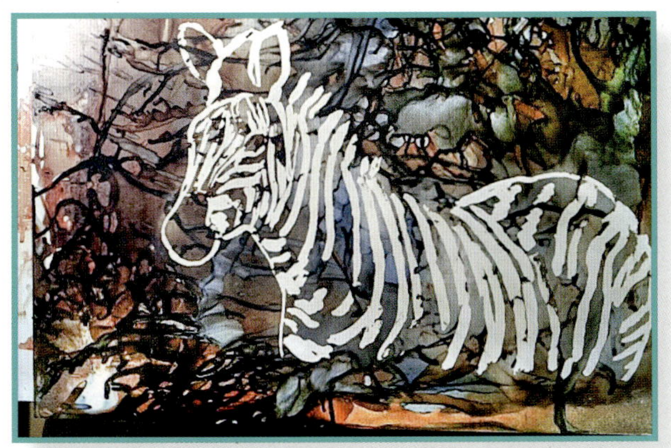

3. When the ink is dry, remove the masking fluid.

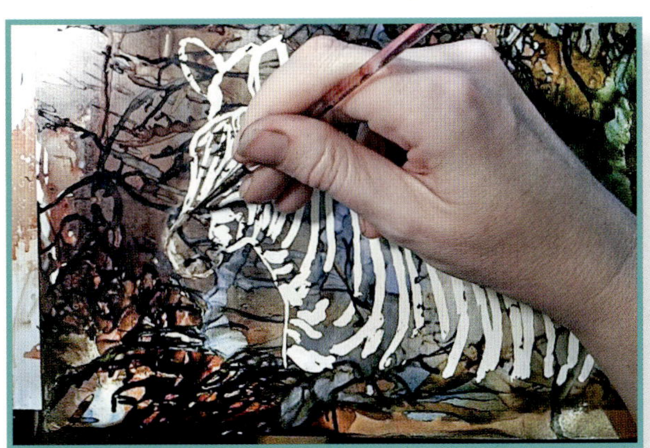

4. Use the brush and alcohol to soften and blend the masked lines as necessary.

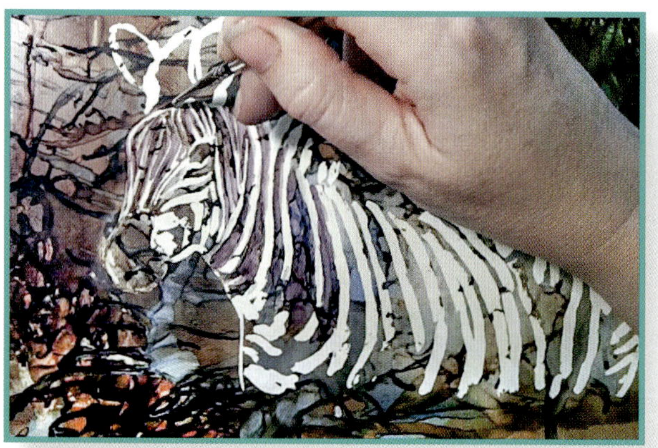

5. Add additional color both in the white and black stripes while continuing to soften and form the zebra.

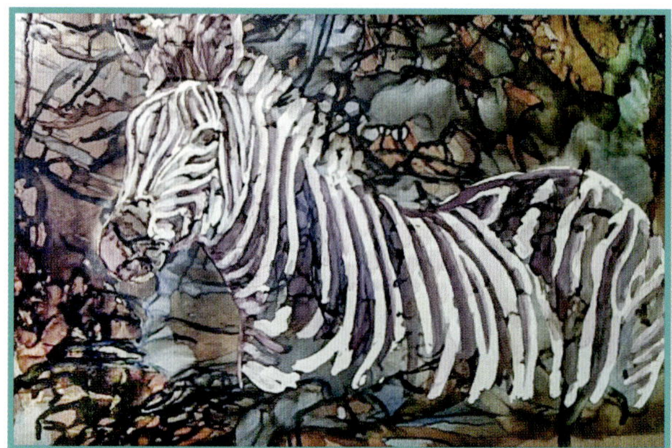

Hidden Zebra - In progress...

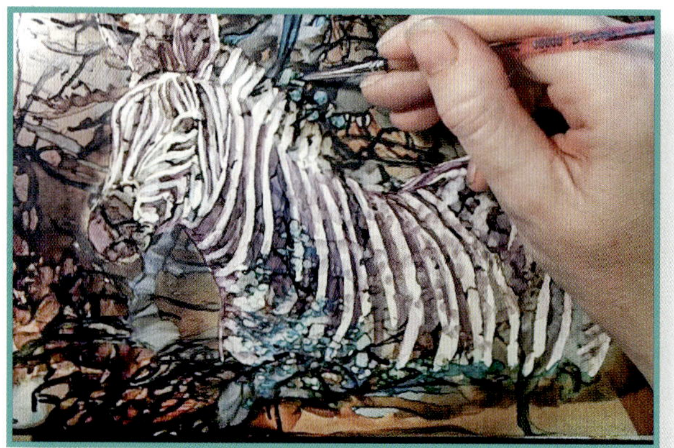

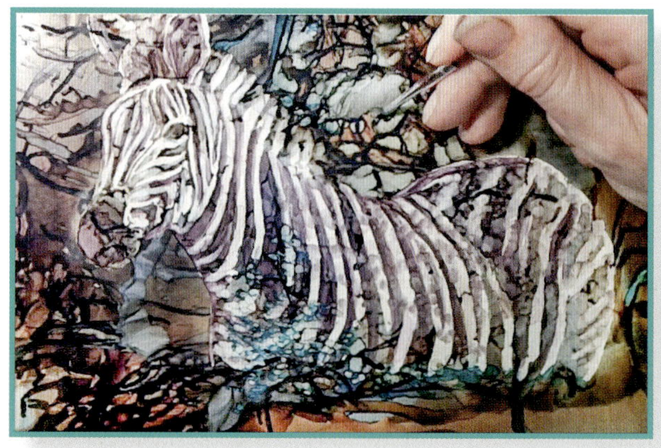

6. Create foliage in the background by adding in green ink and lifting out around the zebra.

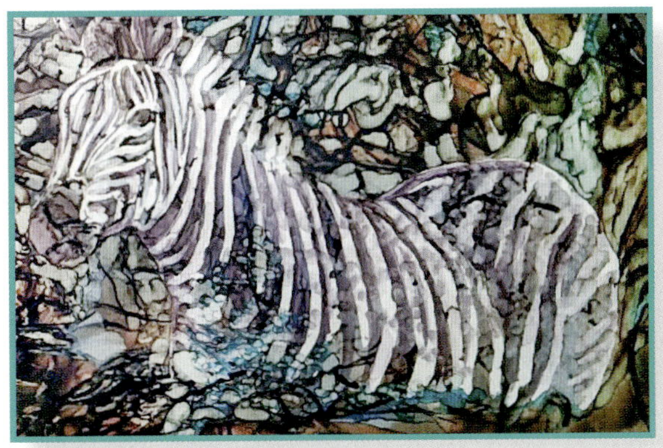

Hidden Zebra - In progress...

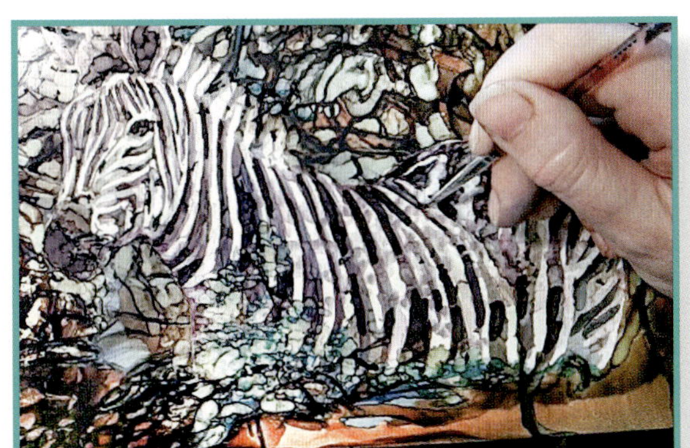

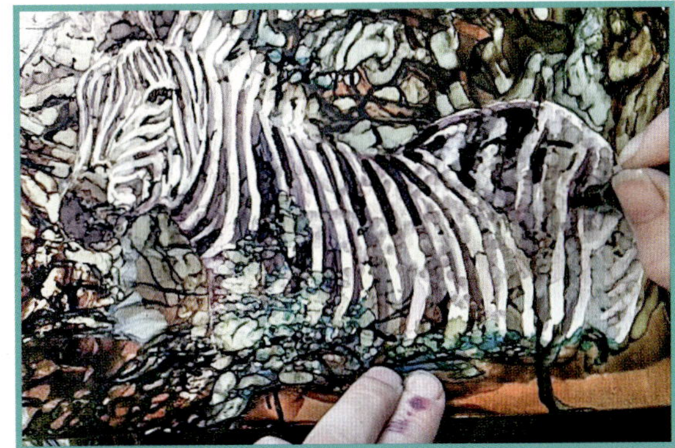

7. Define the darks.

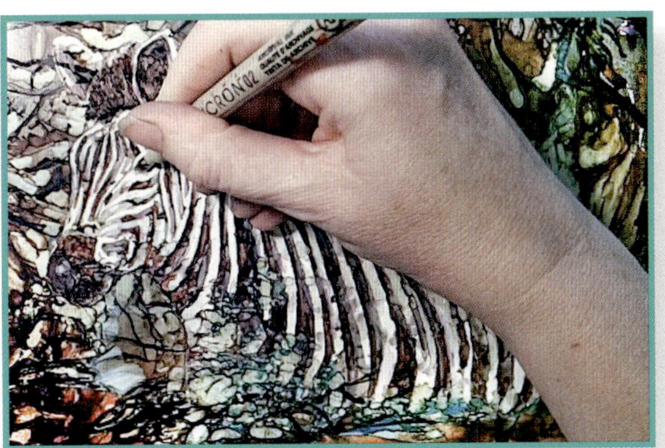

8. Use the fine-tipped pen for details such as the eyes and fur.

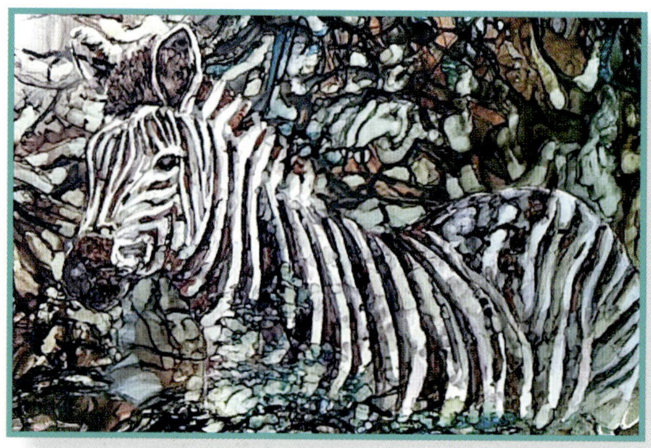

Hidden Zebra - In progress...

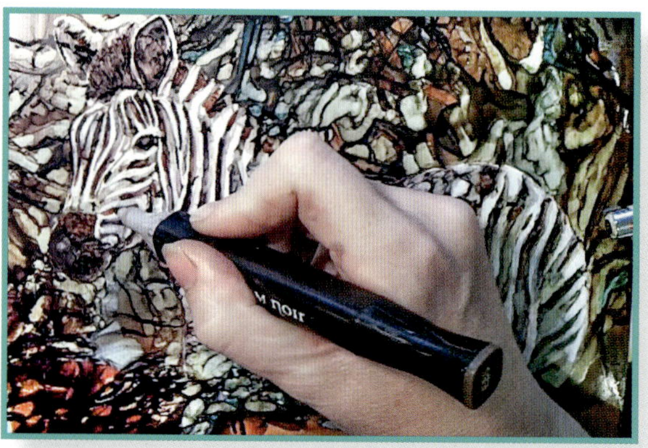

9. Add additional color to the stripes with the alcohol ink marker.

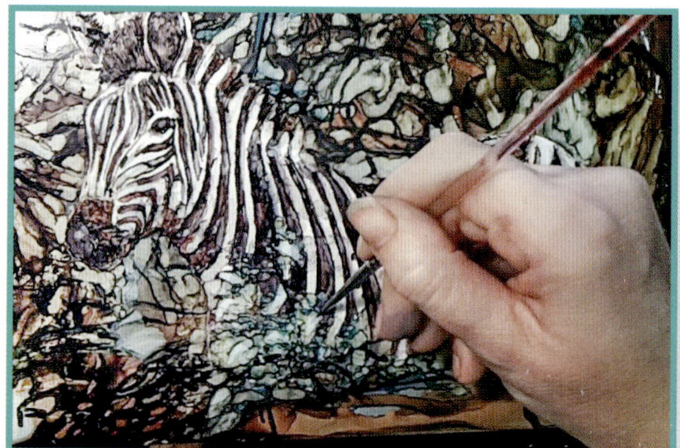

10. Add finishing touches to the foliage.

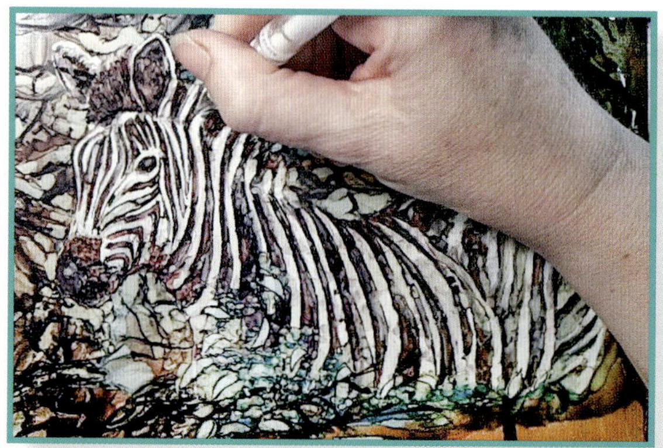

11. Use the white pen for highlights in the fur.

Variation: Colorful Zebra

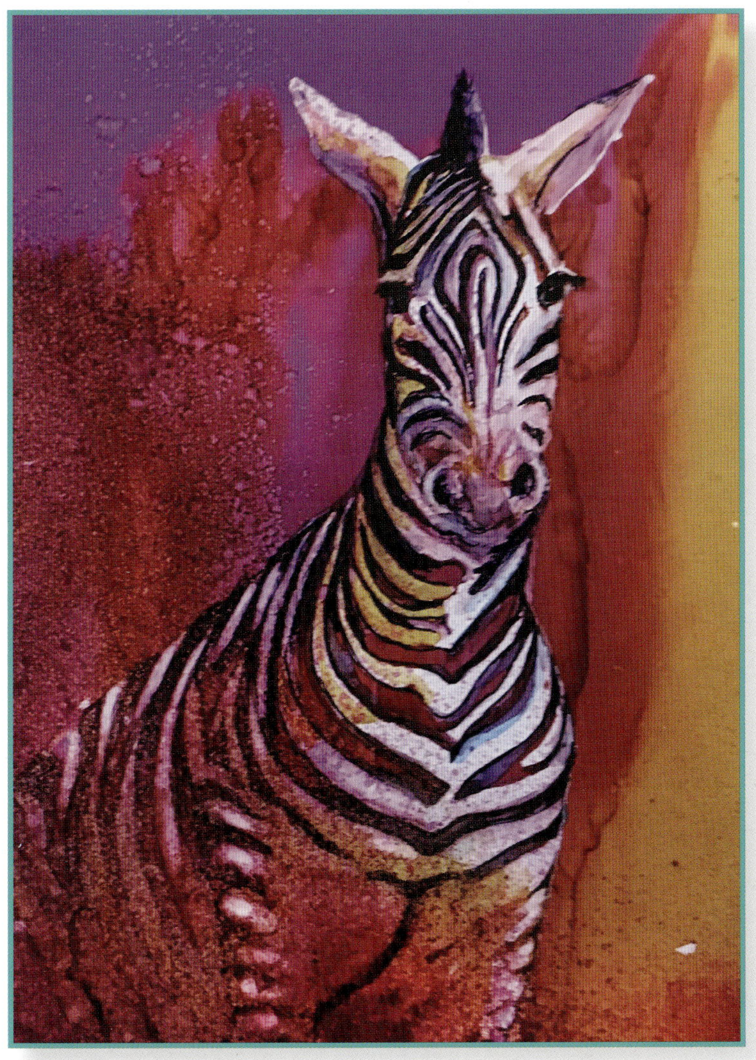

Karen Walker. *Colorful Zebra.*
While there is quite a bit of color in *Hidden Zebra*, the effect is naturalistic. Not so for *Colorful Zebra!* Not only do zebras make great subjects to practice masking, but there are also unlimited possibilities for color and excitement.

5 Vive la France

From monuments to food, the wide-ranging projects in this chapter demonstrate additional techniques and approaches to painting a variety of textures.

Arc de Triomphe: White background with markers

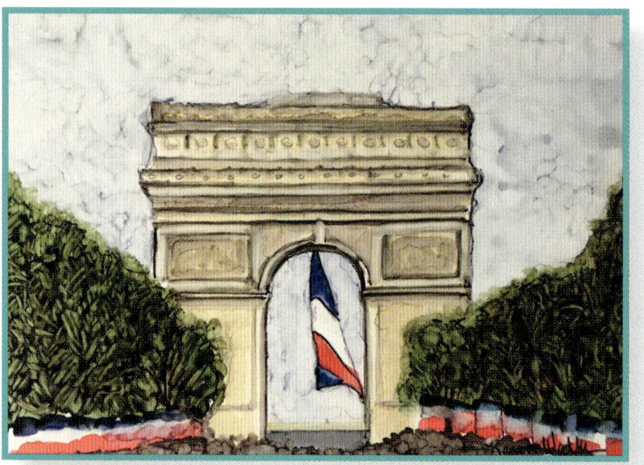

Giverny: Inky background with masking and textures

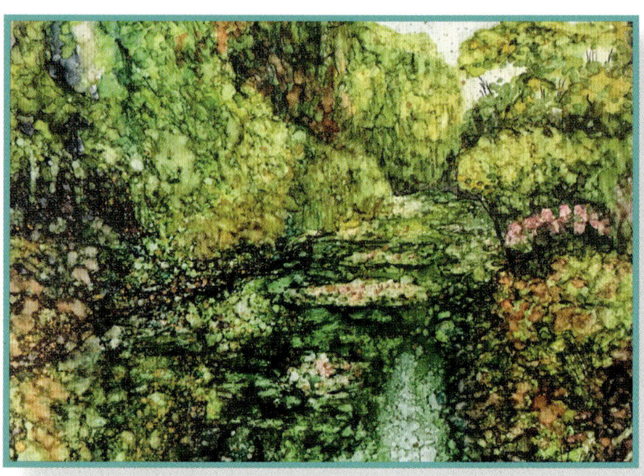

Fig Tart: Stained background with brush and penwork

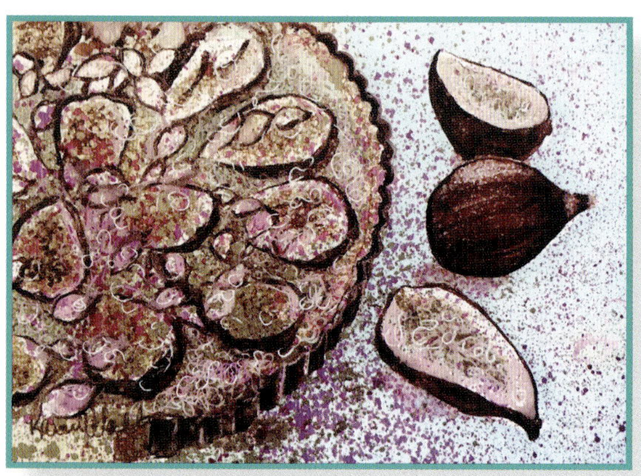

Square du Vert-Galant: Inky background with double masking and textures

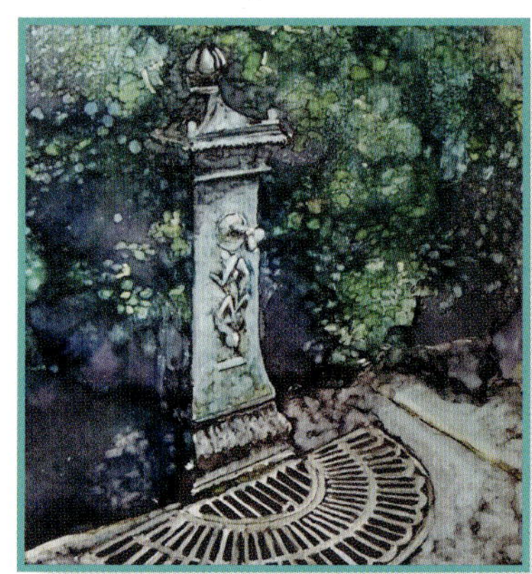

Project 13 - Arc de Triomphe

Karen Walker. *Arc de Triomphe.*

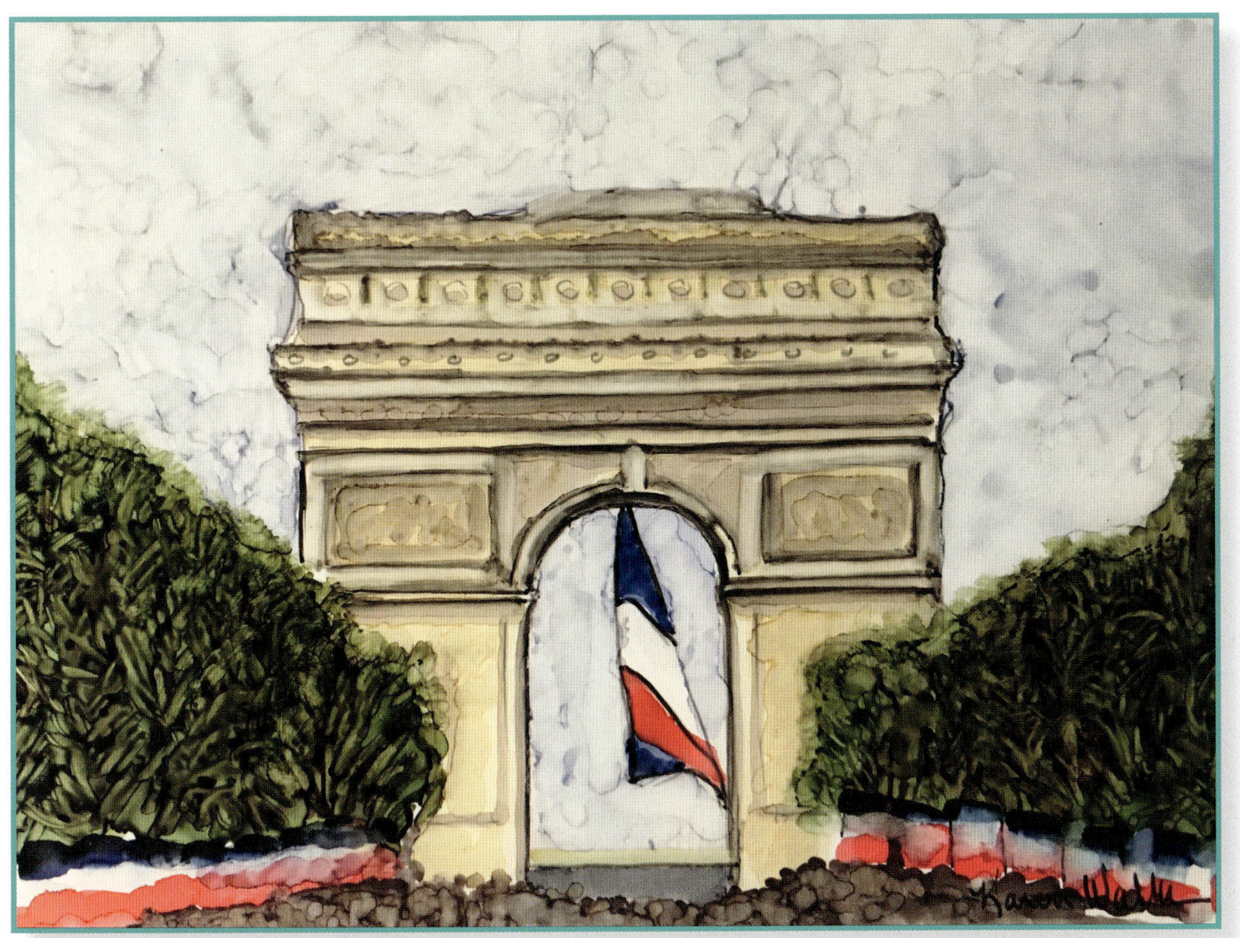

Can you make an ink painting without bottled ink? Yes—this painting was created with markers, fine-tipped pens, and a bit of alcohol to soften.

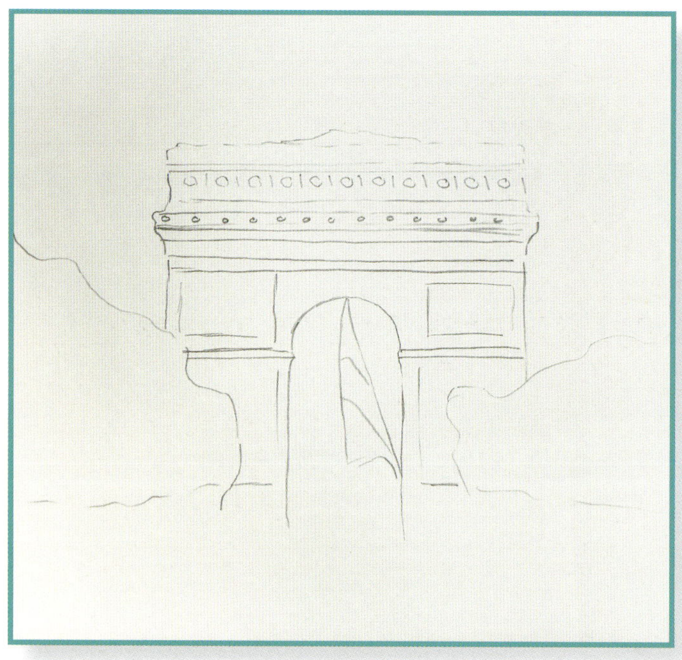

1. Begin with a light sketch.

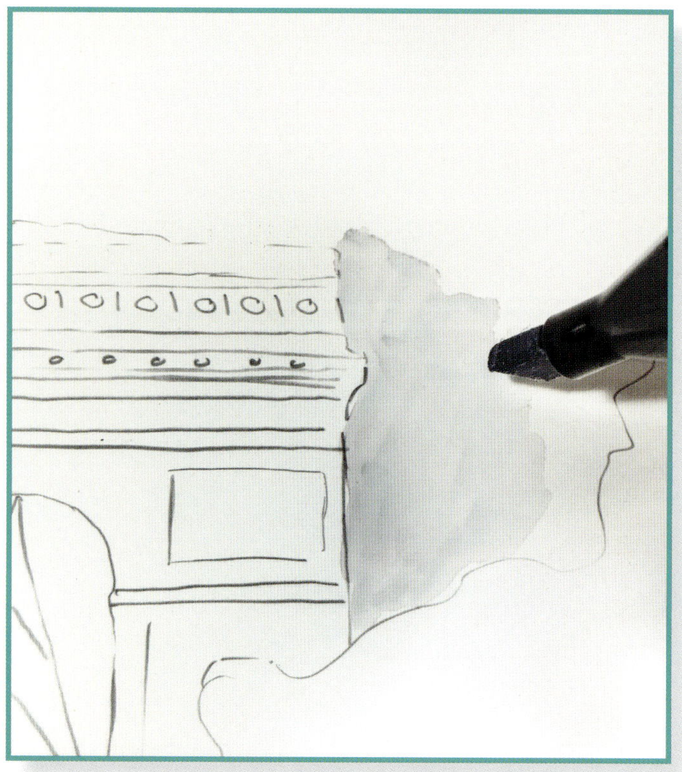

2. Color in the sky with a pale marker.

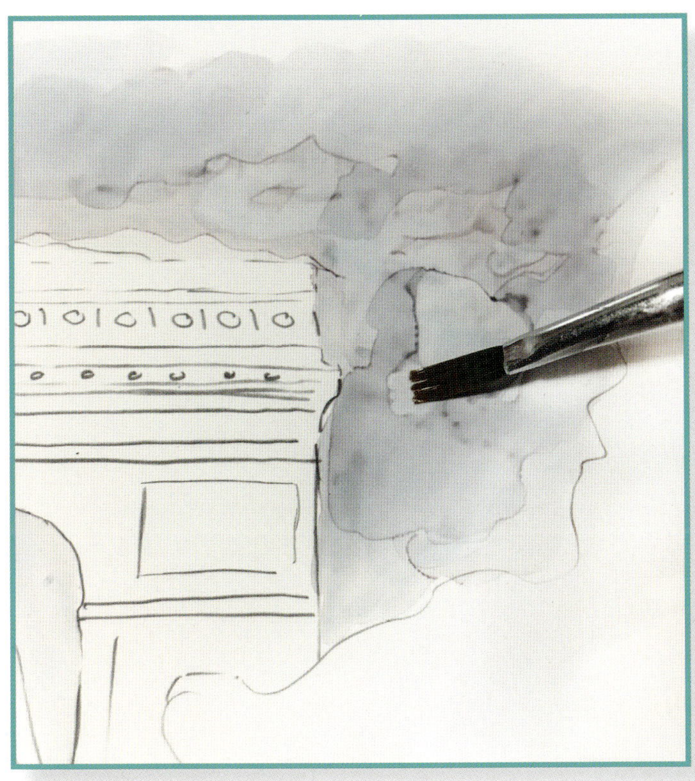

3. Soften the sky by brushing over with alcohol.

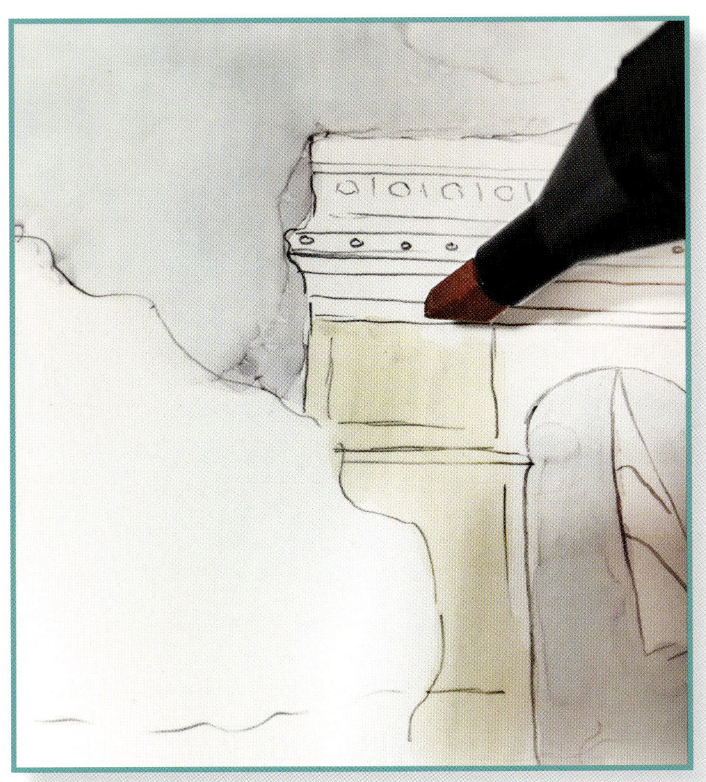

4. Color in the monument.

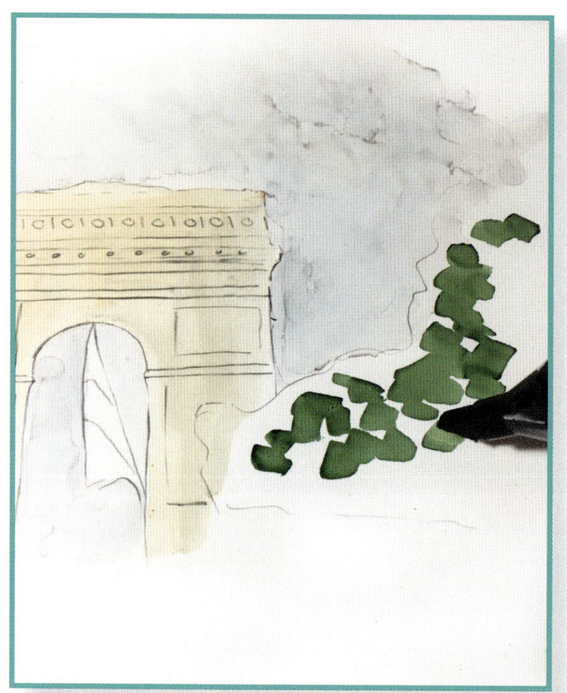

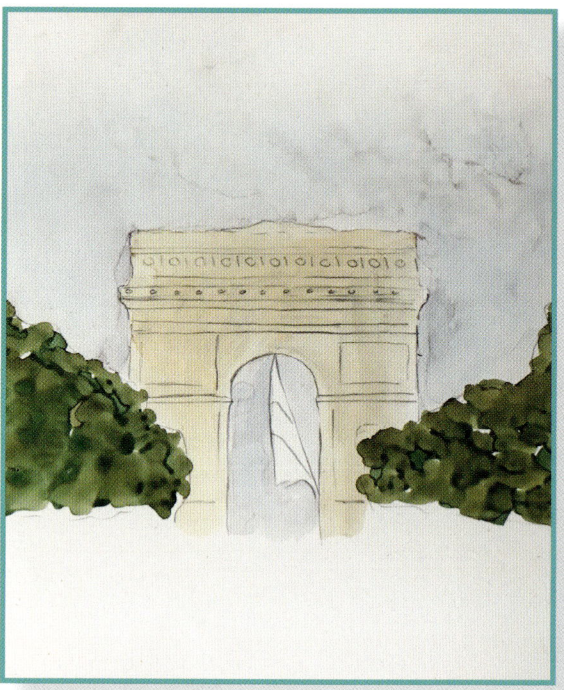

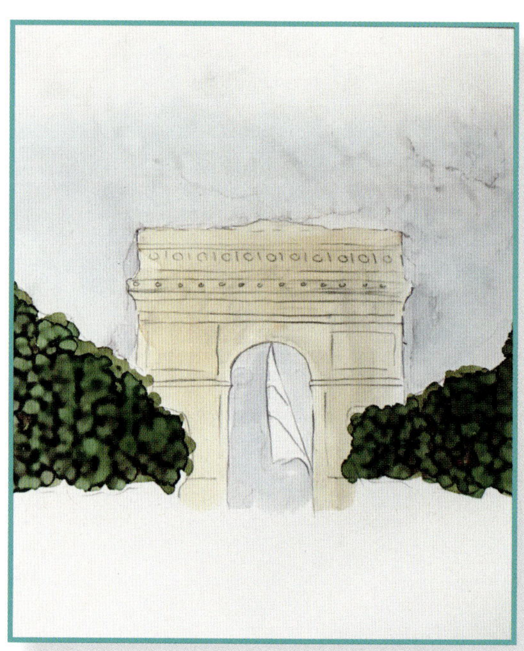

5. Add in foliage with multiple colors of green, then soften with alcohol.

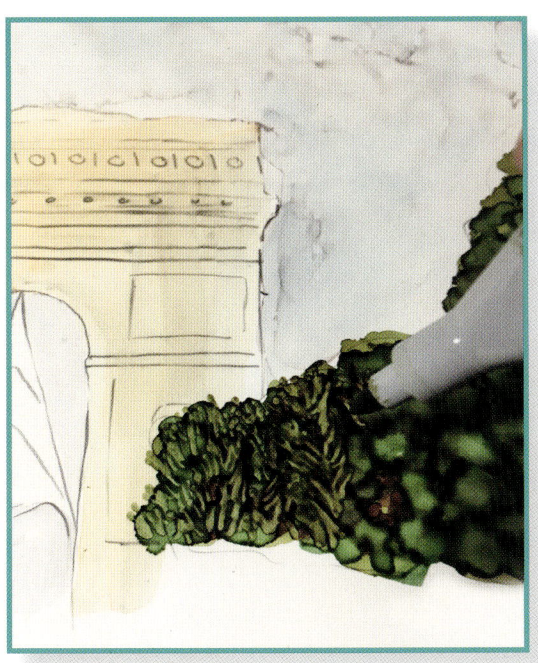

6. Use the smaller nib of the marker to lift ink and draw in tree branches.

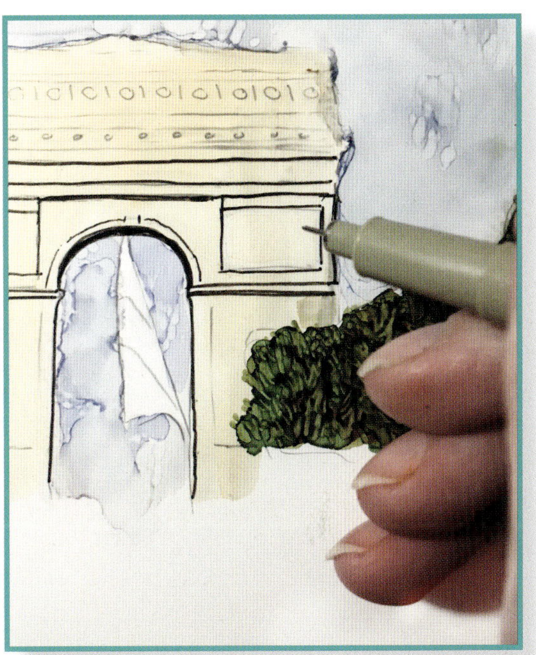

7. With the fine-tipped black pen, outline the monument and add definition.

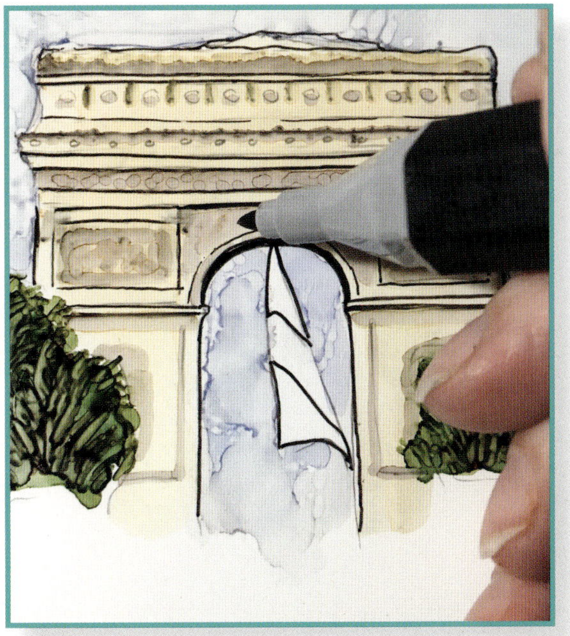

8. Use various shades of alcohol ink markers to create dimensionality and to soften the black pen.

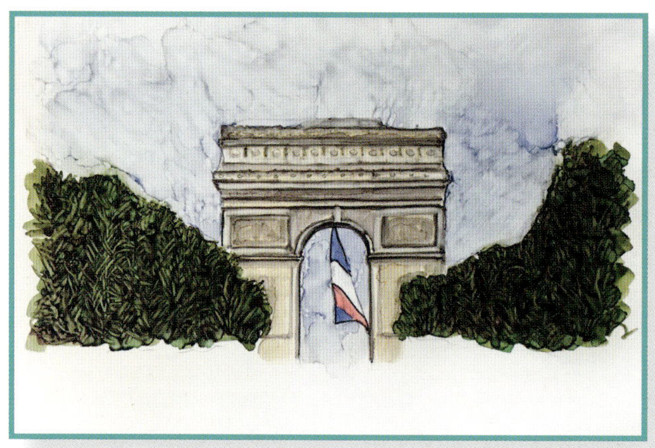

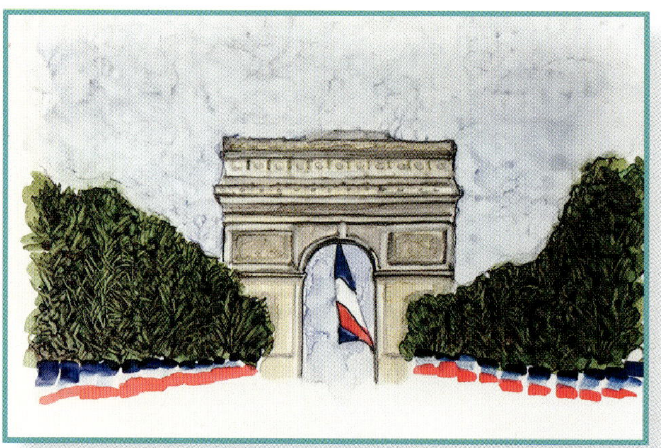

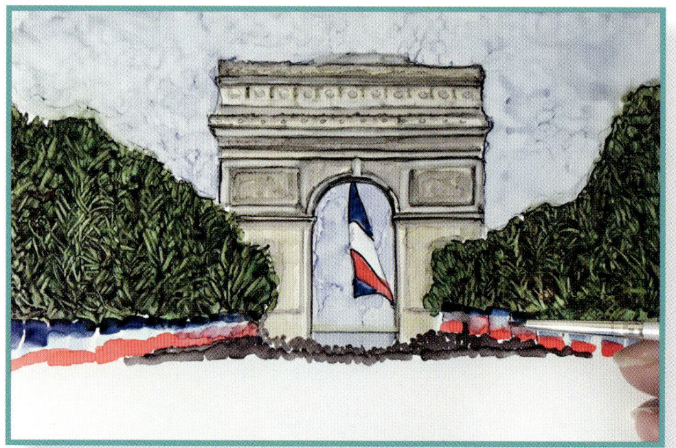

9. Add more details, including the flags and texture in the sky, with markers and the brush with alcohol.

Variation: Under the Eiffel Tower

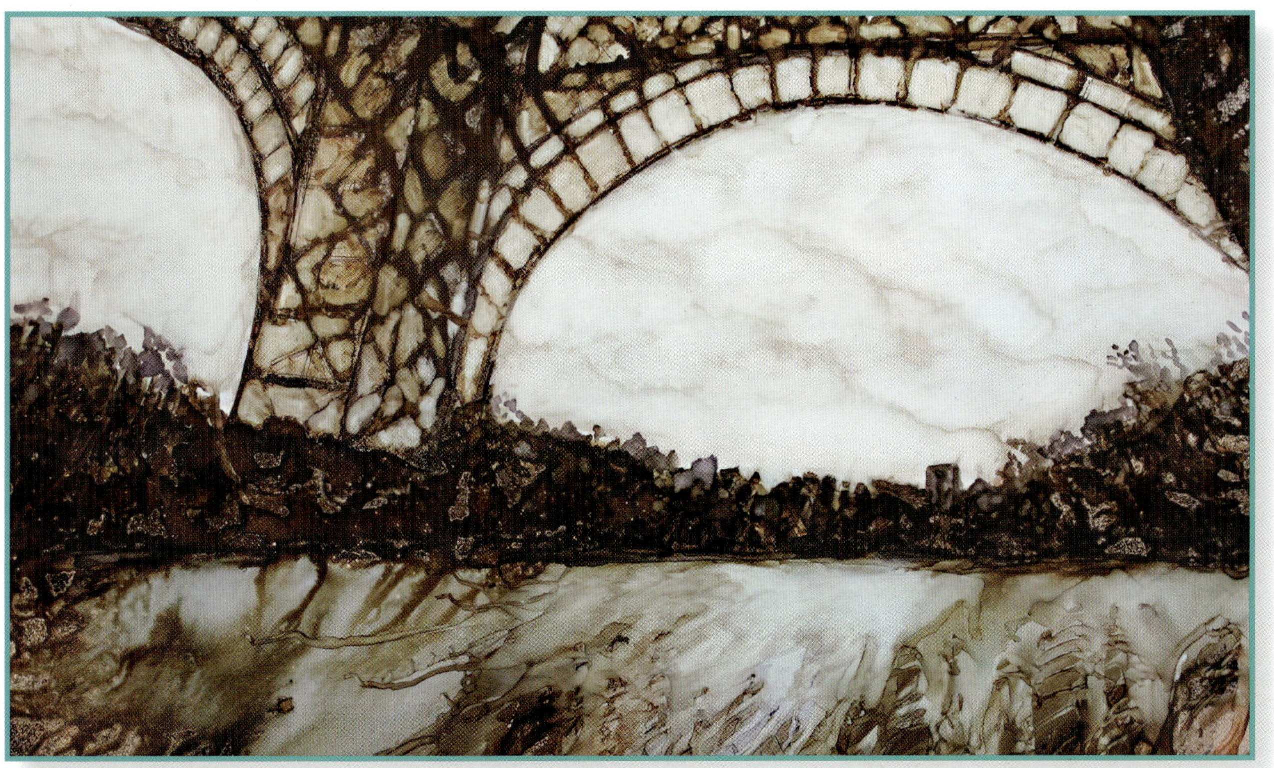

Karen Walker. *Under the Eiffel Tower.*
The controlled effect of the *Arc de Triomphe* created by using markers is in sharp contrast to this version of another Paris monument. The fluidity of *Under the Eiffel Tower* evokes the feelings of a rainy day, not uncommon for Paris.

Project 14 - Giverny

Karen Walker. *Giverny.*

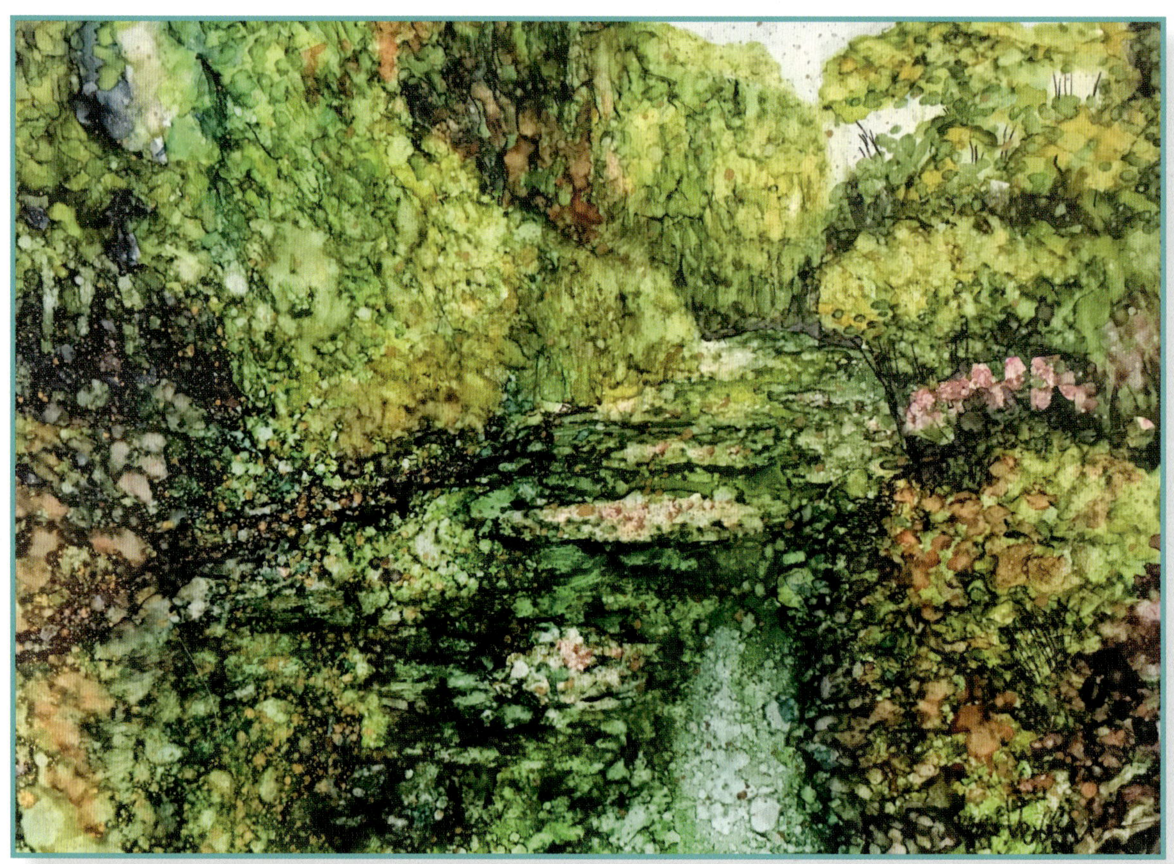

Splattered alcohol and a lot of texture give this garden painting an impressionist feel. My trip to Monet's garden was the highlight of my trip to France.

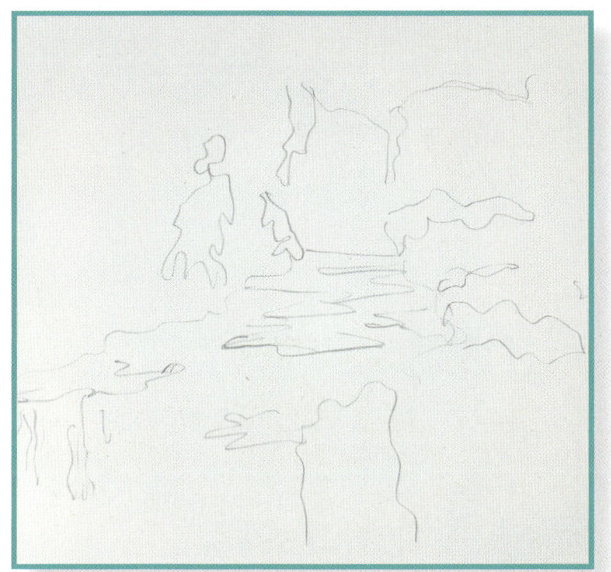

1. Begin with a light sketch, noting the lightest parts of the landscape.

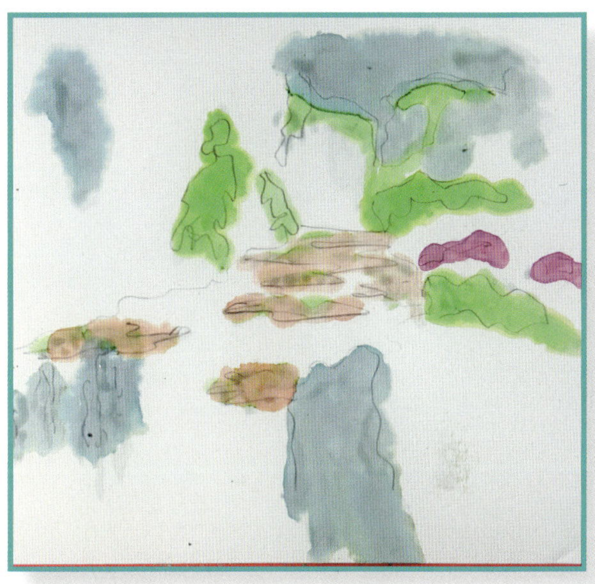

2. For this project, the light areas are toned with colored ink prior to masking. The lightest spots are left white. Mask and let dry.

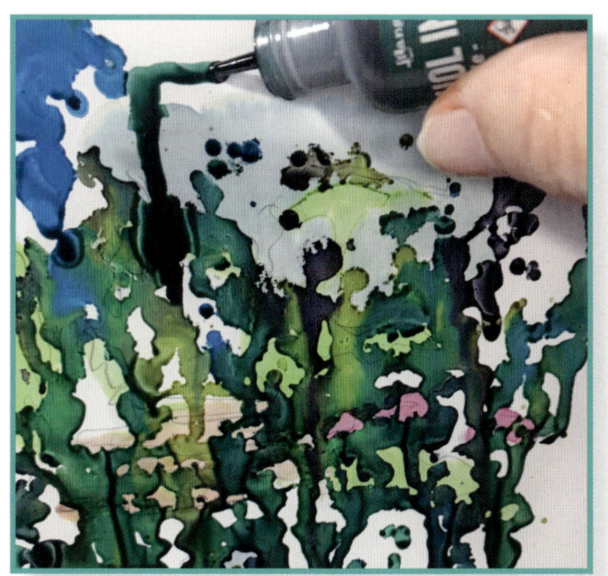

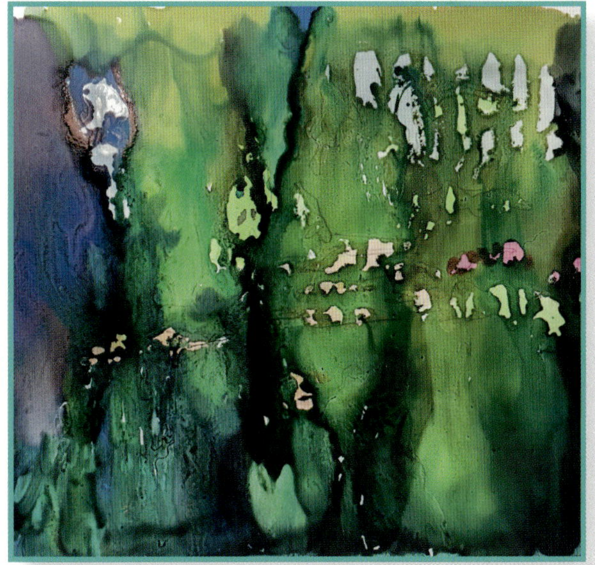

3. Pour an inky background, keeping in mind the colors of the painting particularly regarding the light and dark parts of the landscape.

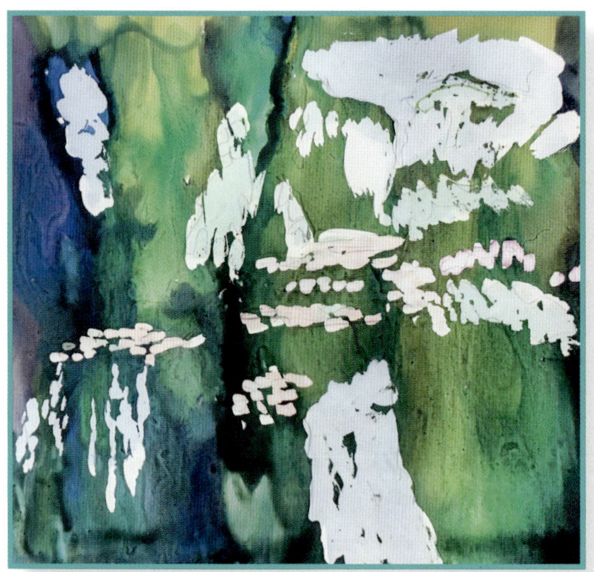

4. Let dry and remove the masking fluid.

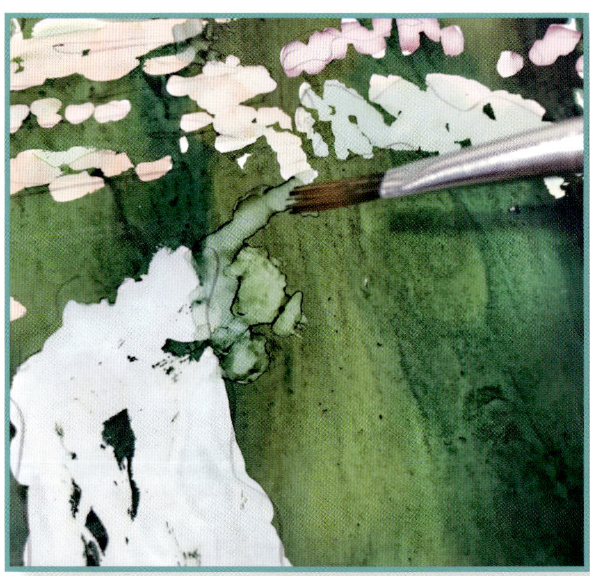

5. Begin to build the structure of the landscape by drawing in the water lines with the brush and alcohol.

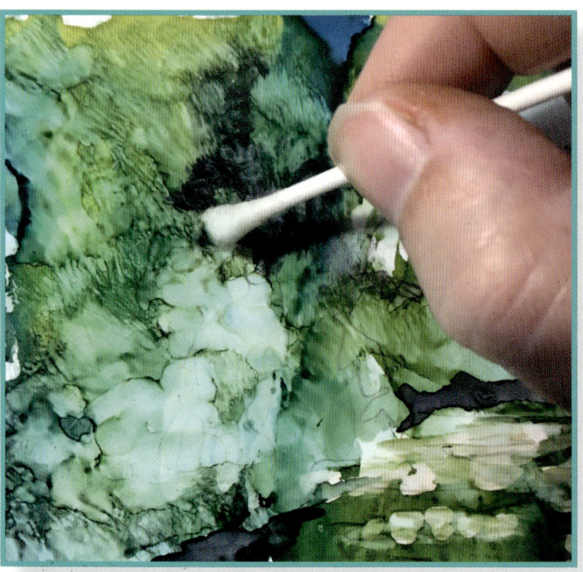

6. Use the cotton swab and alcohol to lift out the bush and tree forms.

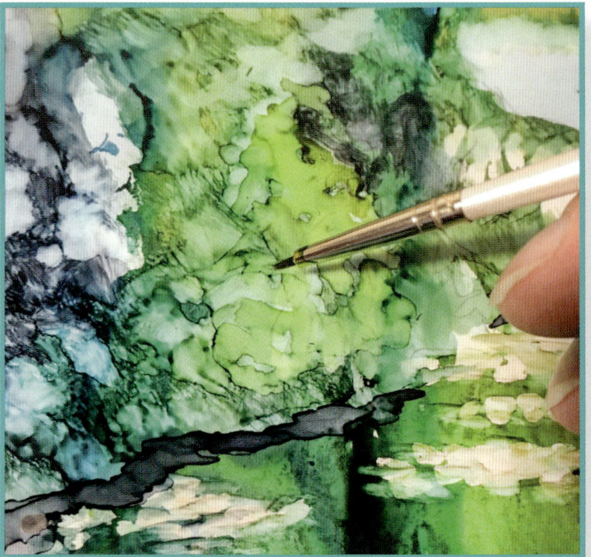

7. Paint in foliage with the brush and ink.

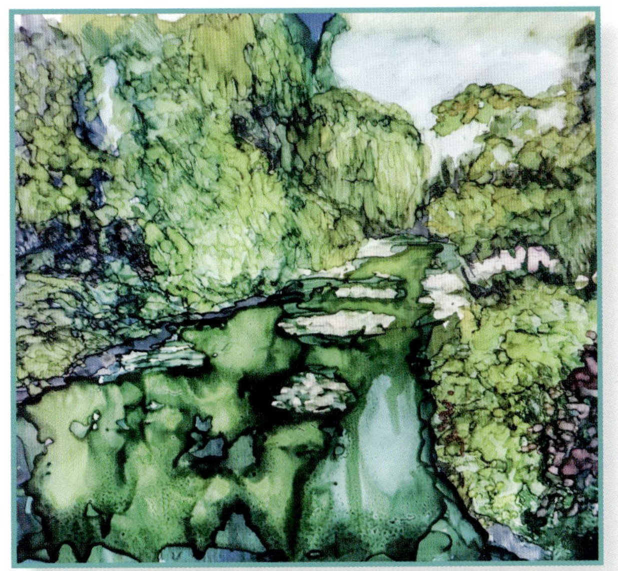

8. At this stage, review the painting and the landscape. Add more ink to deepen and unify the water.

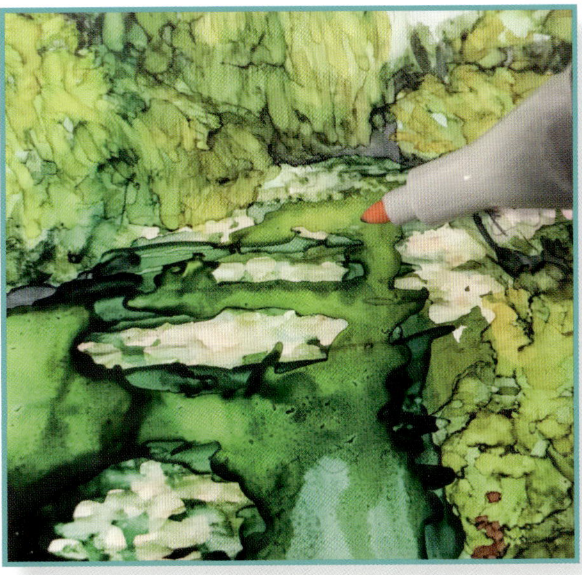

9. Use the pink marker to lift out the water lilies.

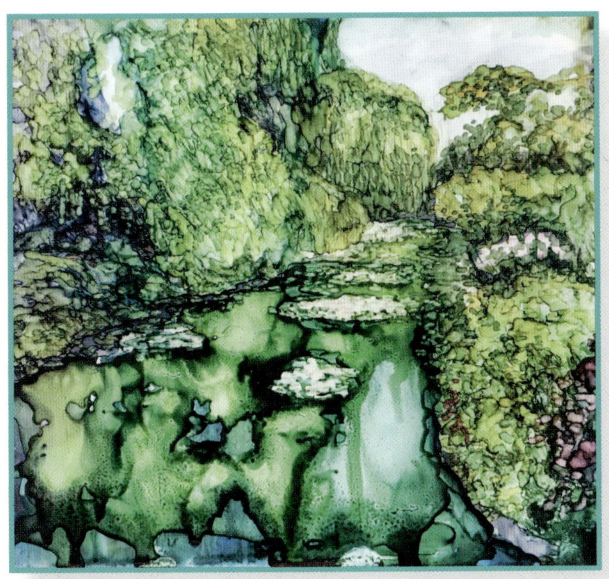

Giverny - In progress...

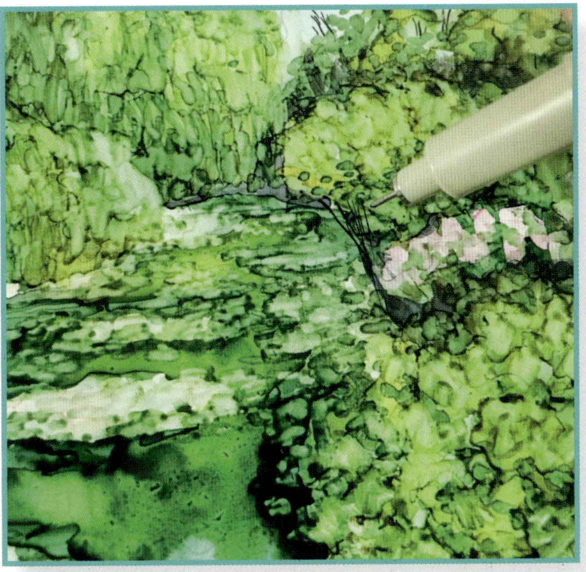

10. Add tree trunks and details with the fine-tipped black marker.

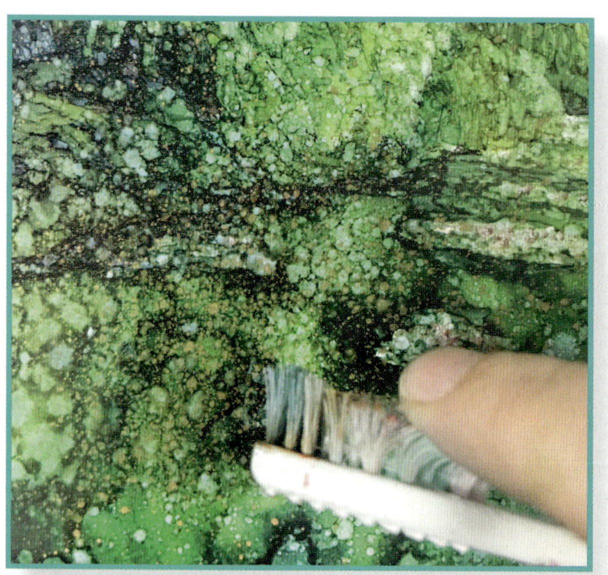

11. Add an impressionistic feel by using the toothbrush to splatter the painting with alcohol, gold, and colored ink.

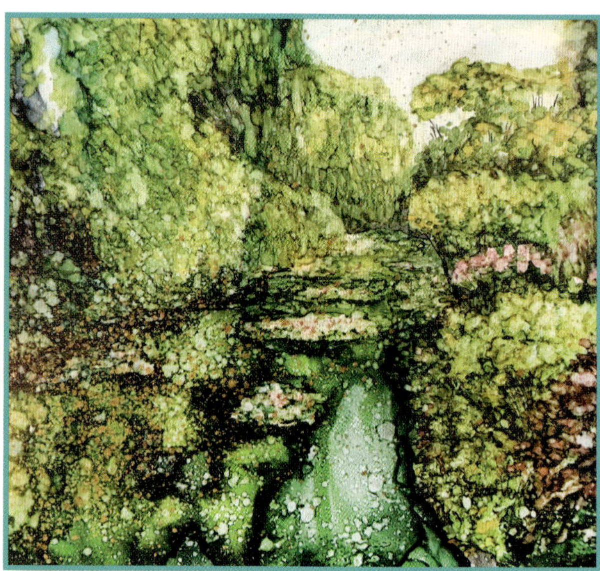

Giverny - In progress...

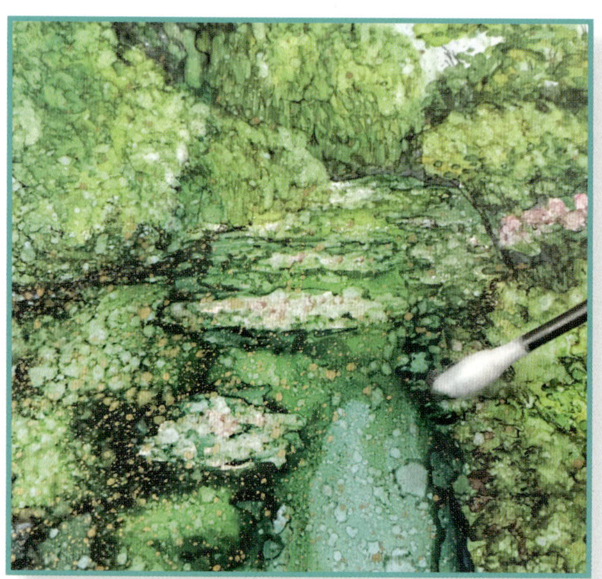

12. Use the cotton swab to remove any unwanted dark lines.

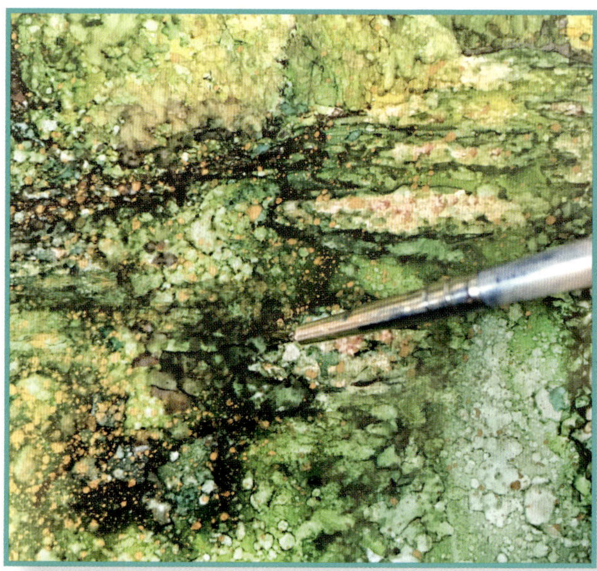

13. Add a few finishing touches with the brush.

Variation: Chinese Bridge

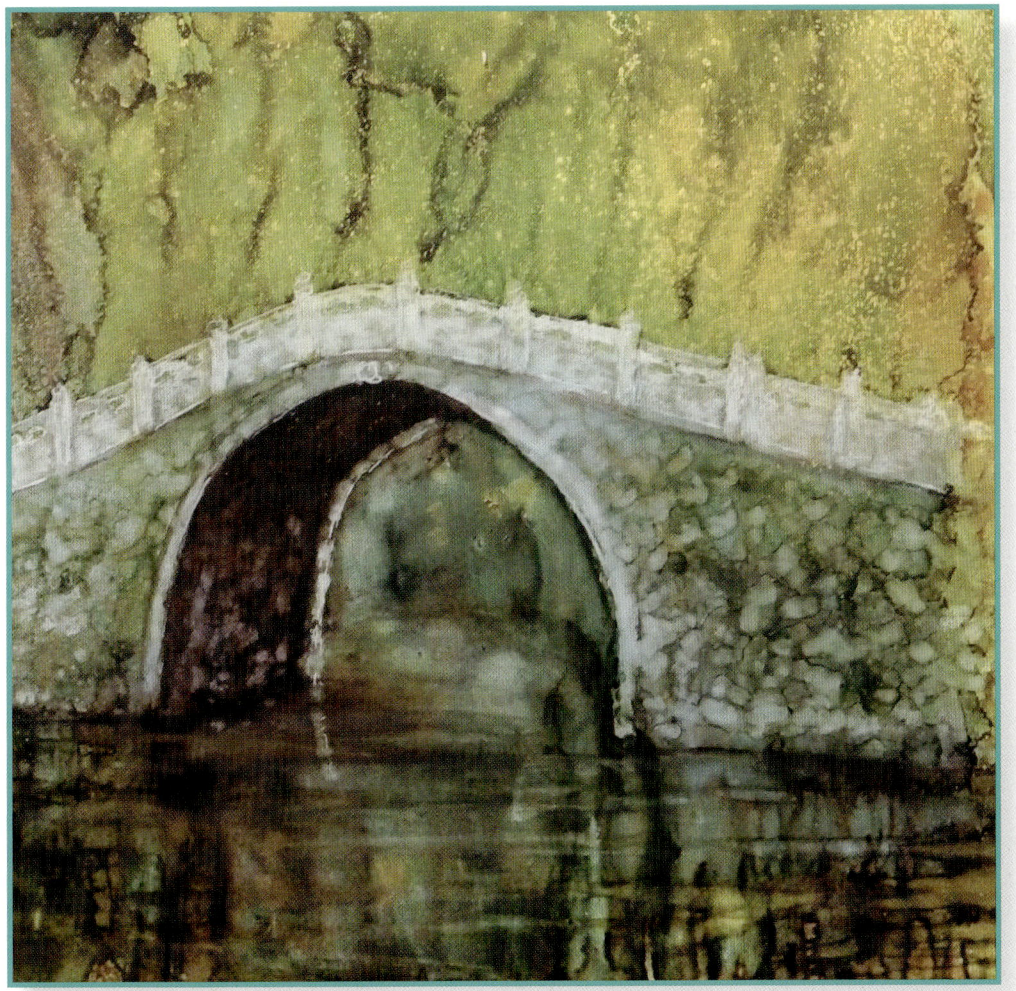

Karen Walker. *Chinese Bridge*.
Like the painting of the garden at Giverny, *Chinese Bridge* features water and is nearly monochromatically green. While the impressionistic style of *Giverny* yields small texture and broken color, the inky passages in the *Chinese Bridge* are much larger.

Project 15 - Fig Tart

Karen Walker. *Fig Tart.*

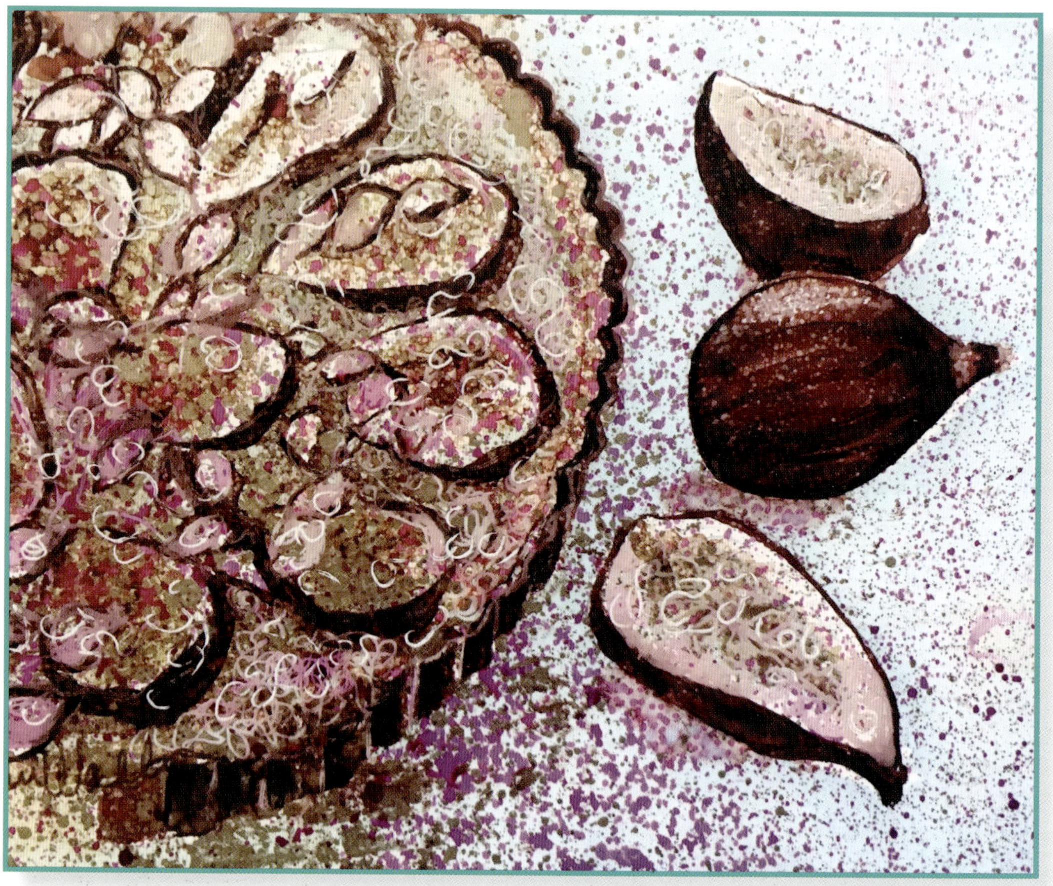

This whimsical rendition of a fig tart was inspired by my cousin Daisy's food blog recipe for a fig, almond frangipane, and orange tart. This painting features a pale background, created by lifting the ink to leave just the stain, and a fair amount of detailed painting with thickened ink.

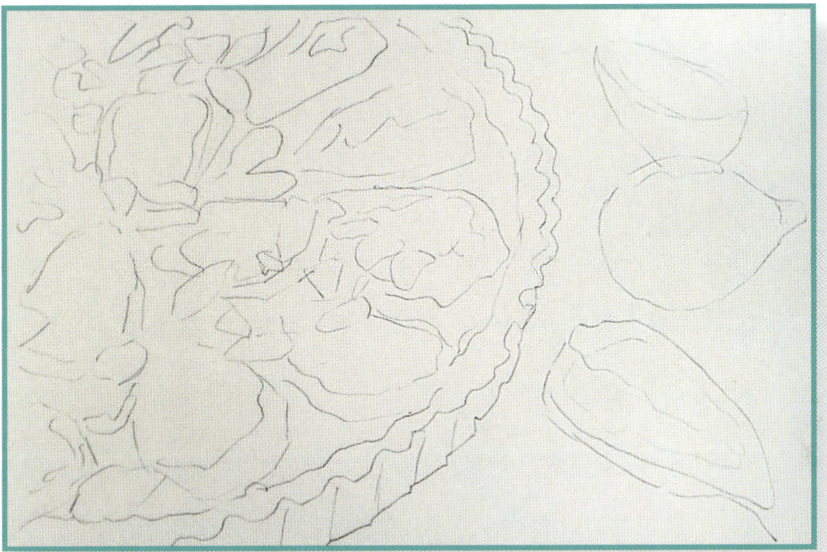

1. Lightly sketch the design in pencil.

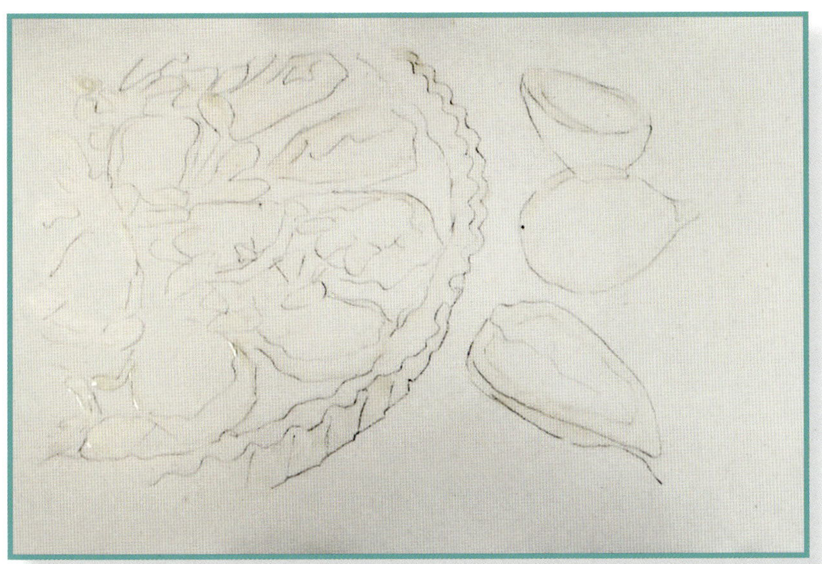

2. Partially mask the outlines of the figs and tart as well as areas to be left light.

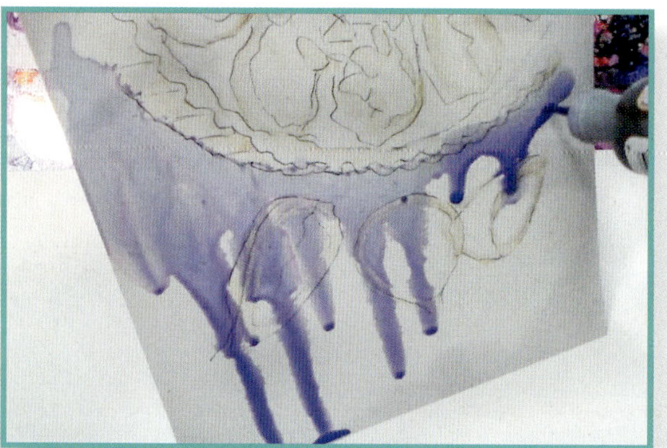

3. Ink the background by holding the paper vertically and following around the tart so the ink flows away from the tart.

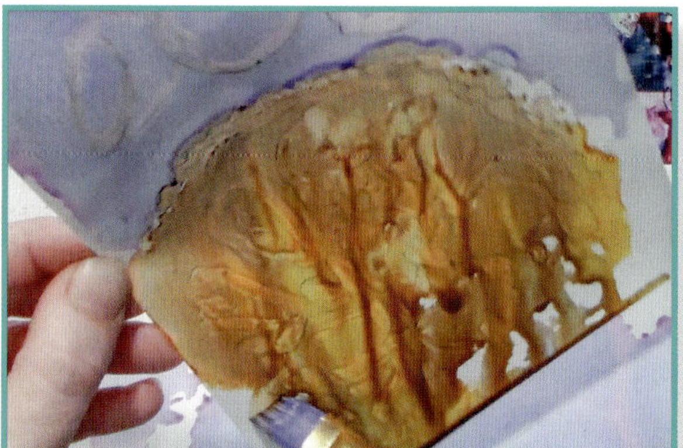

4. Ink the tart by holding the paper vertically in the opposite direction. Use the brush to direct the ink to fill in any white spots while it is still wet.

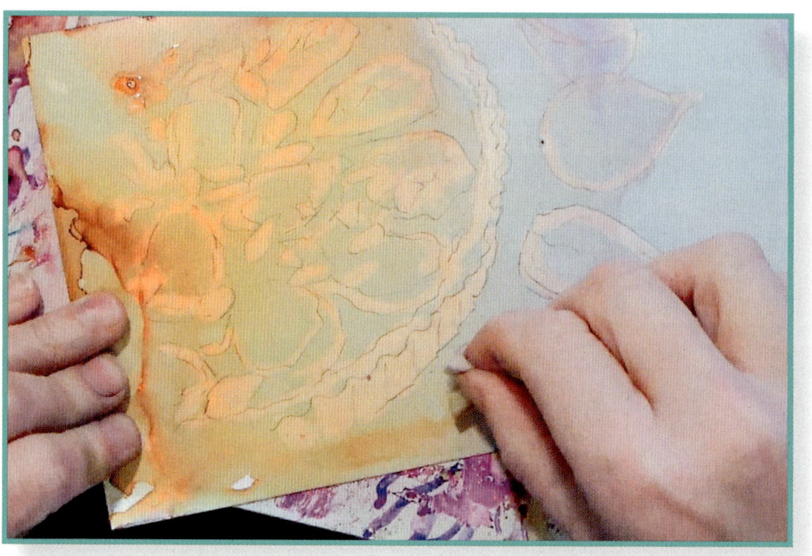

5. Use felt to remove the ink and lighten the background to just the stain of the paper.

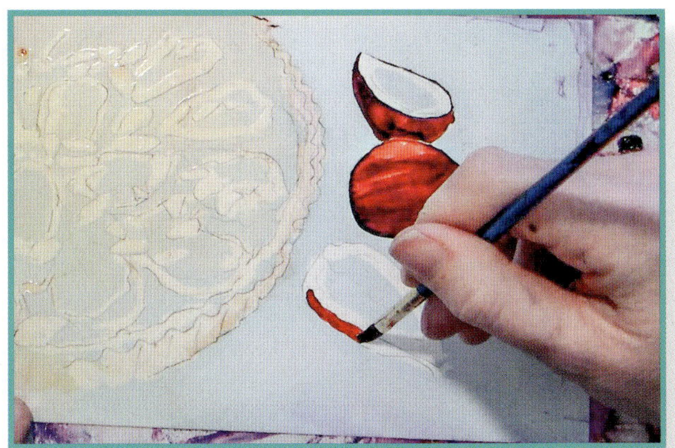

6. Remove the masking fluid from the figs and paint them in, using the brush and thickened ink (to thicken, allow ink to partially evaporate in the welled palette).

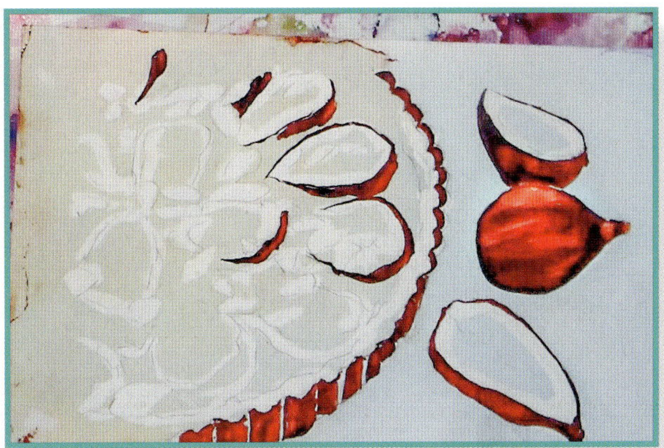

7. Begin painting in the tart by removing the masking fluid and brushing in brown ink, as with the figs.

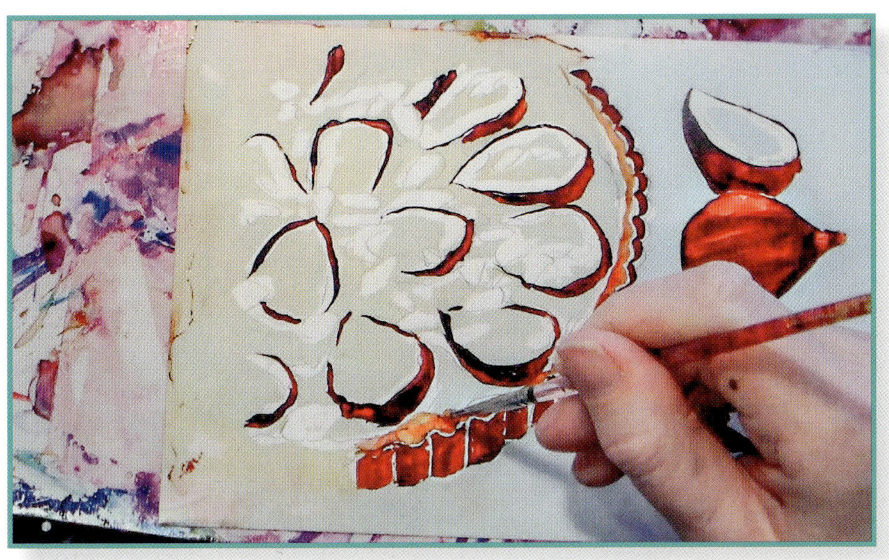

8. Use the brush to fill in lighter shades.

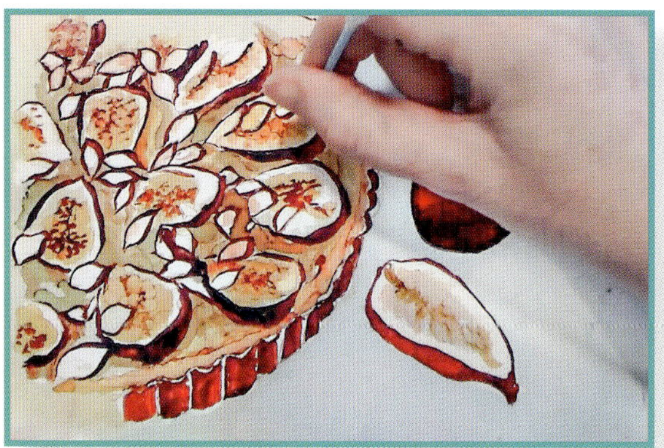

9. Use a cotton swab to soften edges.

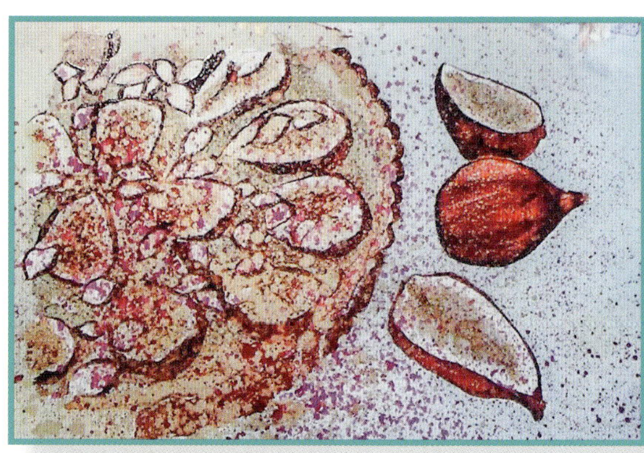

10. Splatter ink (gold and pink) and alcohol.

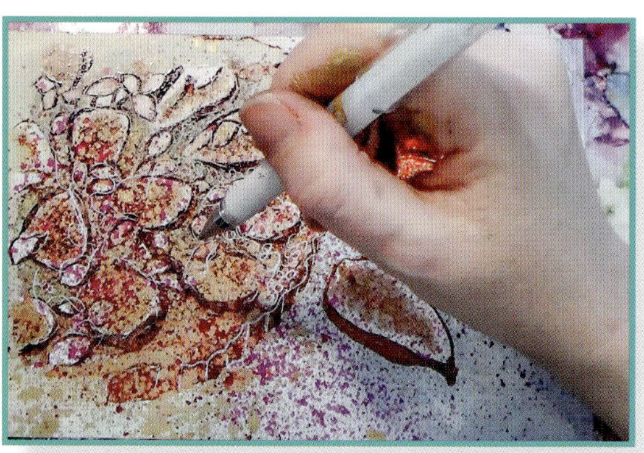

11. Use the white pen to create a squiggly design across the tart.

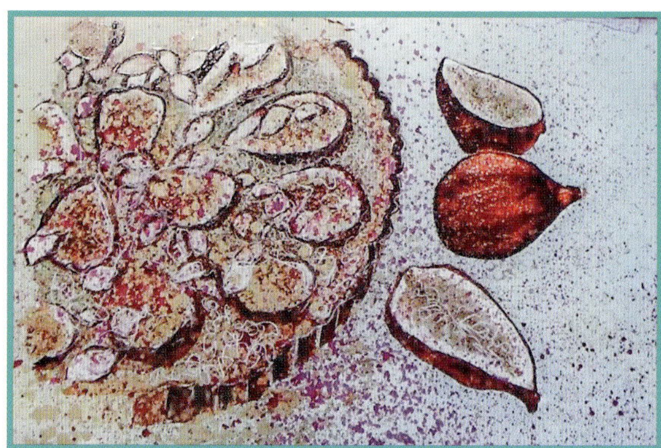

12. Define the edges with the black pen and soften with alcohol to blend.

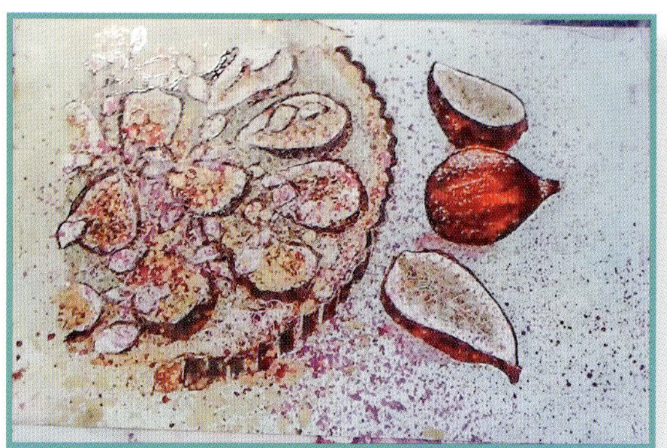

13. Add soft shadows under the figs with alcohol and ink.

Variation: Orchid

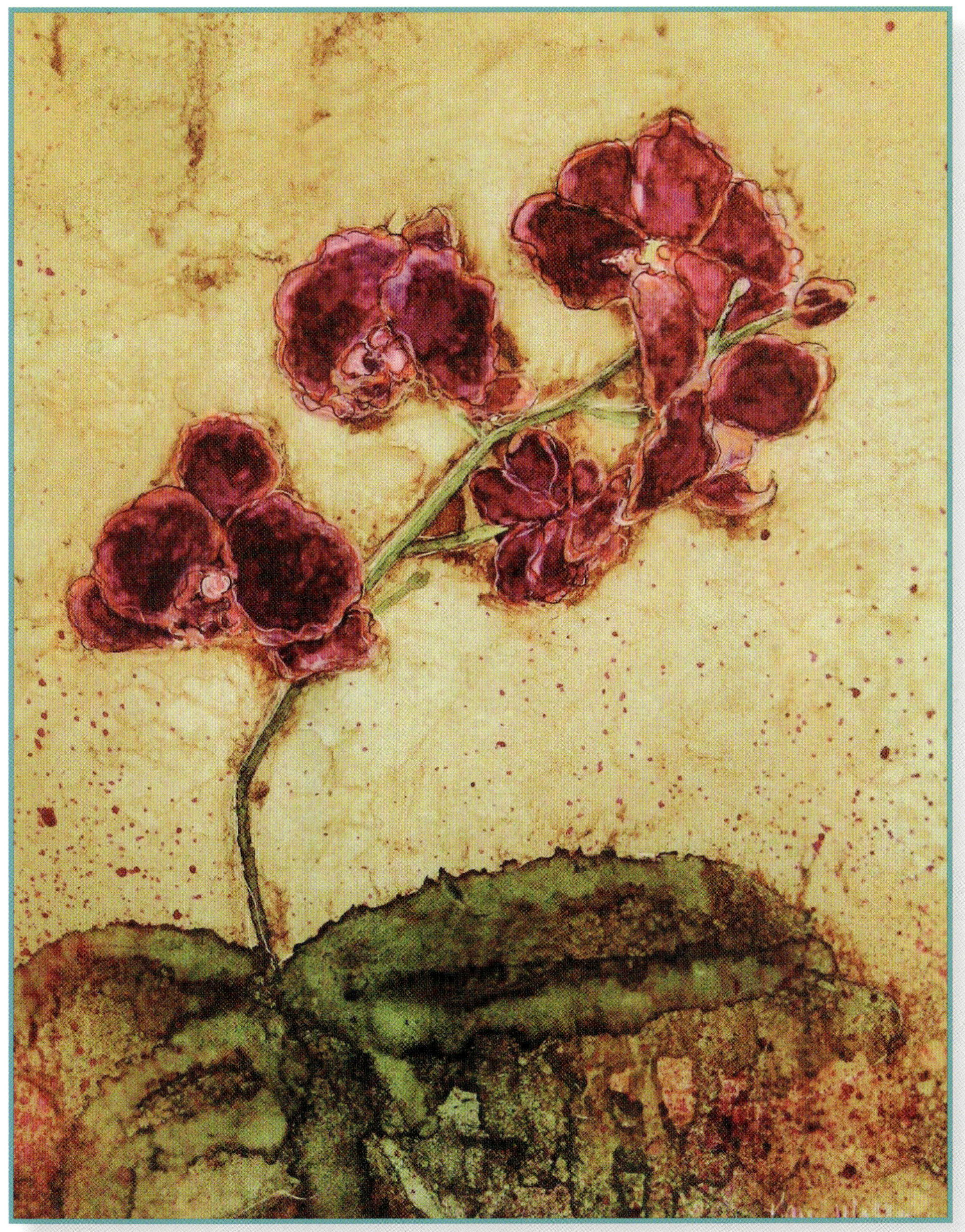

Karen Walker. *Orchid.*
The backgrounds both of *Fig Tart* and the *Orchid* are stained paper created by inking the background and removing most of the ink. For the *Orchid*, a small amount of ink is left to give the impression of parchment.

Project 16 - Square du Vert - Galant

Karen Walker. *Square du Vert-Galant.*

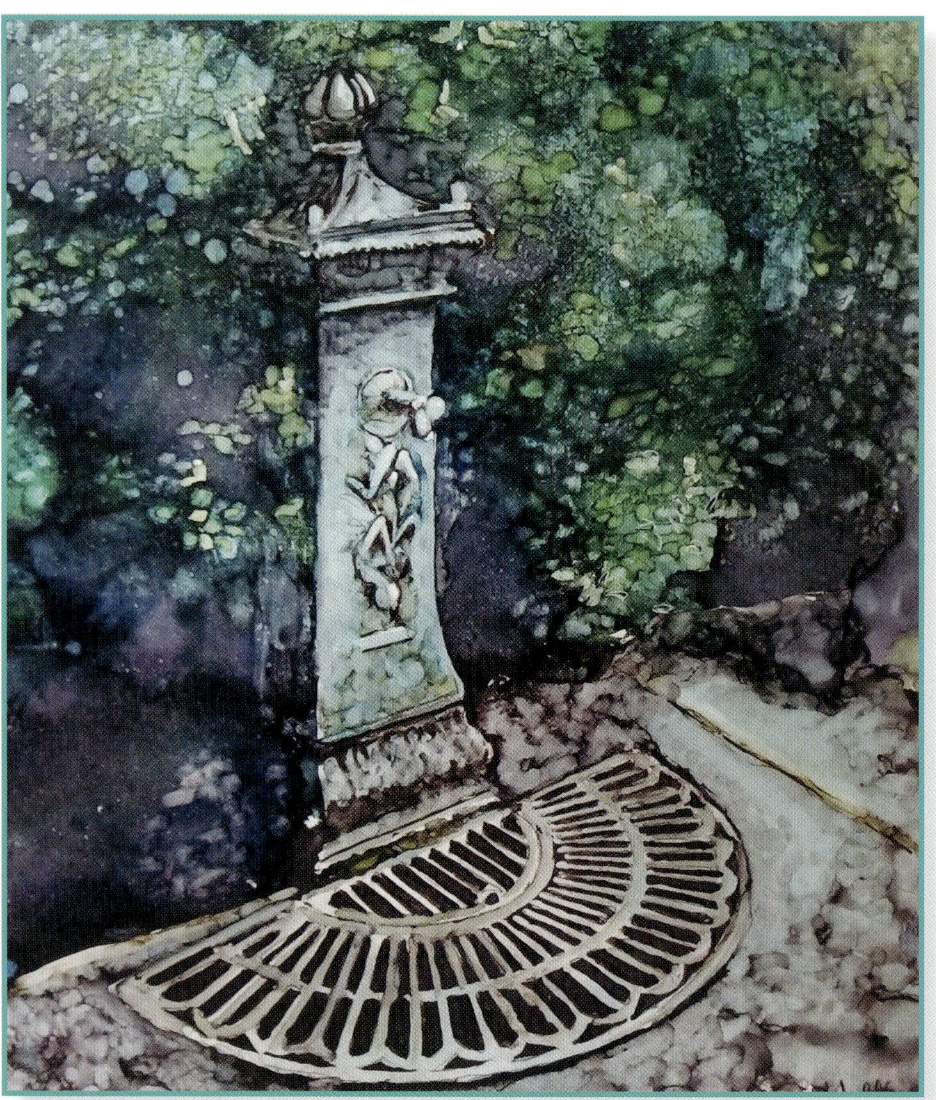

For *Square du Vert-Galant*, the emphasis is on texture—metal, stone, and foliage. This project features two masking steps—one for the lightest lights, and one where the paper is toned for the fountain and grate.

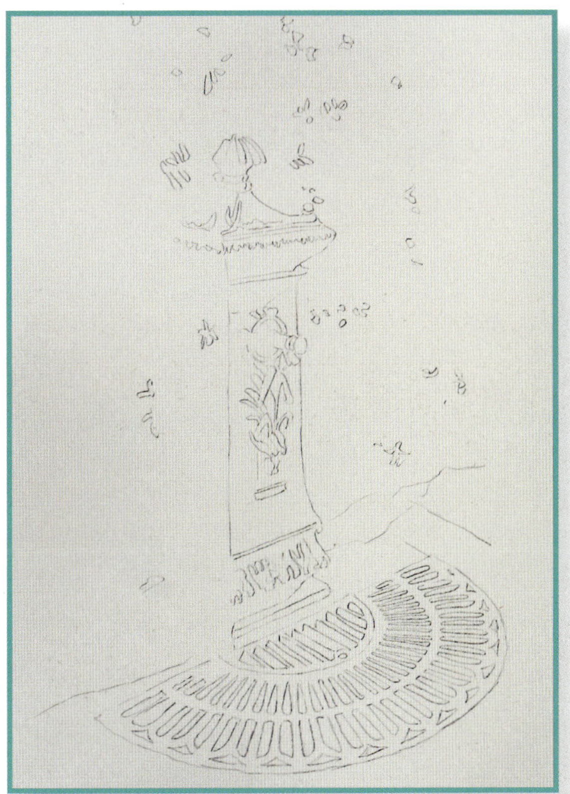

1. Lightly draw the outline and details of the fountain.

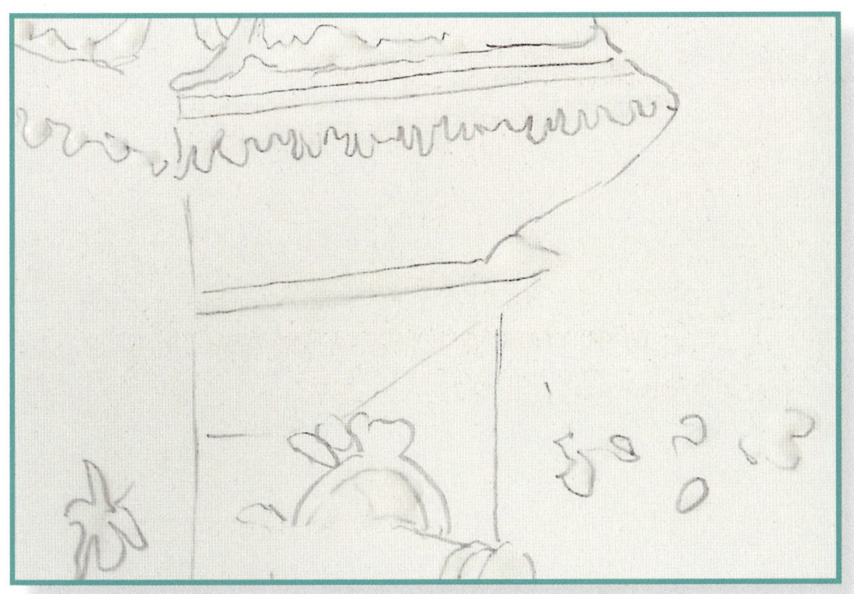

2. Mask the areas to be left white.

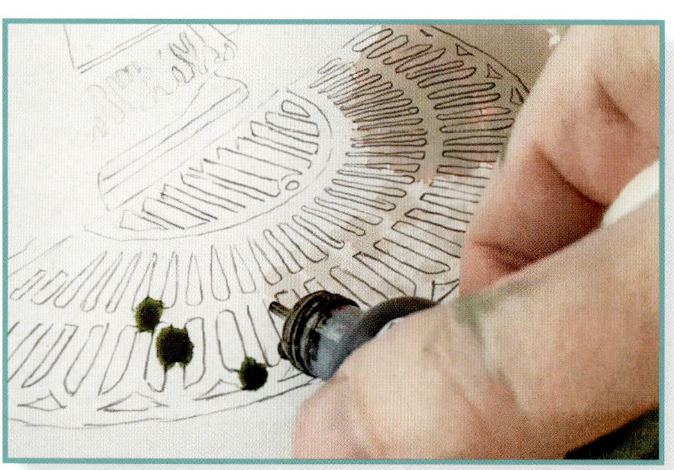

3. Softly tone the areas to be protected in the second masking.

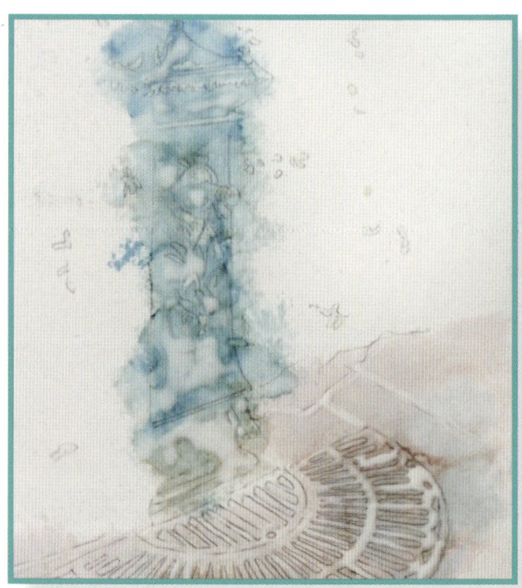

4. Apply the second layer of masking fluid over the fountain and the grate.

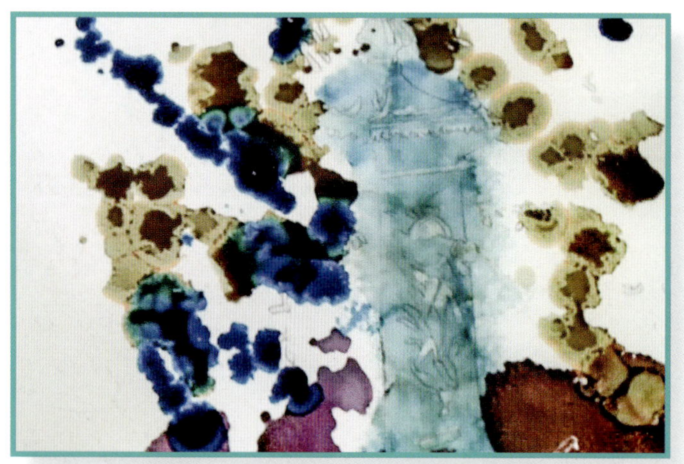

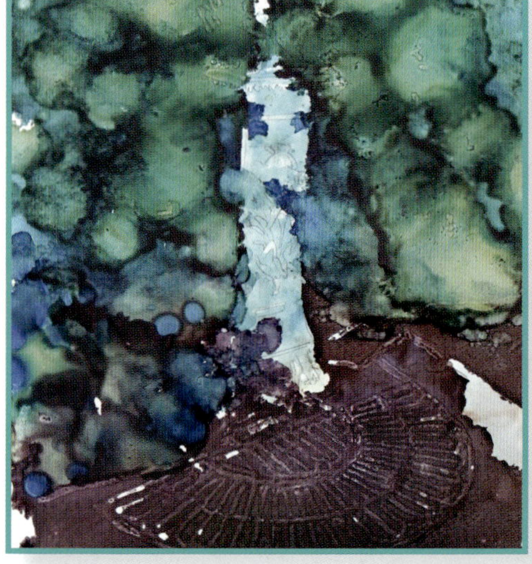

5. Let dry, then apply background ink with mottled colors for the foliage.

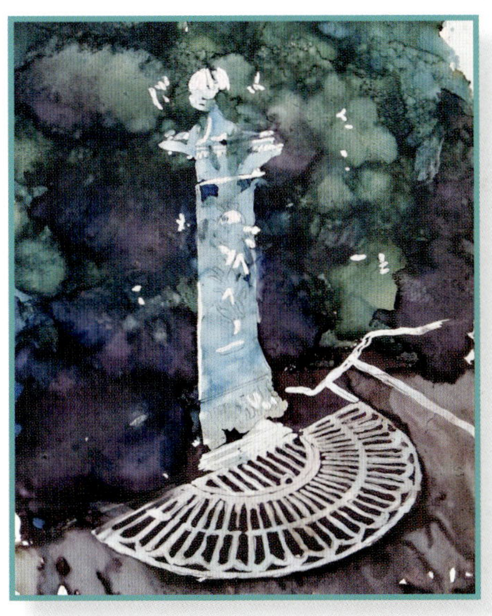

6. Remove the masking fluid.

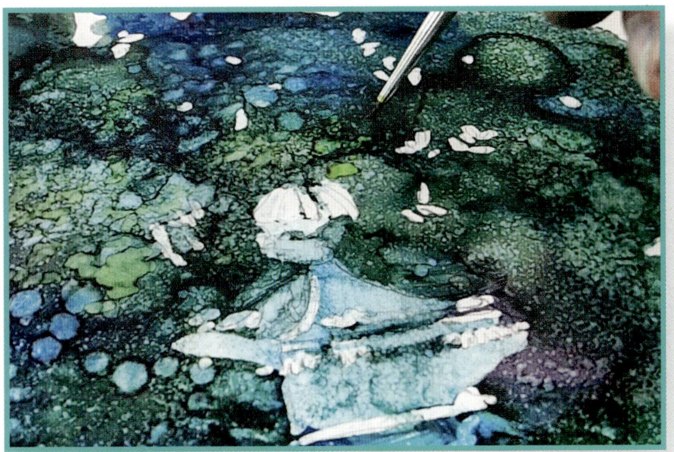

7. After splattering the foliage with alcohol, add ink with the brush to create leaves.

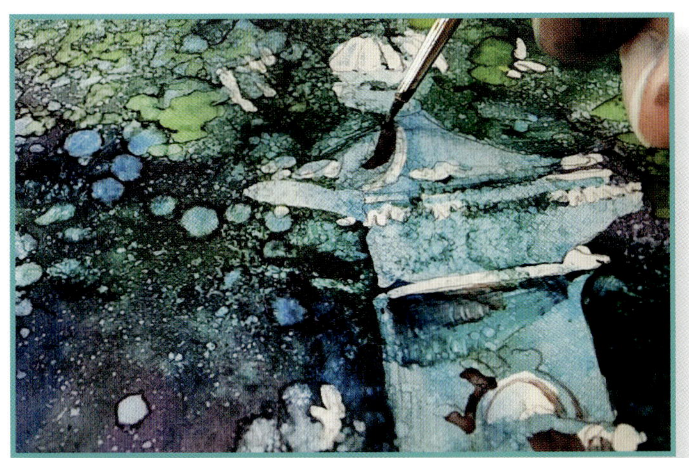

8. Use the brush to apply ink for the darks.

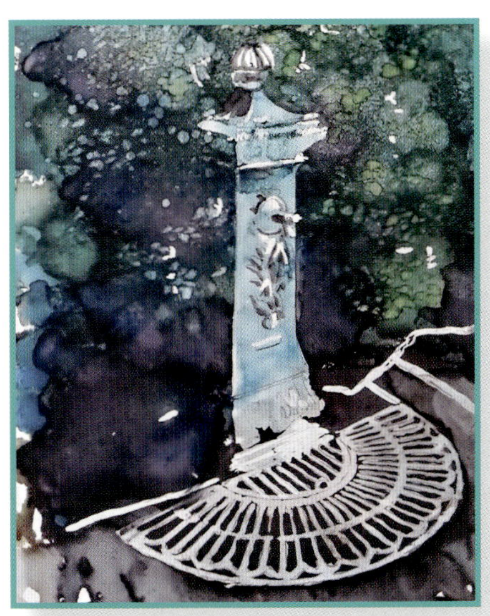

Square du Vert-Galant - In progress...

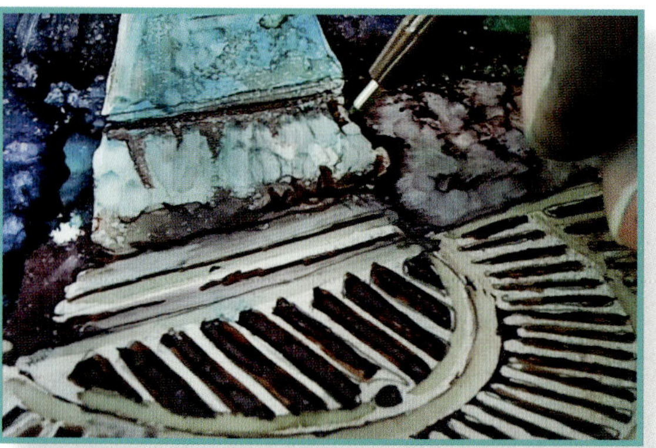

9. Use the sepia pen for details and definition.

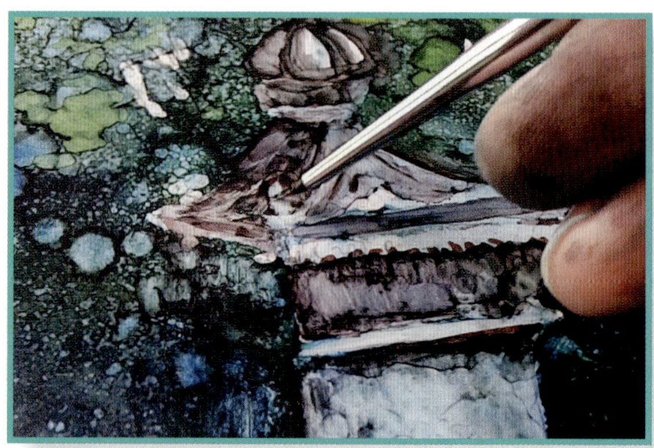

10. Lift out highlights with the brush and alcohol.

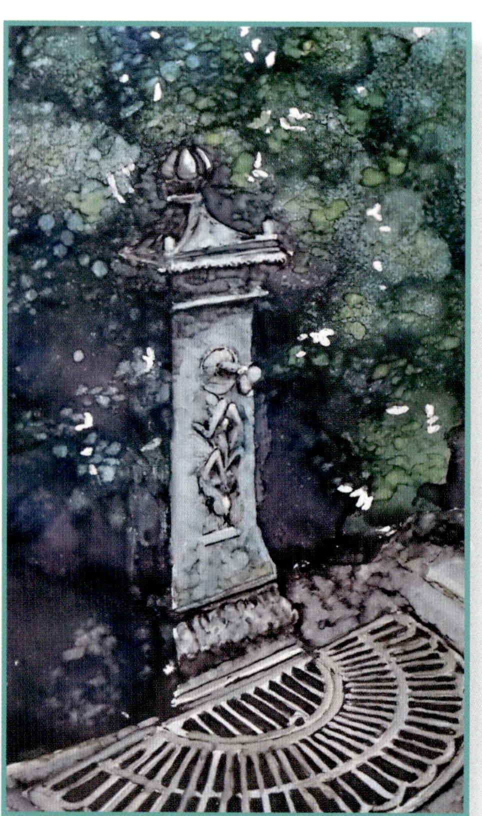

11. Continue to adjust the painting by adding detail with the brush and pens.

Variation: Garden Fountain

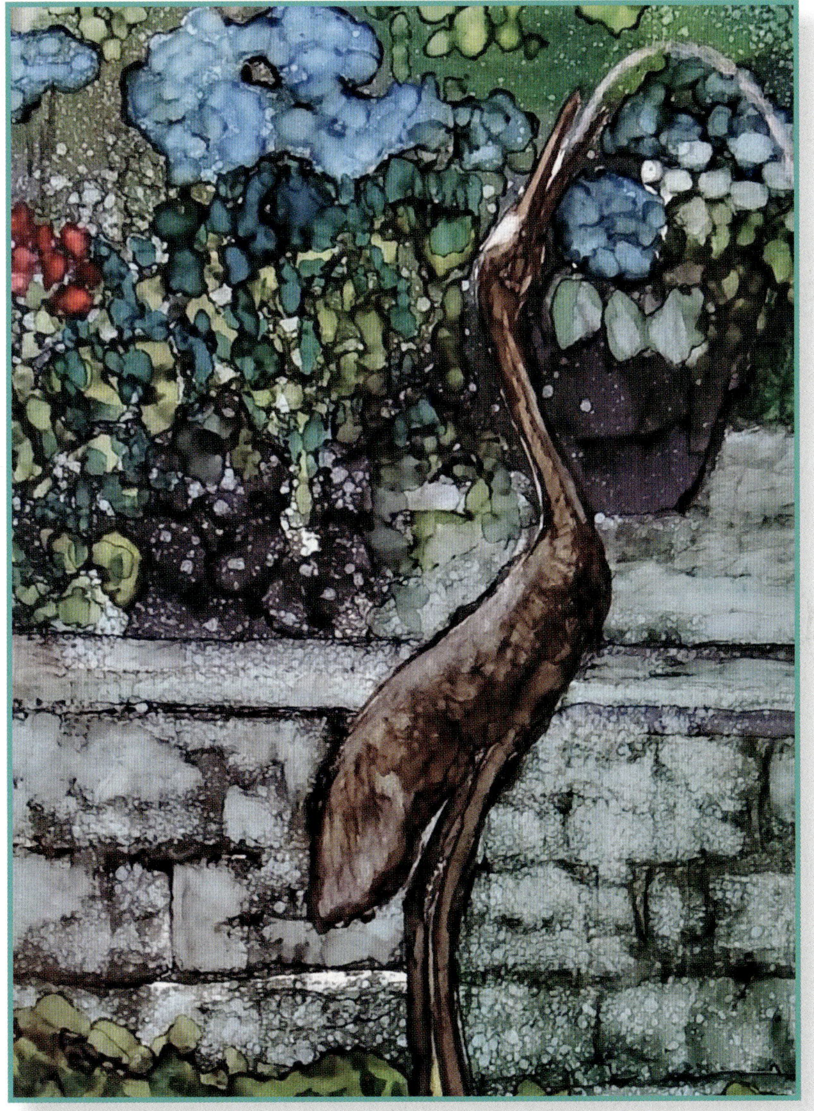

Karen Walker. *Garden Fountain.*
Fountains and other statuary present intriguing focal points for garden scenes. As in the *Square du Vert-Galant*, this piece offers a variety of textures, including stone, metal, and foliage.

6 Coastal Life

All four of the projects in this chapter feature strong and purposed backgrounds. The loose and textured backgrounds of *Shell Secret* and *Tropical Reef* represent a sandy beach and underwater scene, respectively. *Coastal Grasses II* and the *Peggy's Cove Lighthouse* rely on planned landscapes with an intentioned inking process. A benefit to this deliberate approach is that once the background is completed, the entire painting is nearly finished.

Coastal Grasses II: Planned inky landscape background with masking

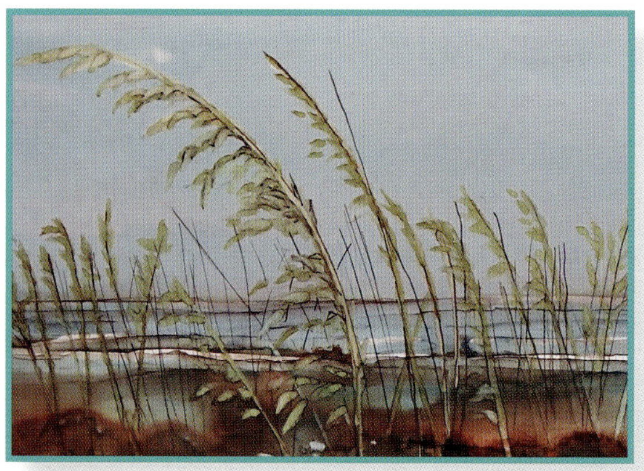

Shell Secret: Textured background with lifting

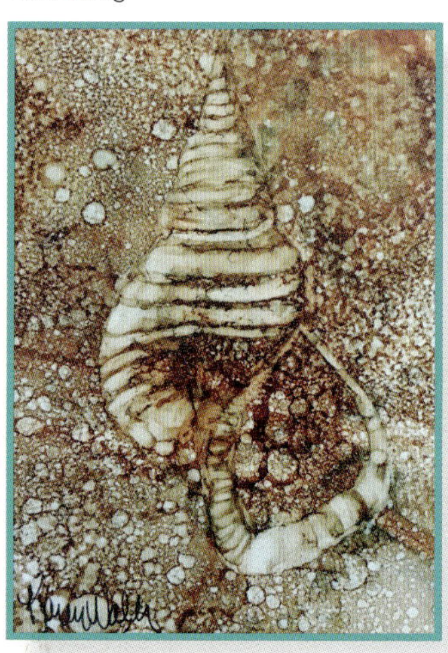

Peggy's Cove Lighthouse: Planned landscape background with solid wash plus masking and direct painting

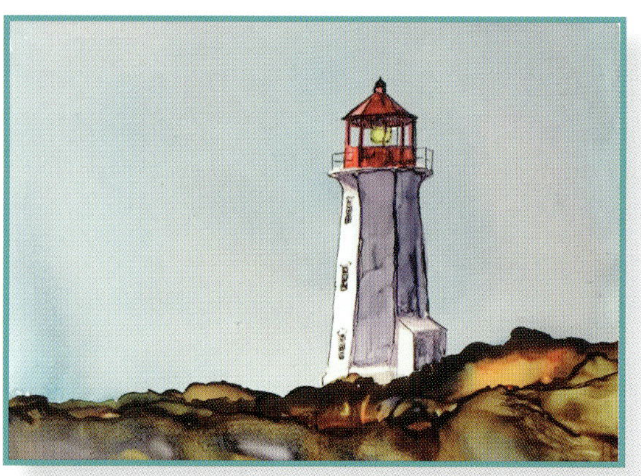

Tropical Reef: Inky underwater background and masking

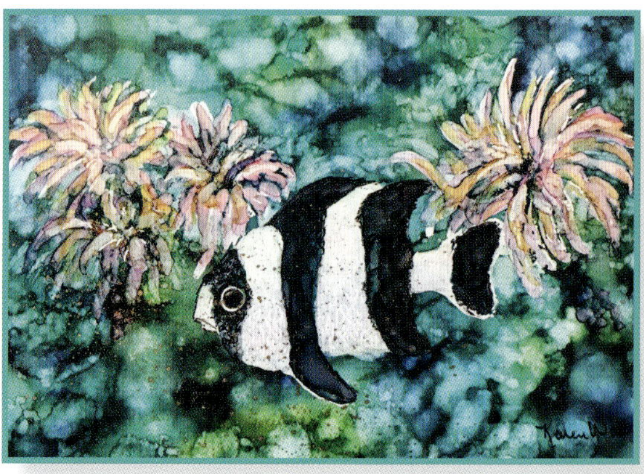

Project 17 - Coastal Grasses II

Karen Walker. *Coastal Grasses II.*

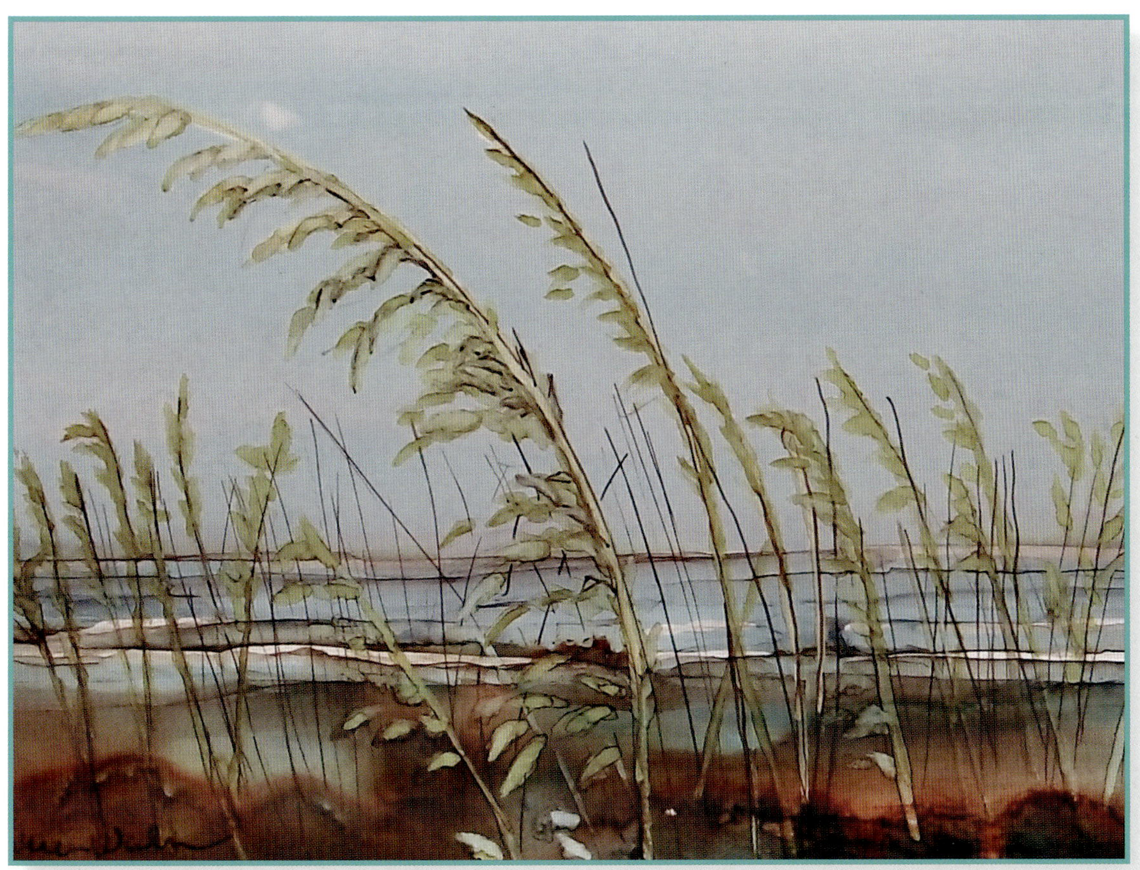

The light and airy feel of *Coastal Grasses II* is largely created by a planned background that was inked to form the sky, ocean, and sand. A few key sea oats were masked ahead of time.

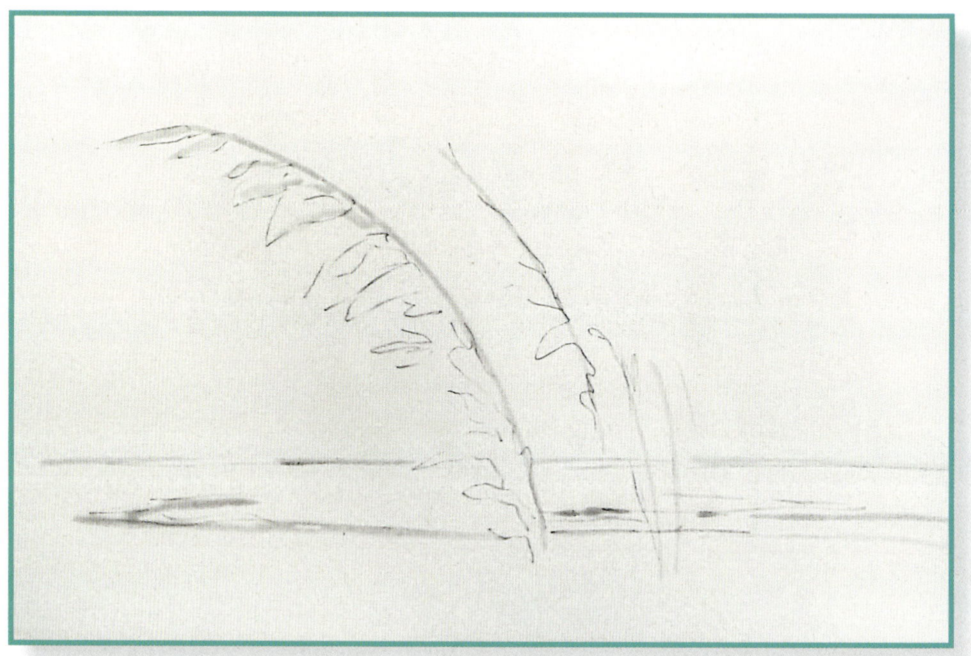

1. Lightly sketch and mask a pencil drawing.

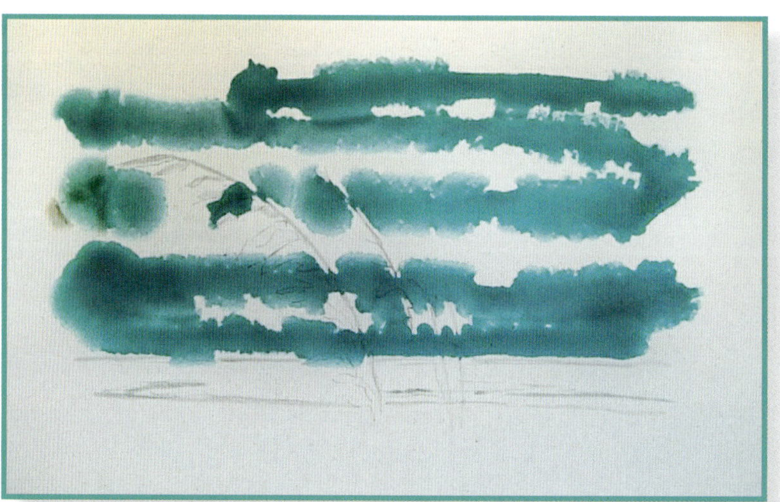

2. Create the sky and ocean by dropping blue and gray ink on the flat paper.

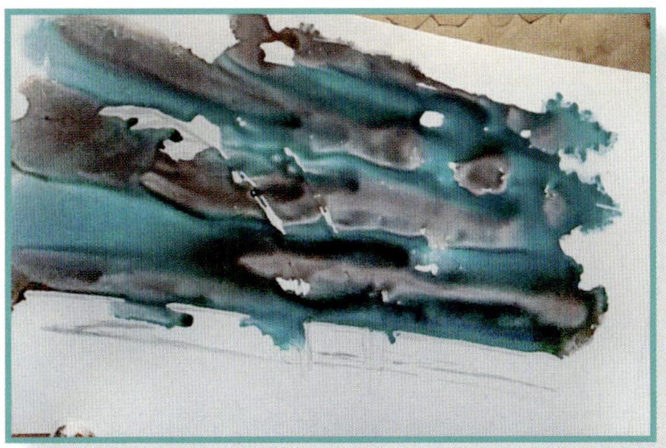

3. Tilt to mix.

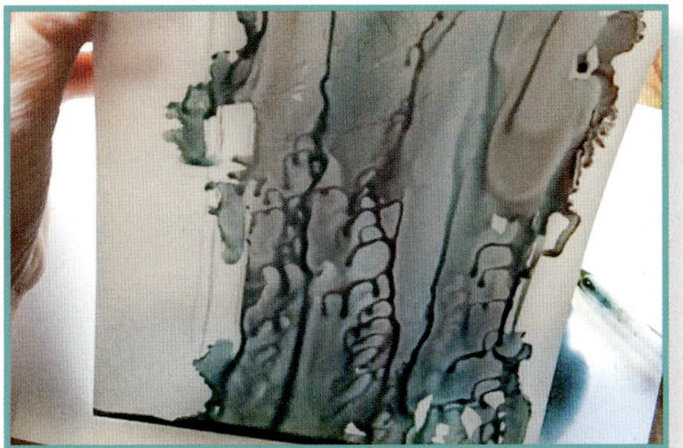

4. Turn the paper 90 degrees and hold vertically. Drop in alcohol and allow the ink to flow downward to create subtle bands of color.

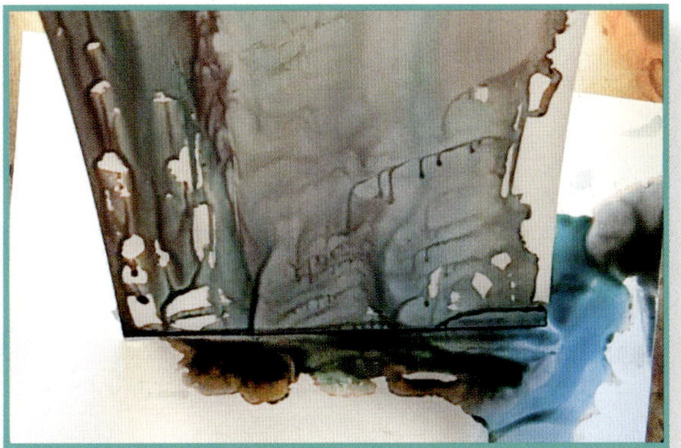

5. Create the ocean by adding darker inks and continuing to let the ink flow down.

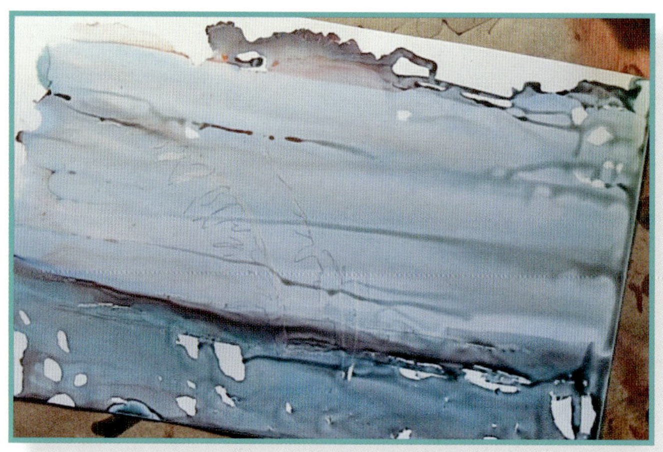

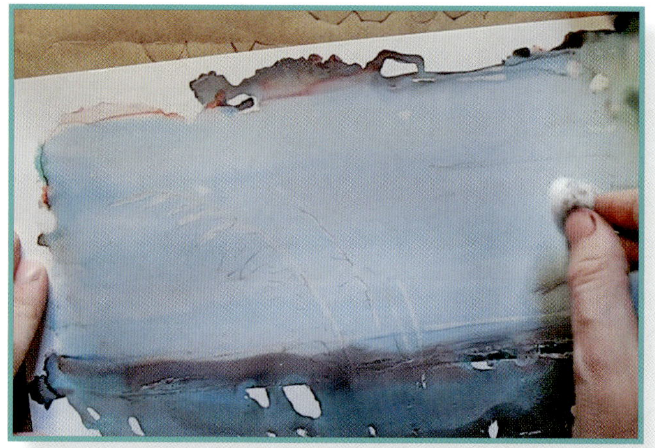

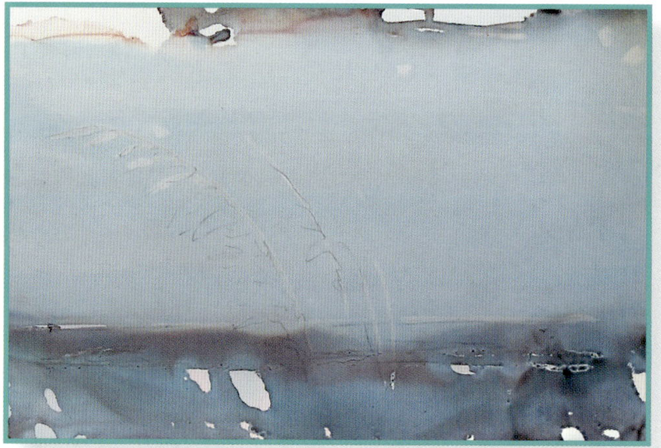

6. Lay the paper flat and use a cotton ball to remove excess ink from the sky.

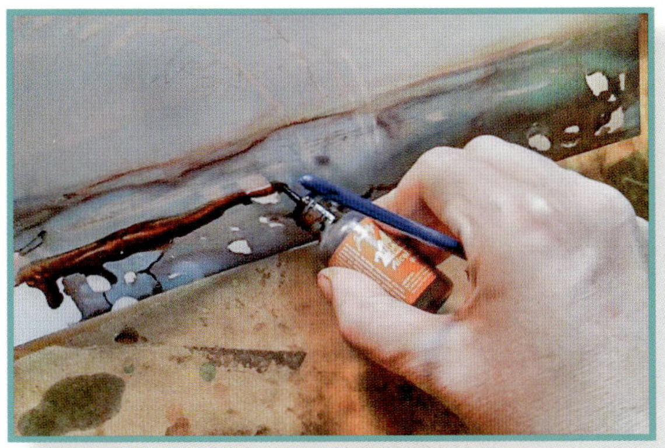

7. Add additional ink to define the shoreline.

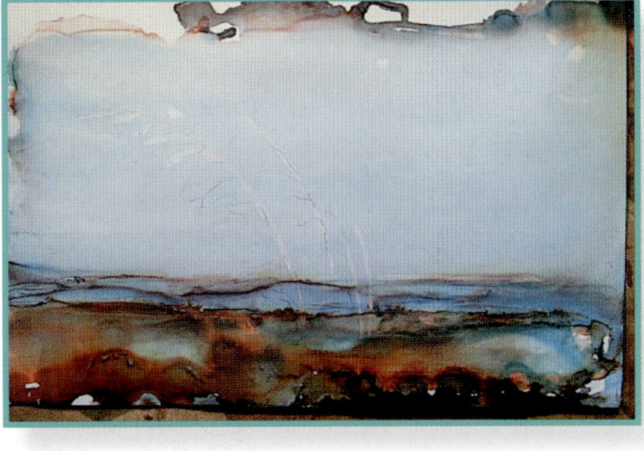

8. Create the sandy beach with additional ink. For an even blend, use a brush to guide the ink while still wet. Let dry.

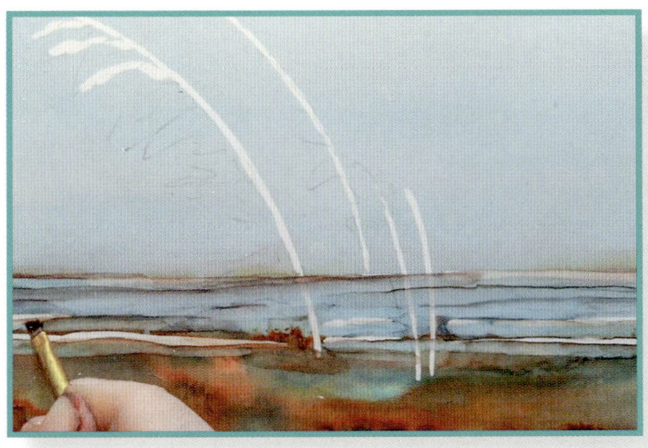

9. Remove the masking fluid and use alcohol to define the waves.

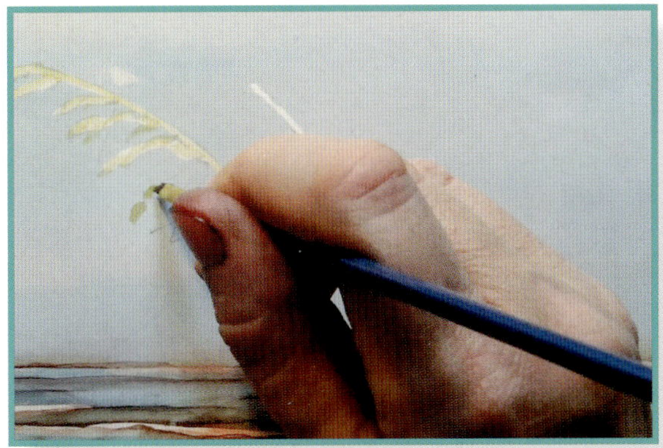

10. Paint in the grasses by using the brush and several shades of ink.

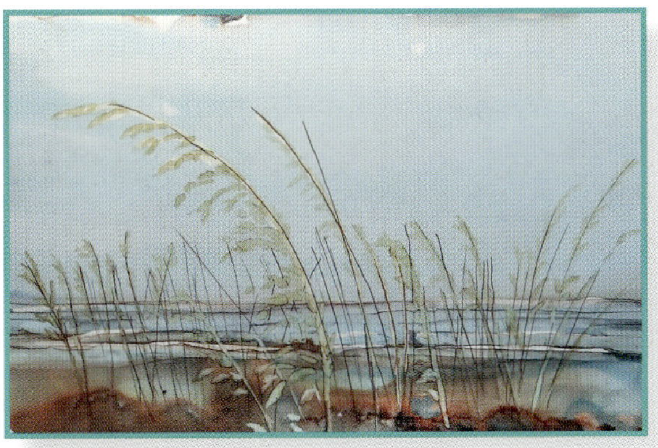

11. Use the sepia pen to add additional stalks and grasses.

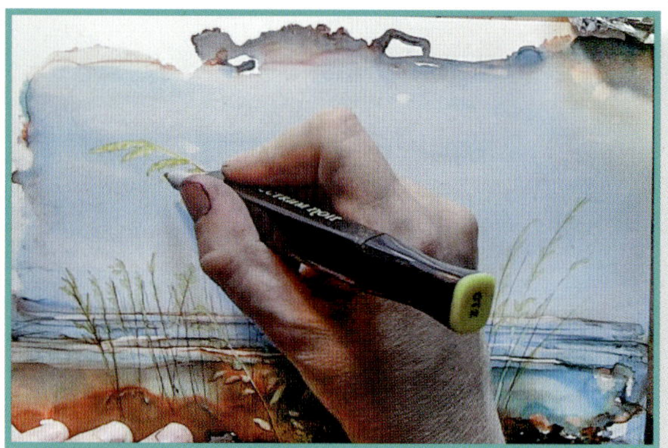

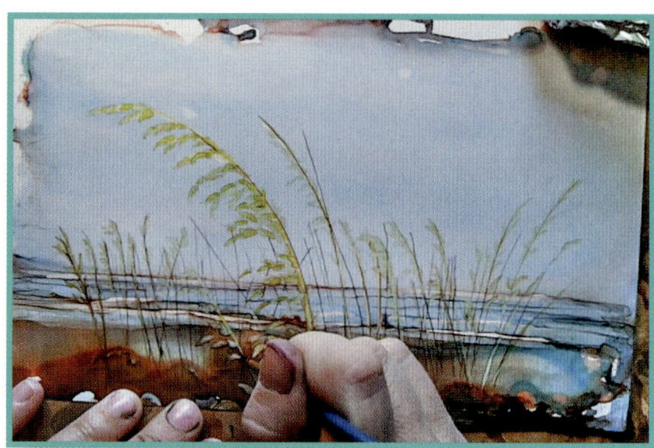

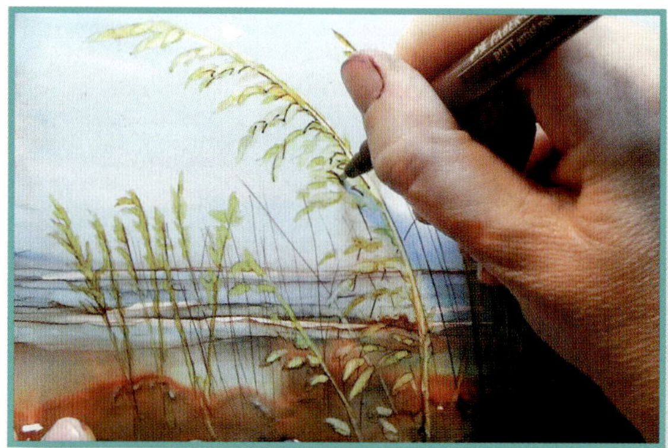

12. Continue adding to the grasses with the alcohol ink marker and sepia pen.

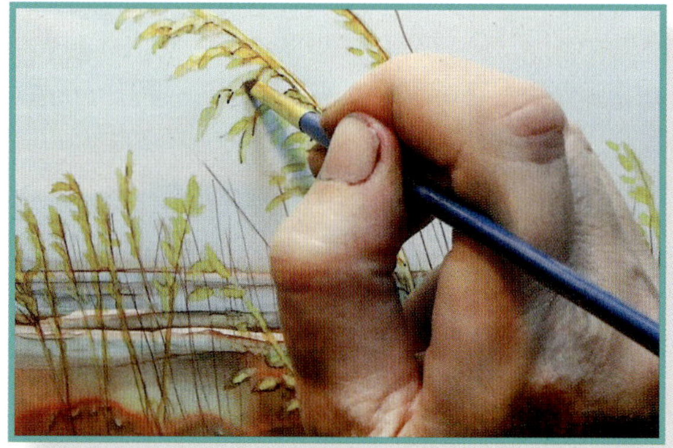

13. Soften the edges with the brush and alcohol.

Variation: Coastal Grasses

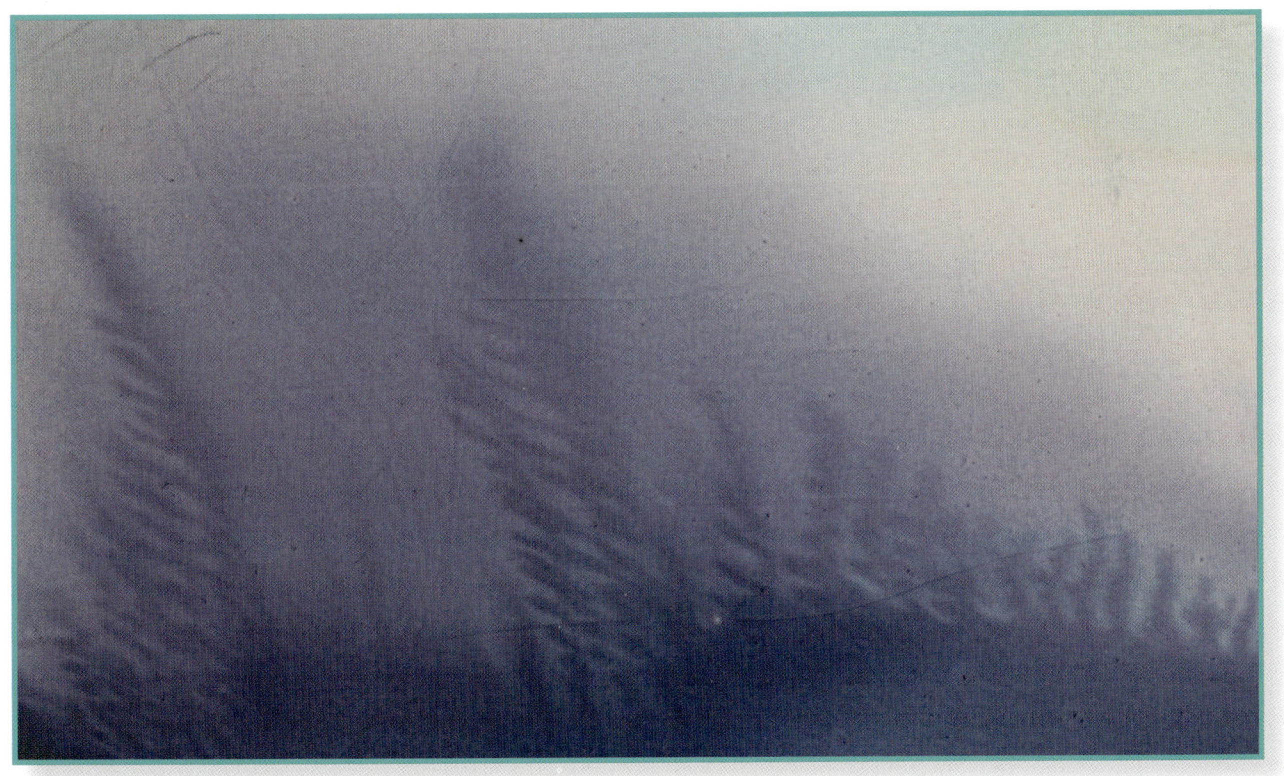

Karen Walker. *Coastal Grasses*.
This ink flow version of *Coastal Grasses* was created entirely by accident. The natural patterns of the ink formed the grasses and landscape; the only artistic touch beyond directing the ink flow was knowing when to stop.

Project 18 - Shell Secret

Karen Walker. *Shell Secret.*

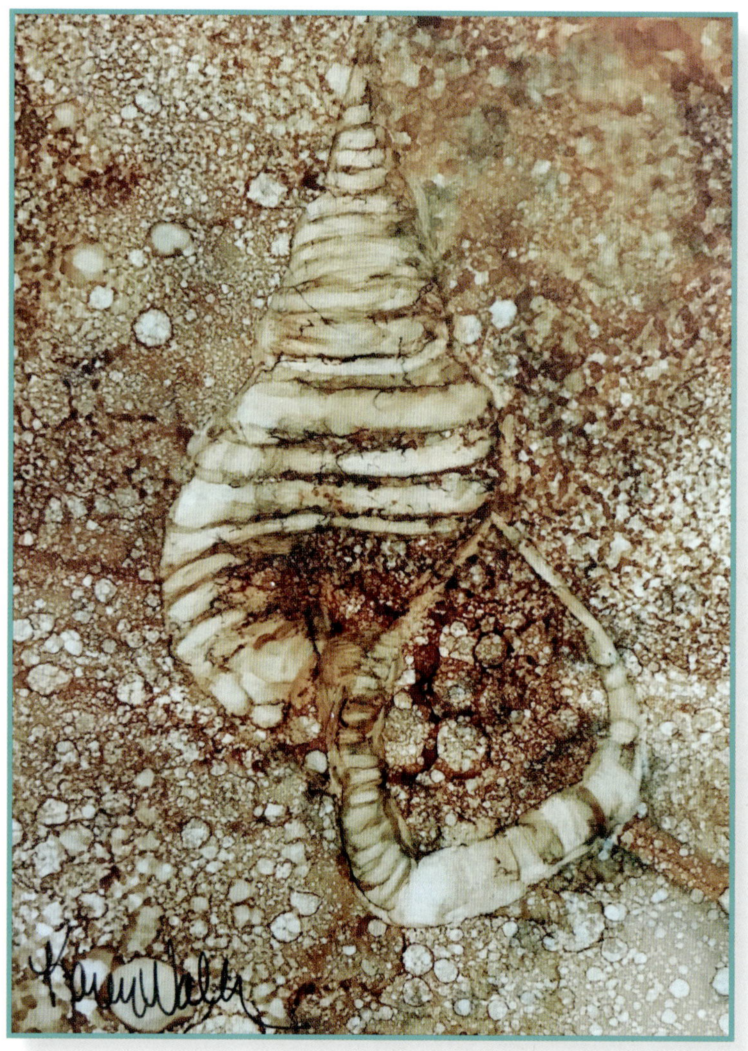

For this shell, I lifted the image out of a sandy background and left plenty of the background showing through for a more fluid, inky effect. While the warm earth tone inks lift well, the painting could also be lifted out of a dynamic colorful background!

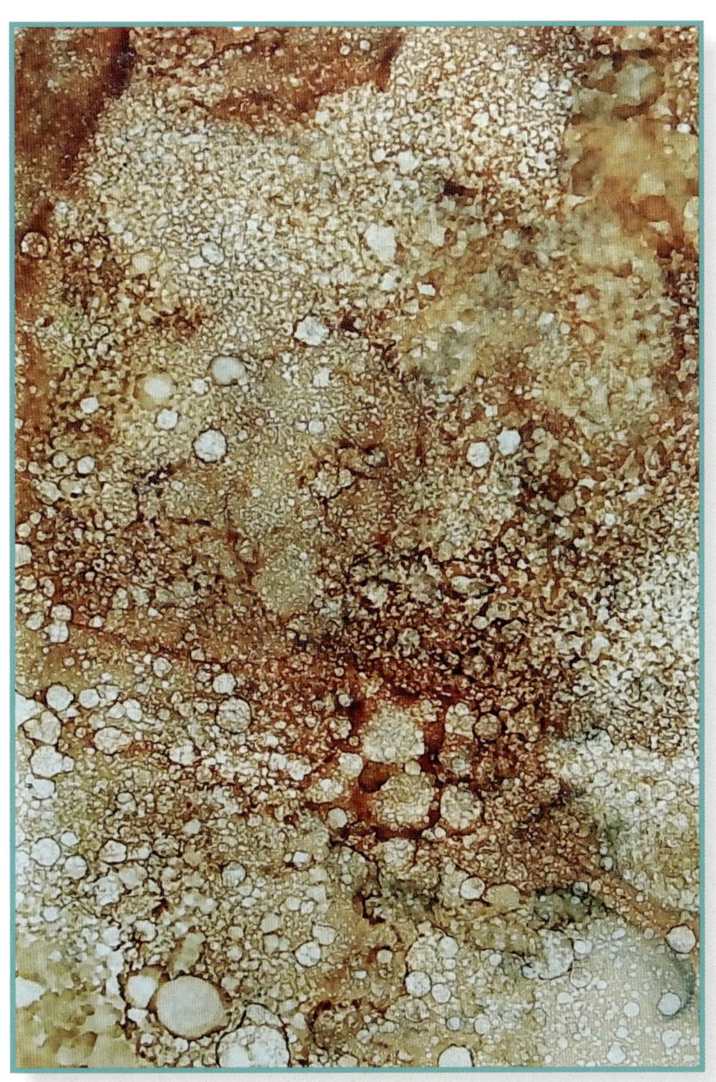

1. Begin with a textured background.

2. Lift the outline of the shell by using the brush and alcohol with a paper cutout as a guide.

To make a cutout of the reference drawing, use your reference photo or copy the outline of the subject to a separate piece of paper. Cut out the shape and use the negative space to trace by lifting.

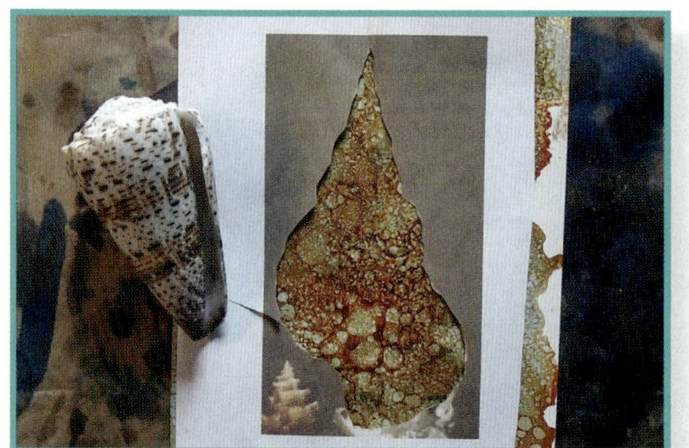

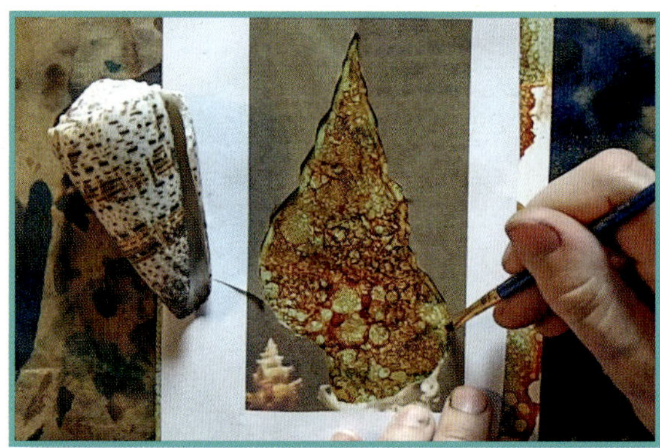

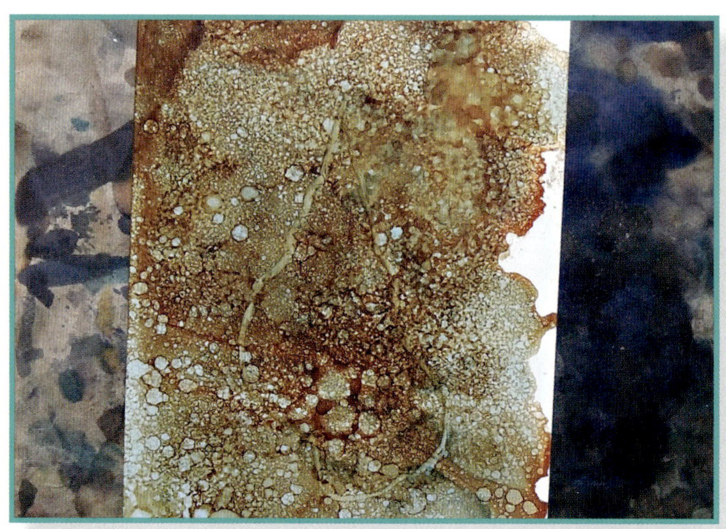

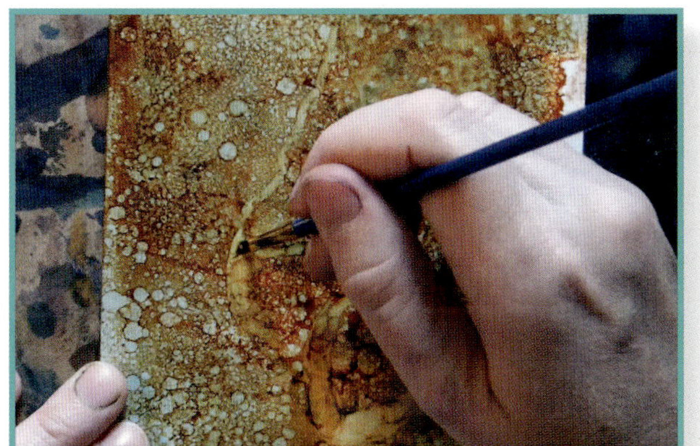

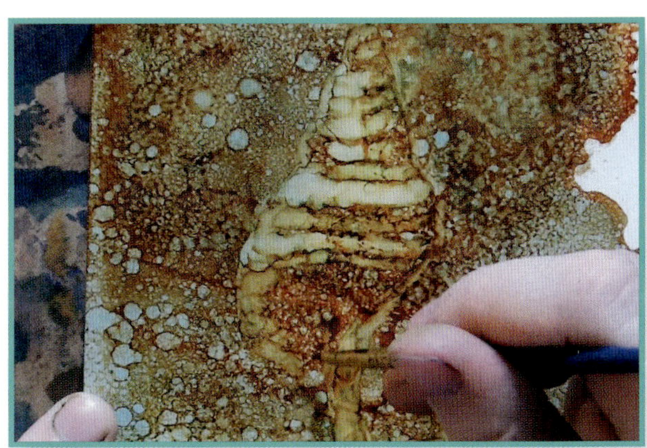

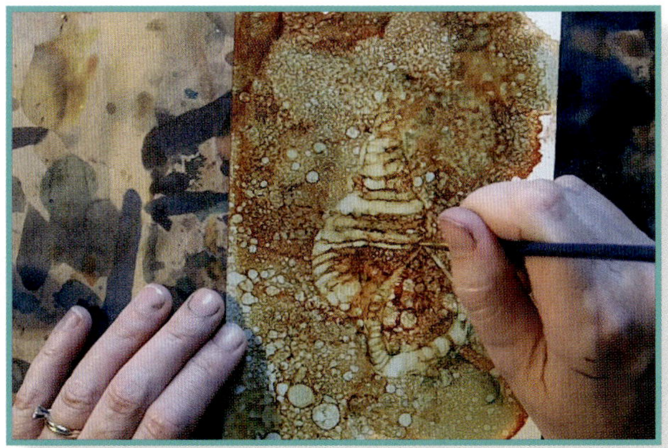

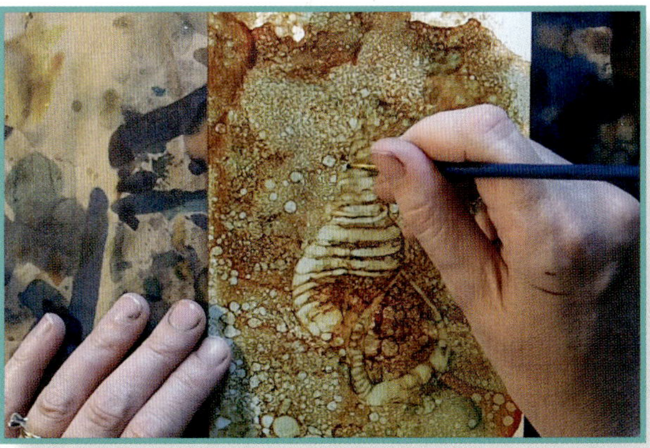

3. Continue to use alcohol and the brush to lift out the design. No pen required.

Variation: Grazing Sheep

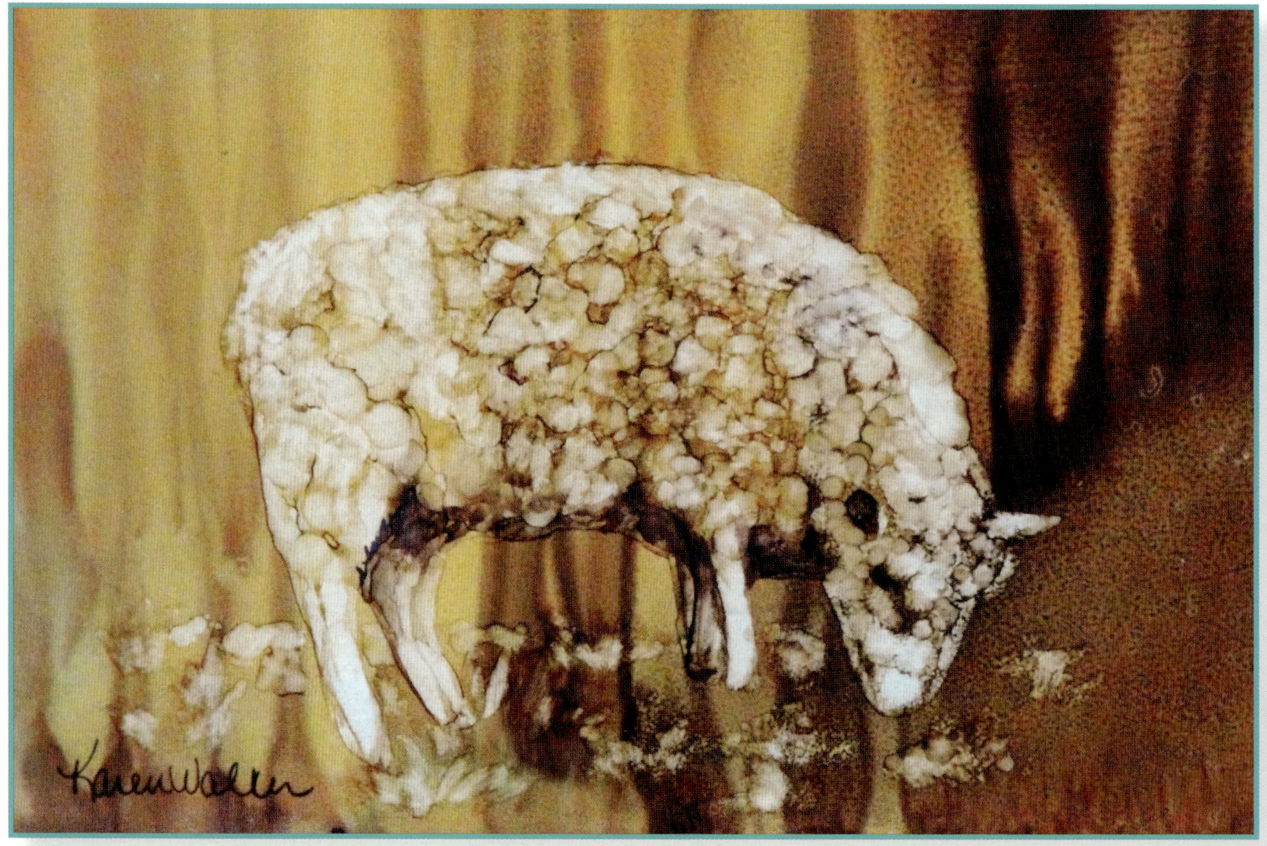

Karen Walker. *Grazing Sheep*.
Grazing Sheep was painted in the same manner as *Shell Secret*. The outline of the sheep was drawn in alcohol by using the cutout shape method, and the remainder of the painting was lifted out with alcohol. The cotton swab gives woolly texture.

Project 19 - Peggy's Cove Lighthouse

Karen Walker. *Peggy's Cove Lighthouse.*

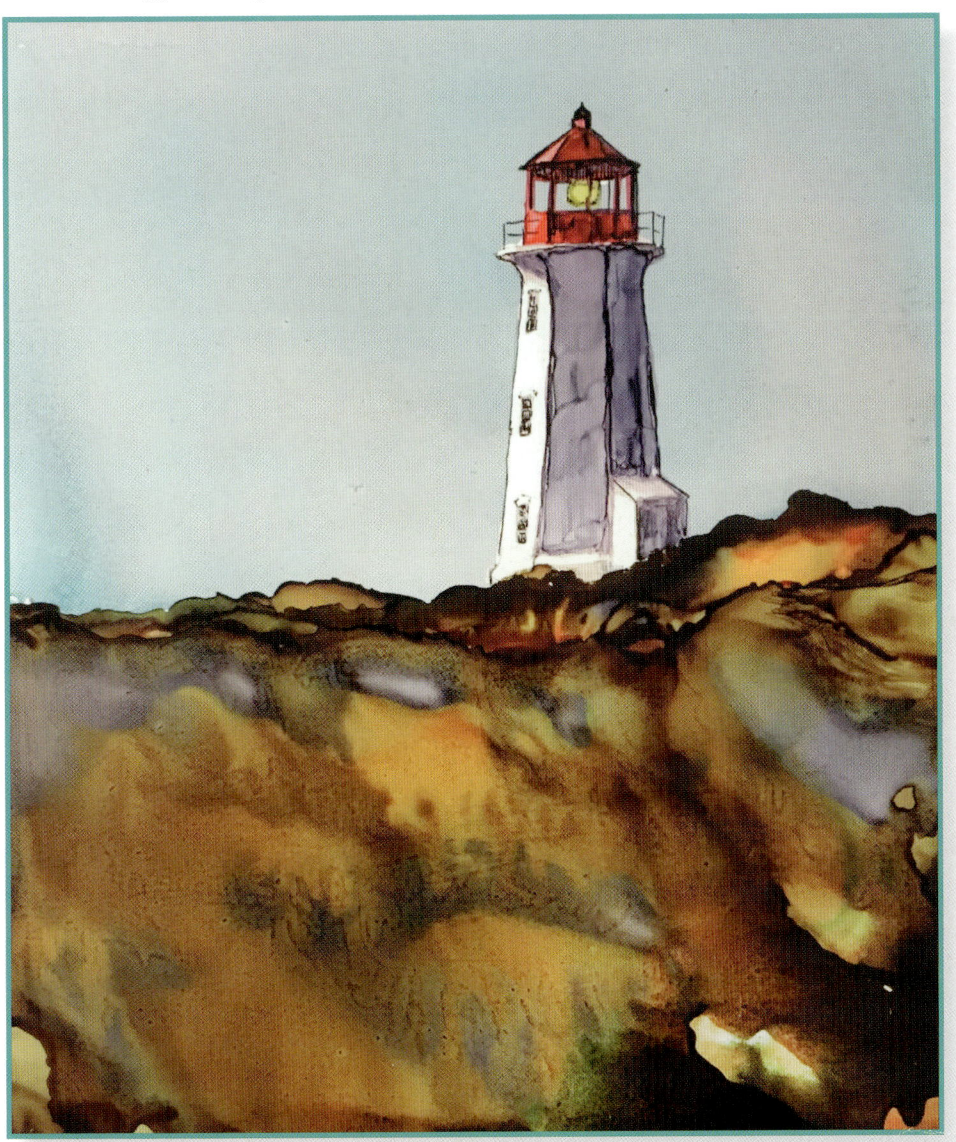

Simplicity reigns with this painting of the lighthouse at Peggy's Cove in Nova Scotia, Canada. The sky was created by an undisturbed ink wash, and the rocky foreground was formed by dropping multiple colors of ink and letting them flow.

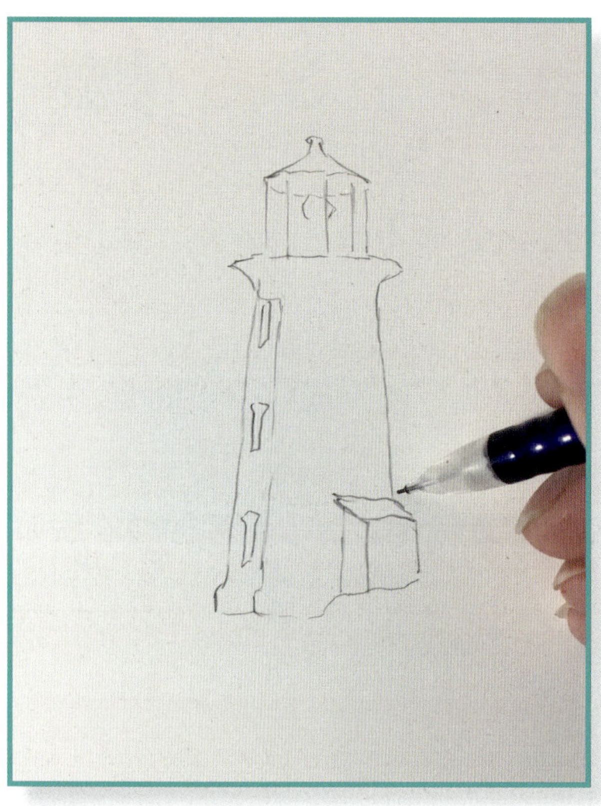

1. Lightly sketch the lighthouse in pencil.

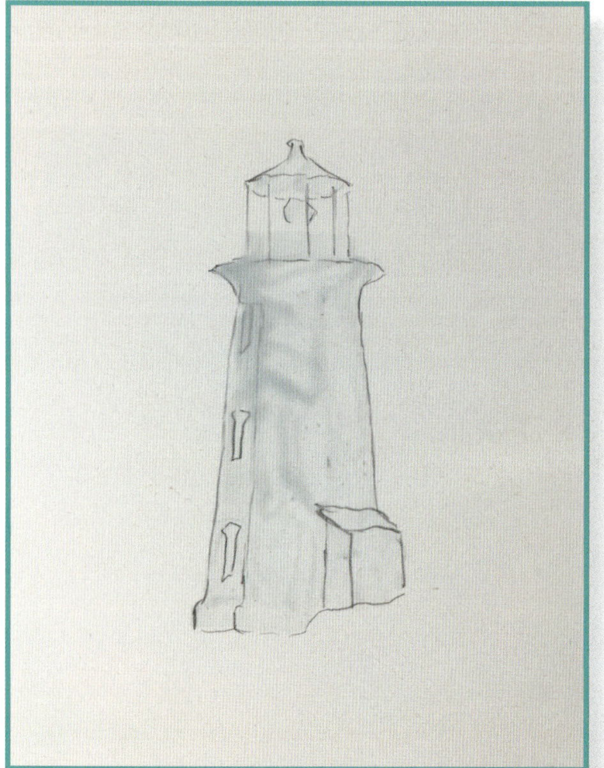

2. Mask the entire lighthouse, skipping the area where the sky shows through the top. Let dry.

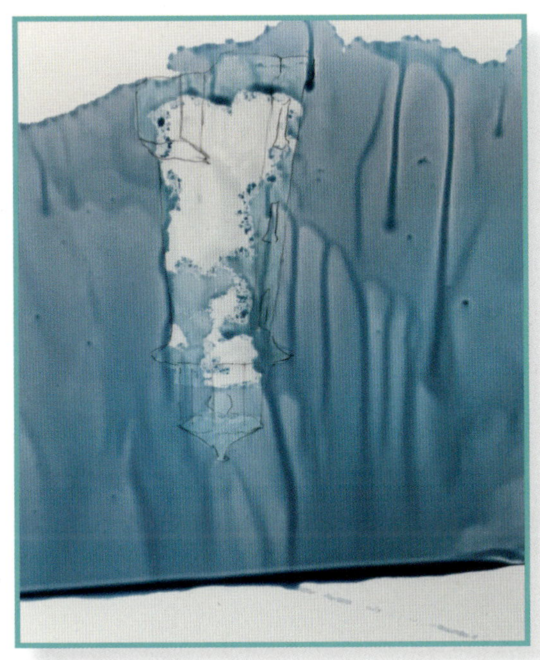

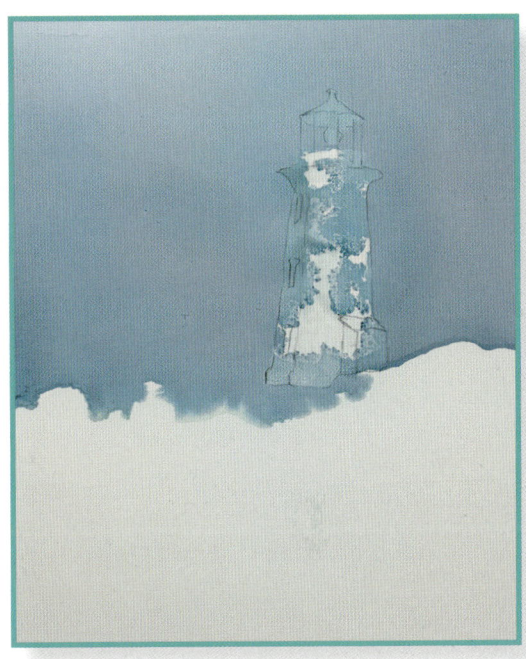

3. Ink the sky by holding the painting upside down and letting the dropped ink and alcohol flow away from the rocky ground. Be sure to use the brush to tap away any white spots while the ink is still wet. Allow to completely dry before proceeding.

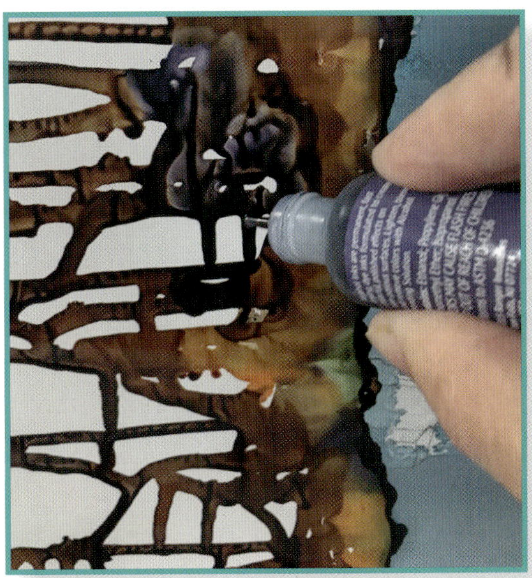

4. Create the rocky ground by dropping various colors of ink directly from the bottle. Control the flow of the ink away from the sky by holding the paper vertically and tilting as desired.

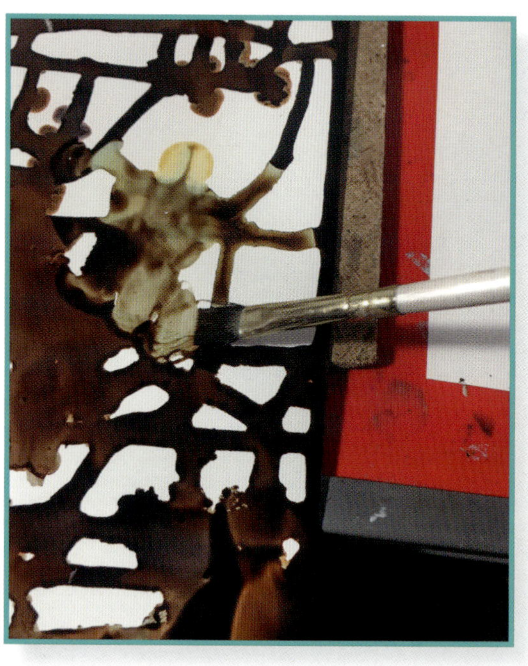

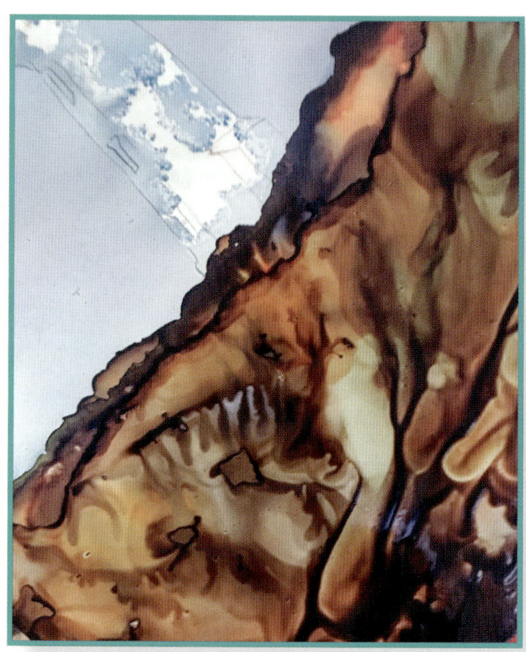

5. Use the brush to fill in any areas where the ink is not flowing, and continue to add more ink, alcohol, or both until an attractive rocky pattern is achieved.

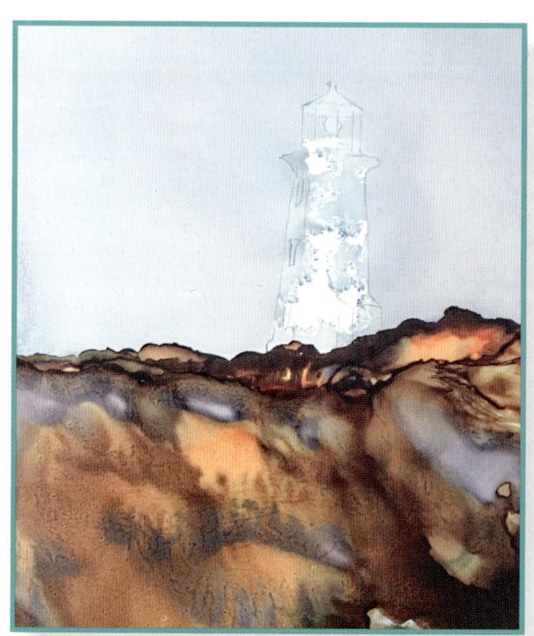

6. Let dry.

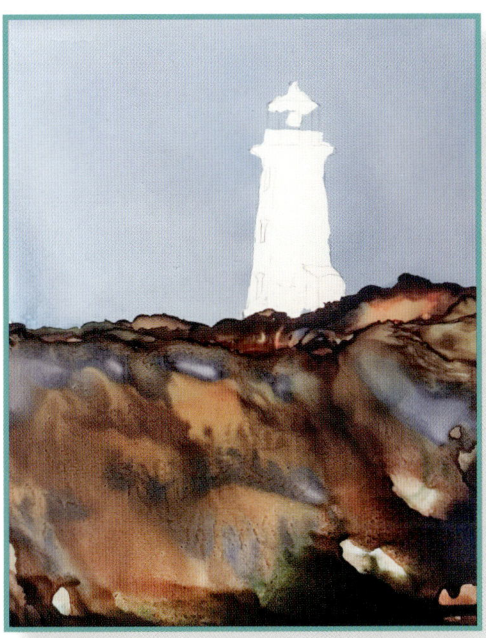

7. Remove the masking fluid.

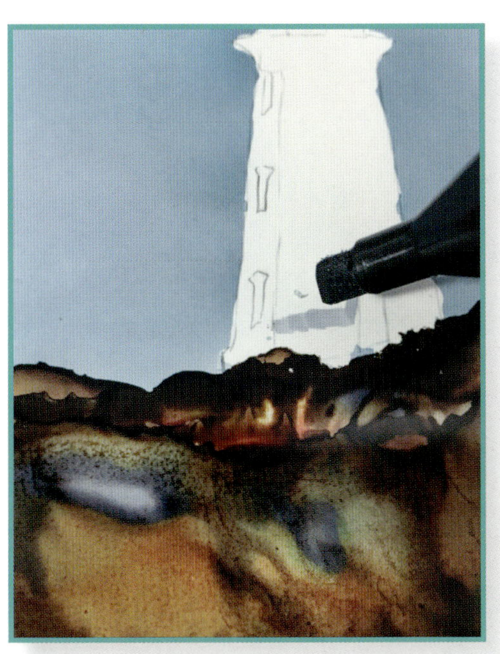

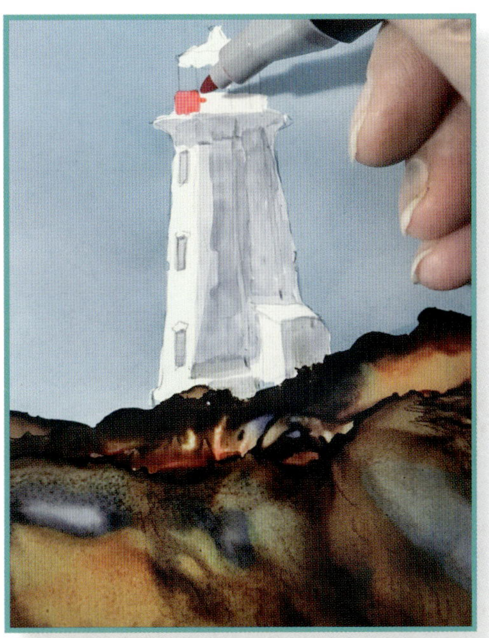

8. Cautiously paint in the lighthouse, taking care not to disturb either the sky or the rocks. Begin by shading in with a pale alcohol ink marker. Adding a first layer with the marker tends to slow down the flow of later layers of ink.

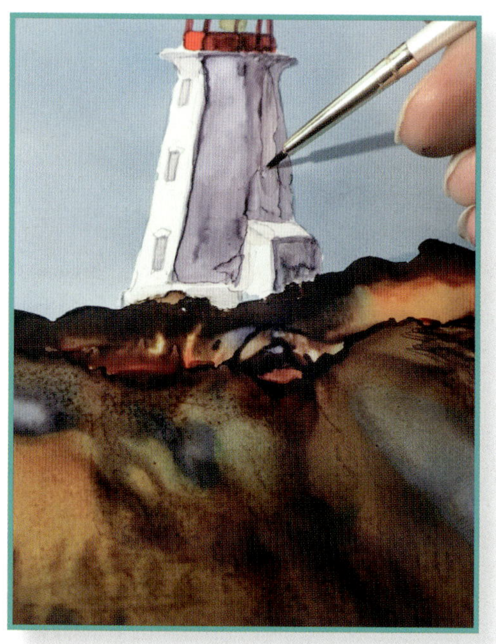

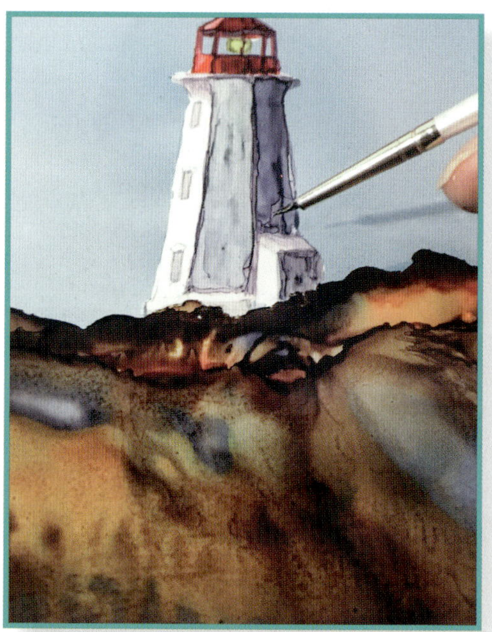

9. Continue painting in with the brush.

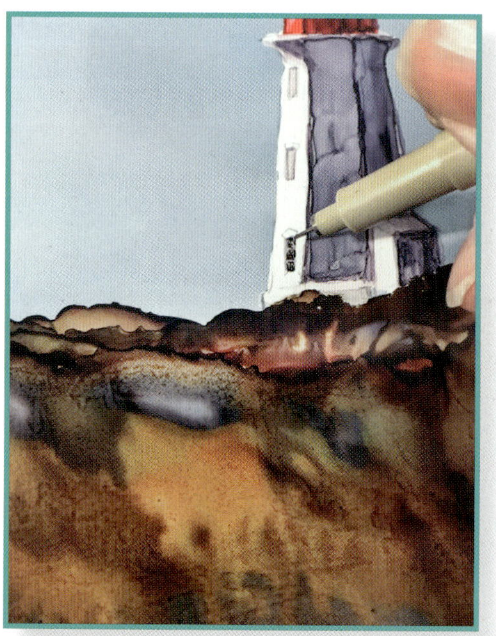

10. Add details with the fine-tipped pen.

Variation: Lover's Cove

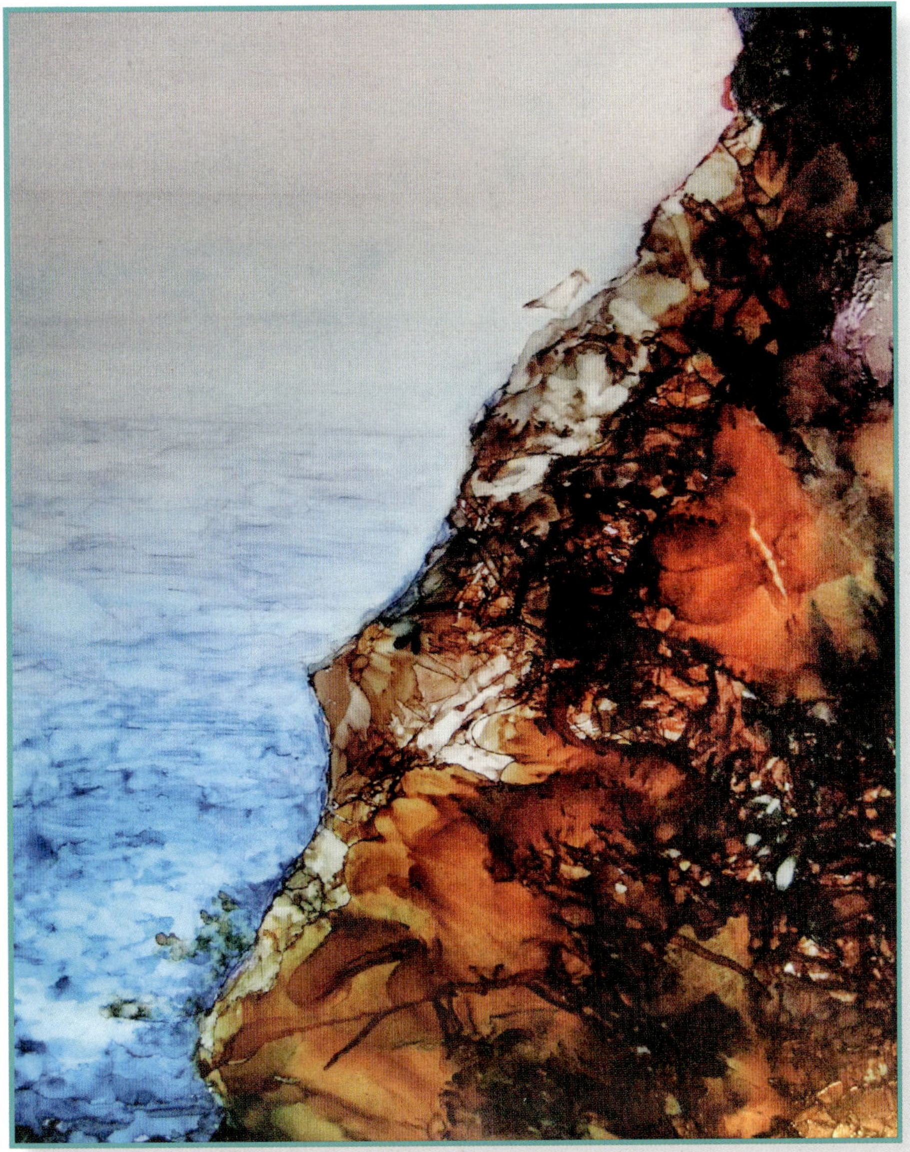

Karen Walker. *Lover's Cove.*
Like the *Peggy's Cove Lighthouse*, the large rock in *Lover's Cove* was created by ink flow. Alternating the direction of the paper and tilting yields interesting rock textures.

Project 20 - Tropical Reef

Karen Walker. *Tropical Reef.*

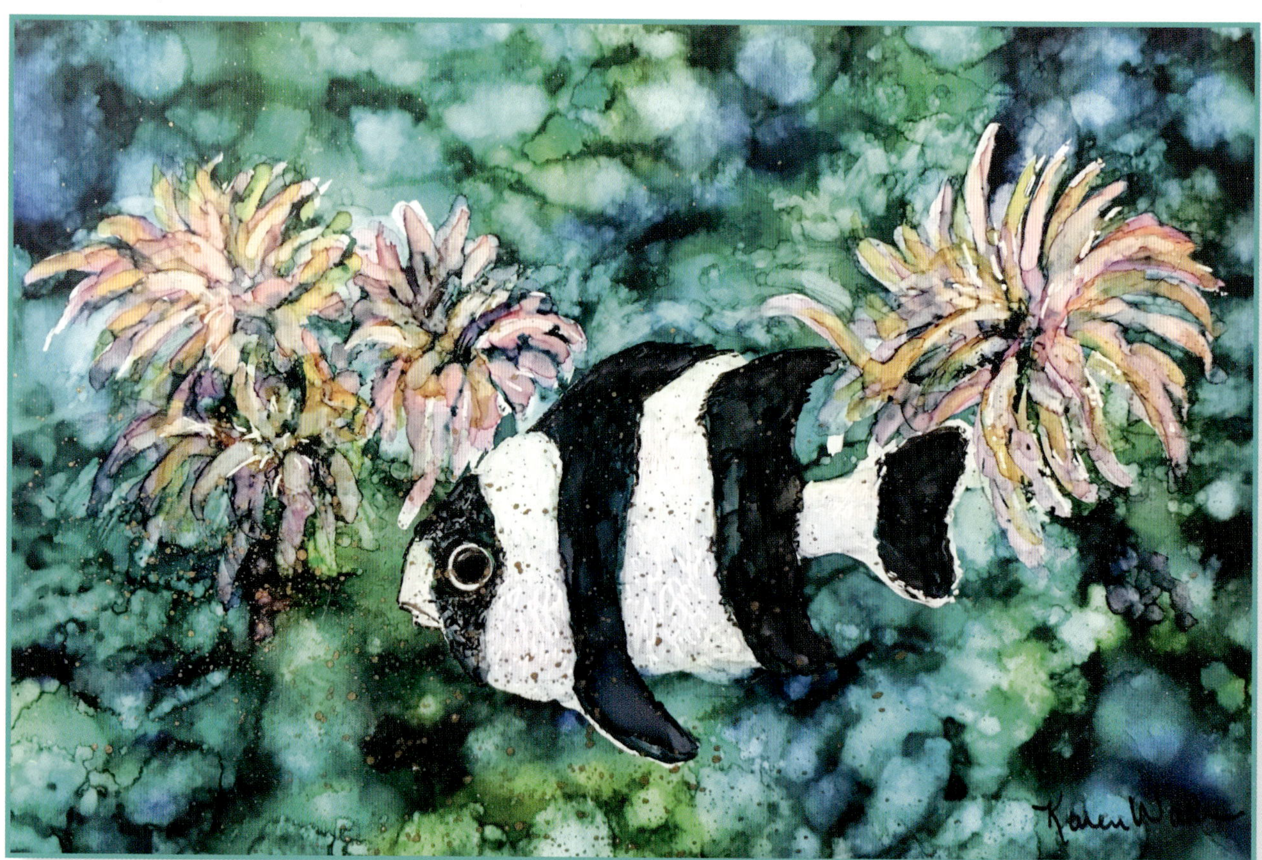

This underwater scene is a classic representational ink painting with a defined subject emerging from a textured, inky, abstract background.

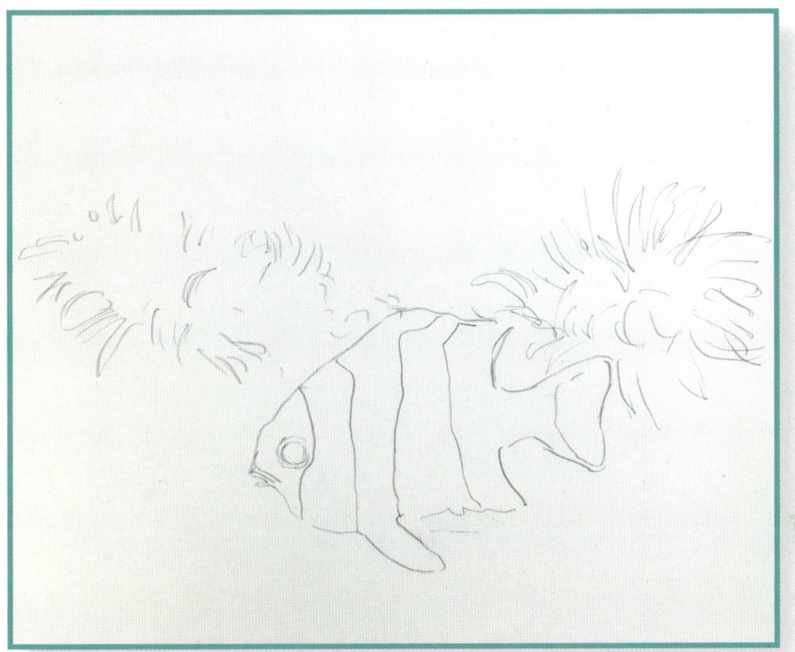

1. Begin with a lightly sketched drawing.

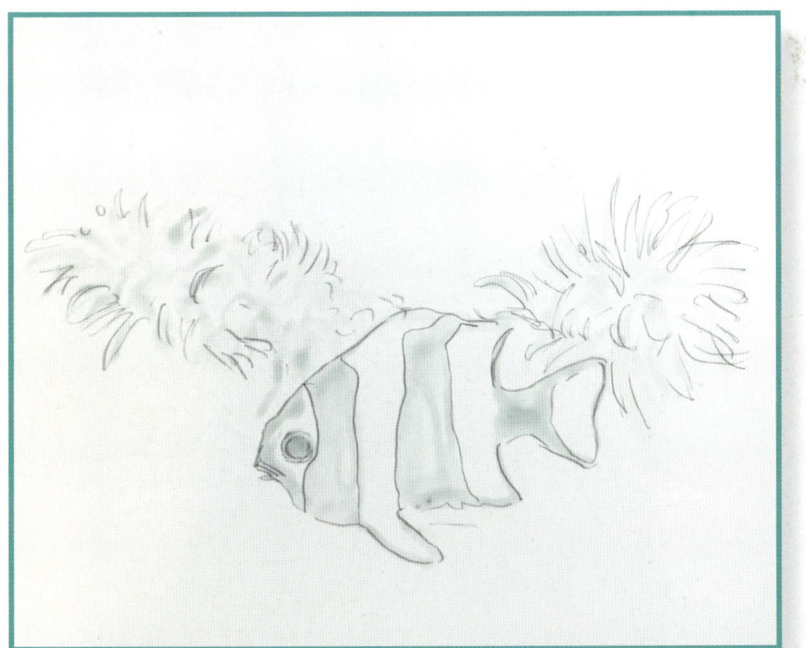

2. Partially mask the sea anemones and the fish, including the outline and white areas of the fish, as well as selective light parts of the sea anemones. Let dry.

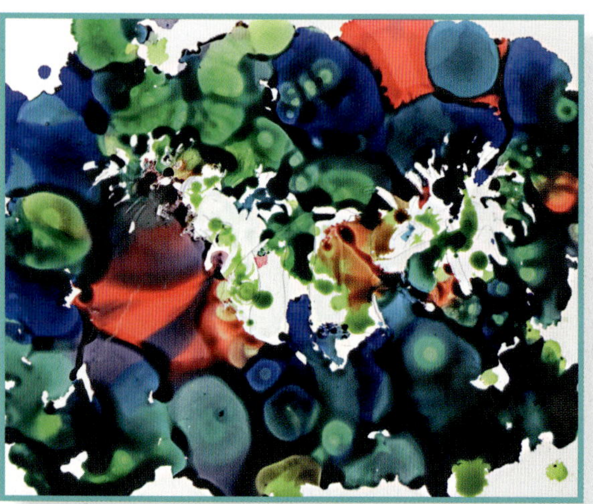

3. Create an inky underwater background by dropping multiple colors of ink over the masked paper.

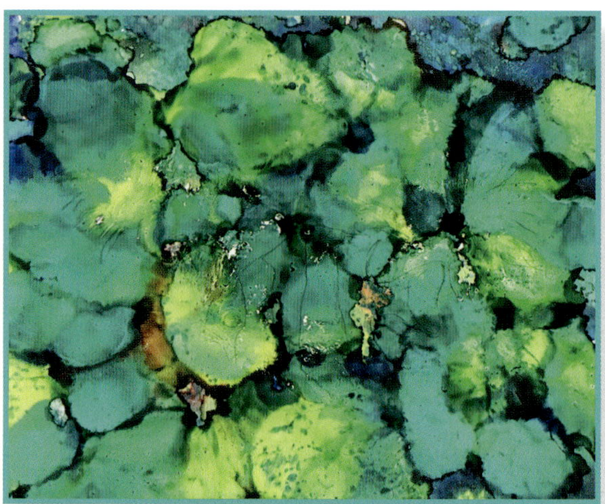

4. Use the cotton ball to make sure that all of the paper is covered. Add more ink as necessary.

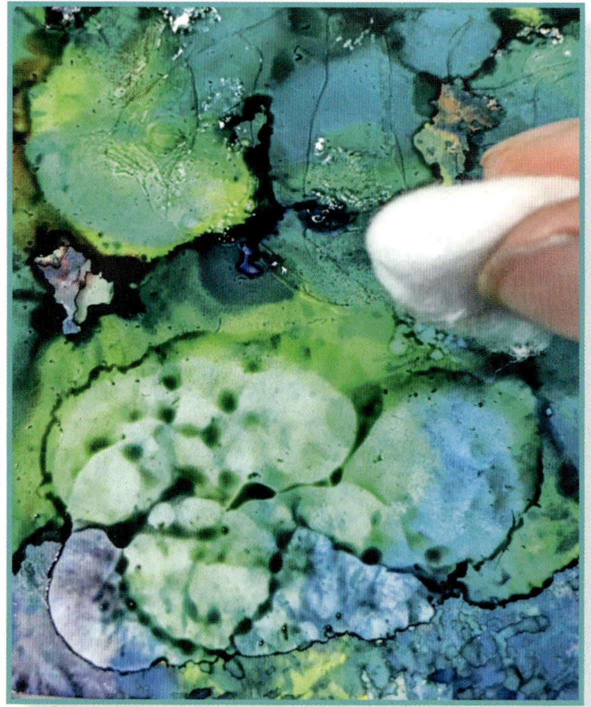

5. Use the cotton ball and alcohol to create watery effects as the ink is drying.

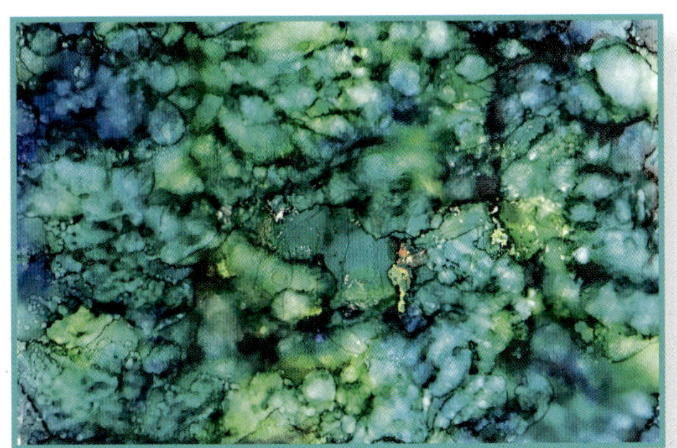

Tropical Reef - In progress...

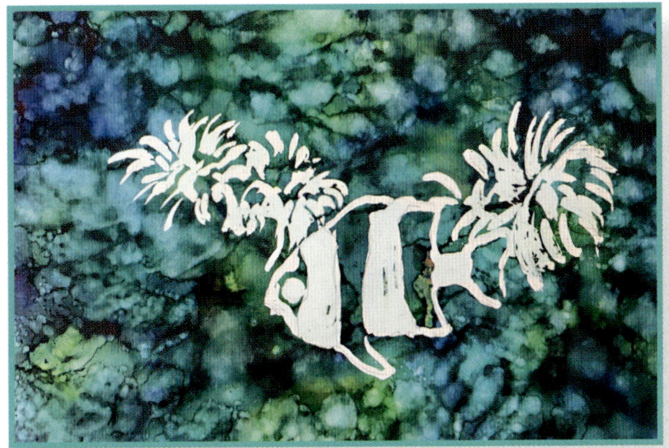

6. When the background is completely dry, remove the masking fluid.

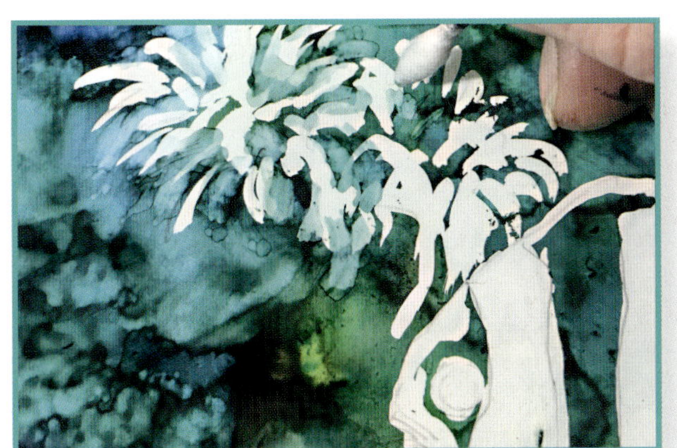

7. Use the cotton swab to lift out more sea anemone tentacles and soften the masked areas.

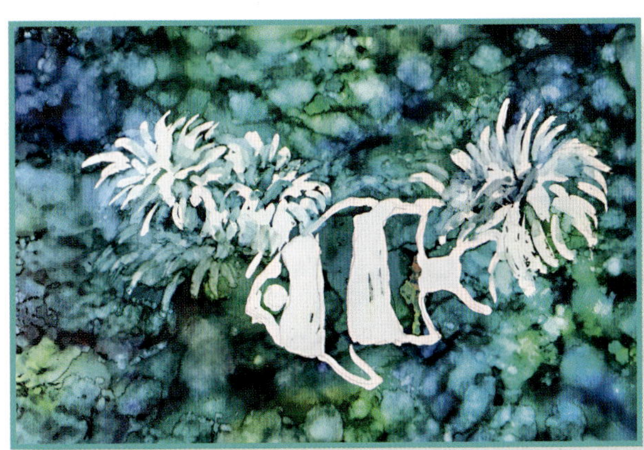

Tropical Reef - In progress...

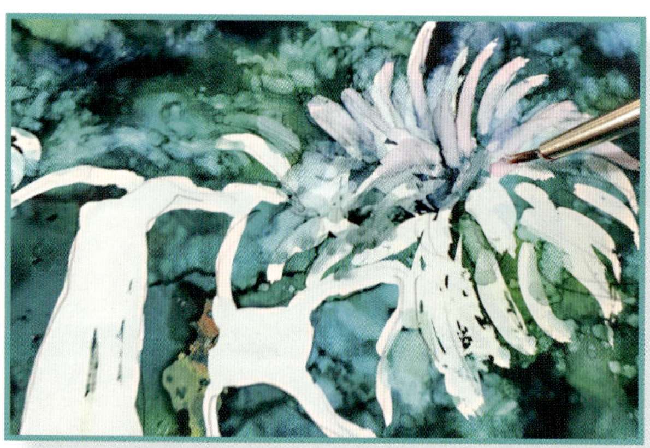

8. Paint in the sea anemones with the brush and ink.

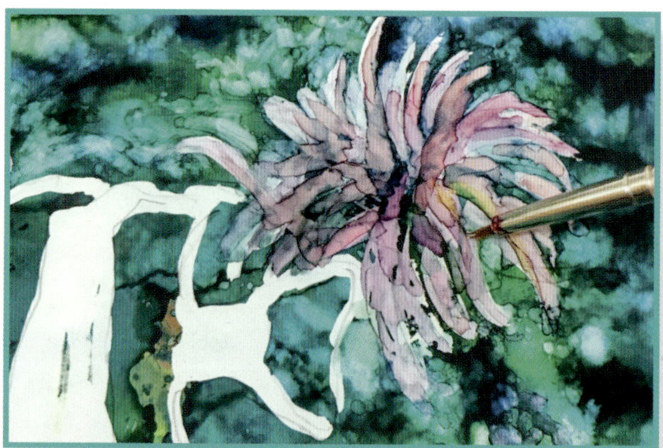

9. Add in several layers and colors of ink.

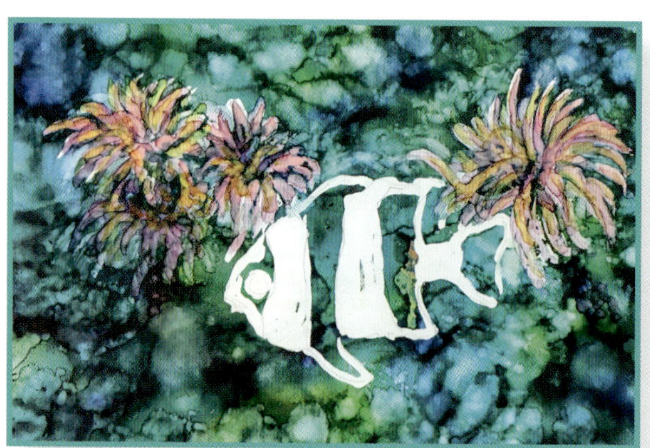

Tropical Reef - In progress...

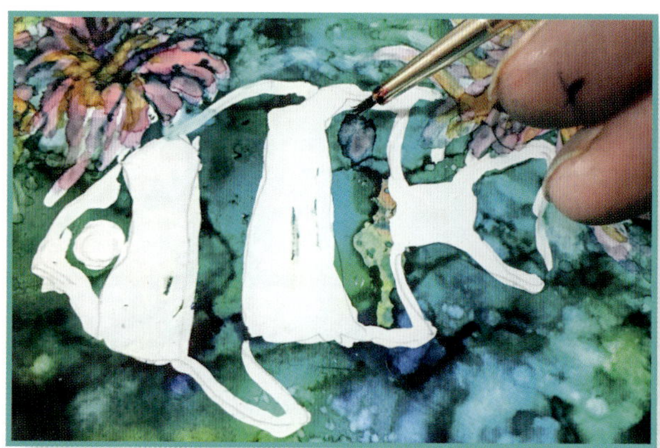

10. Paint in the dark stripes of the fish by adding purple ink directly over the background ink.

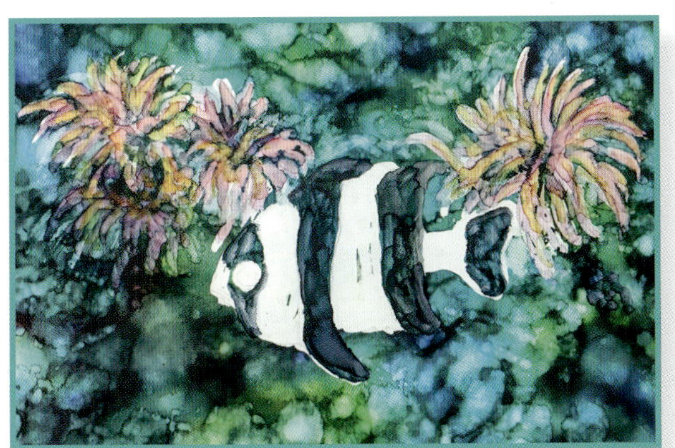

Tropical Reef - In progress...

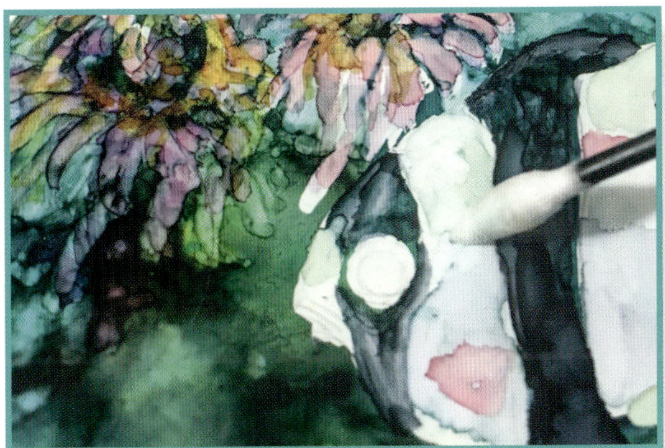

11. For the white stripes of the fish, clean up any masking errors, add in several shades of pale ink, and use the cotton swab with alcohol to blend and soften.

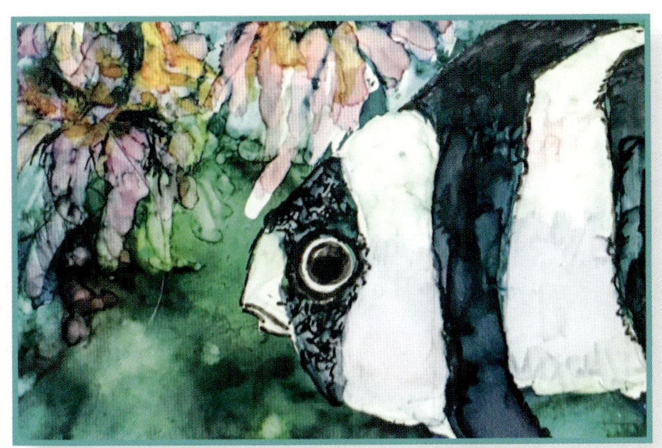

12. Add in the eye and other details with the fine-tipped black pen.

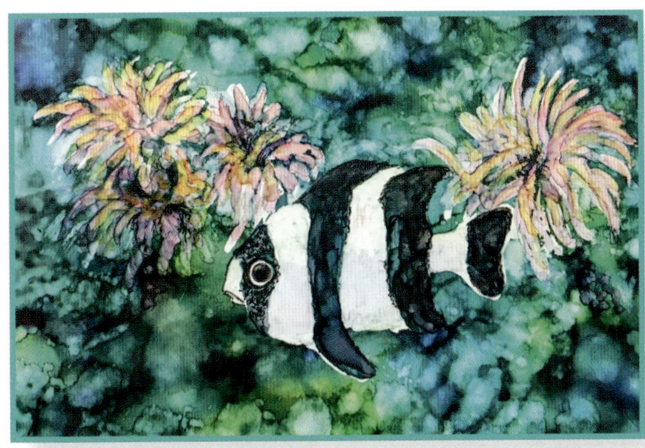

Tropical Reef - In progress...

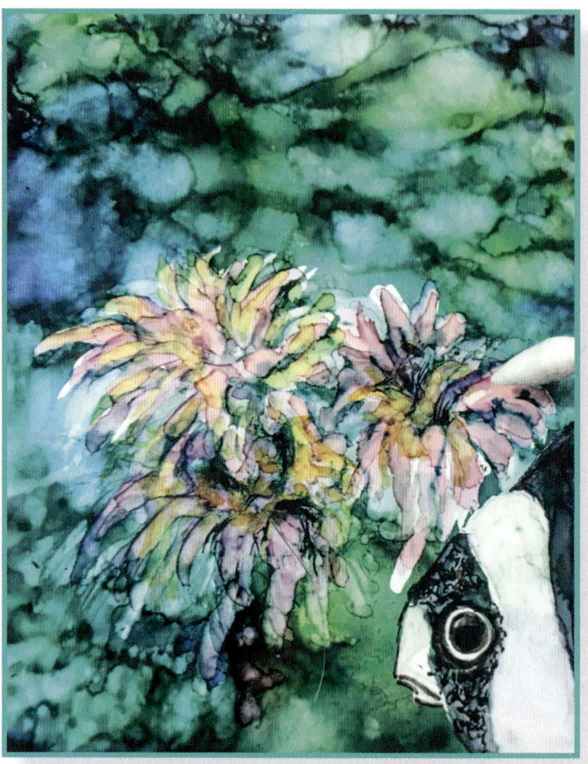

13. Lift highlights in the sea anemones with the cotton swab and alcohol.

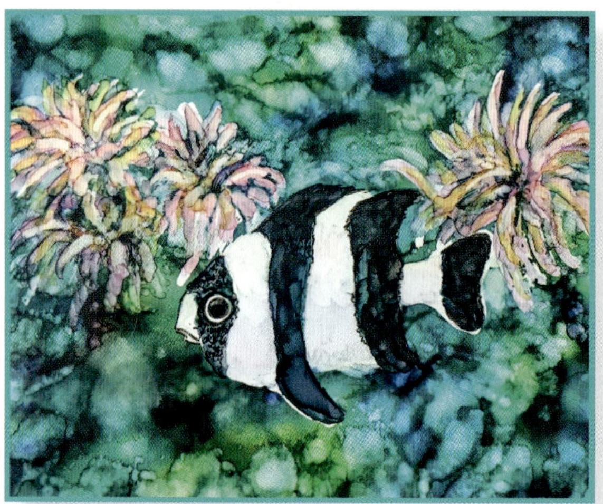

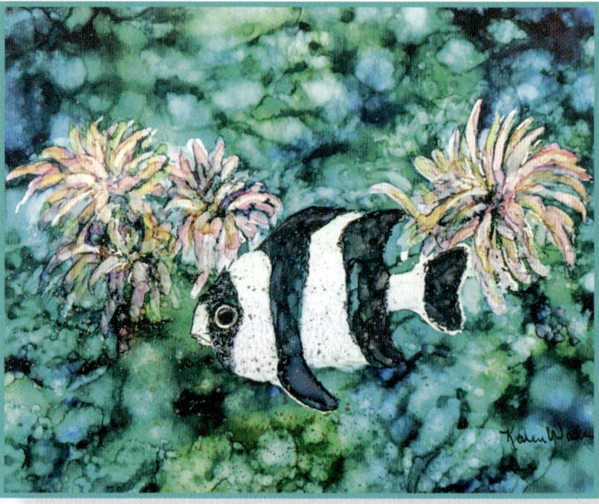

14. Check over the painting and add finishing touches, such as the splattered gold ink.

Variation: Golden Fish

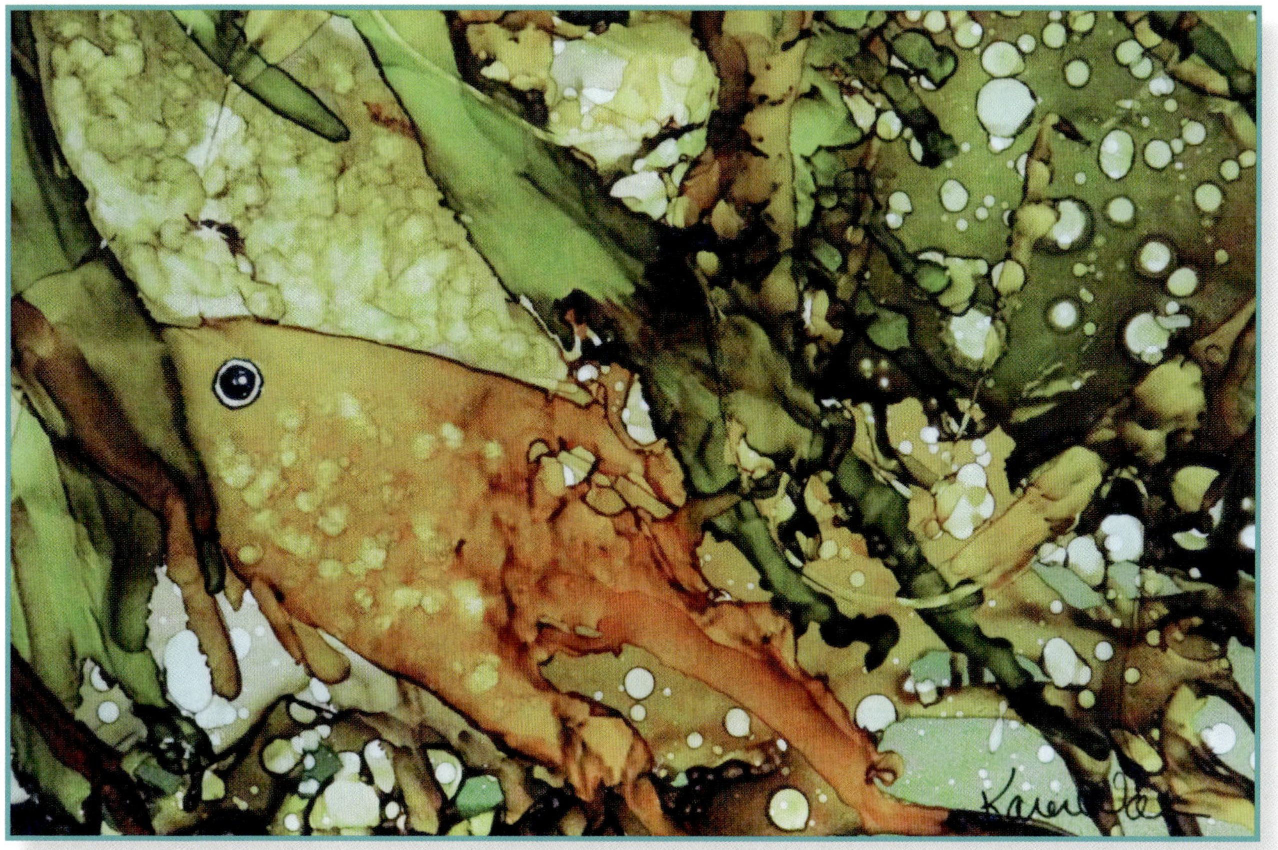

Karen Walker. *Golden Fish*.
While the *Tropical Reef* scene was planned and used masking and an inky textured background, the *Golden Fish* was an unplanned painting. Out of an inky background evocative of kelp and ocean, the yellow fish appeared. Only a small amount of texturing and pen for the eye was needed to develop the piece.

Acknowledgments

A special thank you to Sandy Scott for introducing me to the magic of alcohol inks, and to Cathy Taylor for inviting me to be a part of her beautiful book, *Pigments of Your Imagination*. Thank you to Schiffer Publishing for the opportunity to create this book and for their patience and support along the way. Finally, thank you to all the alcohol ink artists who have enriched my life through their friendship, art, and love of alcohol inks.